Civilizational Dialogue and Political Thought

D1314085

Global Encounters: Studies in Comparative Political Theory
Series Editor: Fred Dallmayr, University of Notre Dame

This series seeks to inaugurate a new field of inquiry and intellectual concern: that of comparative political theory as an inquiry proceeding not from the citadel of a global hegemony but through cross-cultural dialogue and critical interaction. By opening the discourse of political theory—today largely dominated by American and European intellectuals—to voices from across the global spectrum, we hope to contribute to a richer, multifaceted mode of theorizing as well as to a deeper, cross-cultural awareness of the requirements of global justice.

Border Crossings: Toward a Comparative Political Theory
    edited by Fred Dallmayr
Beyond Nationalism? Sovereignty and Citizenship
    edited by Fred Dallmayr and José M. Rosales
Gandhi, Freedom, and Self-Rule
    edited by Anthony J. Parel
Race and Reconciliatiation in South Africa: A Multicultural Dialogue in Comparative Perspective
    edited by William E. Van Vugt and G. Daan Cloete
Comparative Political Culture in the Age of Globalization: An Introductory Anthology
    edited by Hwa Yol Jung

Conversations and Transformations: Toward a New Ethics of Self and Society
    by Ananta Kumar Giri
Hinterlands and Horizons: Excursions in Search of Amity
    by Margaret Chatterjee
New Approaches to Comparative Politics: Insights from Political Theory
    edited by Jennifer S. Holmes
Comparative Political Philosophy: Studies under the Upas Tree
    edited by Anthony J. Parel and Ronald C. Keith
Iran: Between Tradition and Modernity
    edited by Ramin Jahanbegloo
Democratization and Identity: Regimes and Ethnicity in East and Southeast Asia
    edited by Susan J. Henders
The Politics of Affective Relations: East Asia and Beyond
    edited by Daniel Bell and Hahm Chaihark
From the Margins of Globalization: Critical Perspectives on Human Rights
    edited by Neve Gordon
Imagining Brazil
    edited by Jessé Souza and Valter Sinder
Islamic Democratic Discourse: Theory, Debates, and Philosophical Perspectives
    edited by M. A. Muqtedar Khan
Postcolonialism and Political Theory
    edited by Nalini Persram
Remaking Turkey: Globalization, Alternative Modernist, and Democracy
    edited by E. Fuat Keyman
Civilizational Dialogue and Political Thought: Tehran Papers
    edited by Fred Dallmayr and Abbas Manoochehri

Civilizational Dialogue and Political Thought

Tehran Papers

Edited by
Fred Dallmayr and Abbas Manoochehri

LEXINGTON BOOKS
A division of
ROWMAN & LITTLEFIELD PUBLISHERS, INC.
Lanham • Boulder • New York • Toronto • Plymouth, UK

LEXINGTON BOOKS

A division of Rowman & Littlefield Publishers, Inc.
A wholly owned subsidiary of The Rowman & Littlefield Publishing Group, Inc.
4501 Forbes Boulevard, Suite 200
Lanham, MD 20706

Estover Road
Plymouth PL6 7PY
United Kingdom

British Library Cataloguing in Publication Information Available

Library of Congress Cataloging-in-Publication Data

Civilizational dialogue and political thought : Tehran papers / edited by Fred Dallmayr
and Abbas
  Manoochehri.
    p. cm. — (Global encounters)
  ISBN-13: 978-0-7391-2236-5 (cloth : alk. paper)
  ISBN-10: 0-7391-2236-3 (cloth : alk. paper)
  ISBN-13: 978-0-7391-2237-2 (pbk. : alk. paper)
  ISBN-10: 0-7391-2237-1 (pbk. : alk. paper)
    1. International relations and culture. 2. International relations—21st century. I.
Dallmayr, Fred R. (Fred Reinhard), 1928- II. Manoochehri, Abbas, 1956-
JZ1251.C57 2007
327.101—dc22   2007028973

Printed in the United States of America

♾ ™ The paper used in this publication meets the minimum requirements of American
National Standard for Information Sciences—Permanence of Paper for Printed Library
Materials, ANSI/NISO Z39.48-1992.

To the Victims of Bloodshed on a Global Scale

Contents

Foreword

FROM "DIALOGUE" TO THE "DIALOGUE OF CIVILIZATIONS"
PRESIDENT KHATAMI

IN THE NAME OF GOD

The most important function of language is speech, and "dialogue" is the most distinctive type of speech. As contrasted with monologue, dialogue is not solitary speech, nor merely a long talk. Its enduring manifestations can be found in history; hence, its historical background needs to be taken into account. One cannot speak of "dialogue" and ignore its origin back in the Socratic dialogues which exemplify the model most clearly. In his dialogues, Socrates learns from his interlocutors as much as they do learn from him. According to him, "knowledge" resides in the depth of the human being and can be revealed through dialogue.

Also, in various religious traditions, man speaks with his creator by calling him "Thou" and thereby ascends from an isolated "individual" to personhood. Likewise, the cultural heritage of various nations, poetic and literary, has benefited from various forms of dialogue in the explication of human, ethical and social themes. From "Kalileh va Demneh" (*Panjeh Tantra*), which is an ancient book in dialogical style, to the mystical works in the East and West, beautiful and attractive examples of dialogue can be found. Philosophers, mystics and reformers, when seeking to explain the rational, ethical, and social aspects of truth, have turned to dialogue to avoid misunderstanding.

But although an old notion, dialogue is also a new one. The new meaning of dialogue results from changes in human knowledge and from the ups and downs in the movement of modern societies toward democracy, understanding, and peace. There is evidence that the present world is seeking a foundation and a new path for the improvement of human and social relations. The idea of a "Dialogue of Civilizations," which I suggested to the United Nations General Assembly in September 1998, aims at the replacement of "enmity" and "violence" by "mutual understanding" and "dialogue." As such, it can be considered a new paradigm which is not confined to formal political structures and processes. "Dialogue of Civilizations and Cultures" is the expression of a persistent effort to get closer to the truth and achievement of "understanding"; therefore it has a close tie with the philosophical foundations of dialogue. This new foundation and path is a dialogue in which "East" and "West" are not the subject of discussion but are the interlocutors of a dialogue.

Dialogue of Civilizations means a true understanding of the world's cultural map and taking a critical look at the "self" and the "other." It presupposes knowledge of the past heritage while seeking and encouraging new experiences. Dialogue belongs to the needs and necessities which exist in the depth of contemporary human life and perspective. As a new chapter in human history, dialogue of civilizations can upgrade human relations from the stage of negative tolerance to positive cooperation. According to this notion, "others" should not just be tolerated, but be accepted as partners. Dialogue of civilizations starts with toleration and leads to respect for the other's freedom while maintaining self-trust and trust in the world.

Another dimension of the dialogue of civilizations is the attention it draws to the critical relation between tradition and modernity. Anyone who looks at himself/herself as "absolute" and considers himself/herself as absolutely "good" while considering the other as absolutely "evil," not only fails to understand the other, but similarly fails to know himself/herself. By considering the critique of tradition and modernity in the contemporary world as unavoidable, I understand that dialogue of civilizations orients us toward the acceptance of reason's authority in this critique. Obviously, knowing the tradition is a prerequisite for its critique, and knowledge of the foundations of modernity is equally necessary for its critique.

In its underlying premises, dialogue of civilizations belongs to philosophy; but it also opens up a vast field of social and political sciences. The two concepts, "dialogue" and "civilization," both are pregnant with philosophical and social meanings. Naturally, the interrelationship between the two adds to the philosophical and social dimensions of the notion of dialogue of civilizations. The notion of the "clash of civilizations" relies upon the existence of "they" and "them." The interlocutor in a dialogue, however, is essentially different from them, who is the other side of the clash. The idea of the dialogue of civilizations requires a dialogical relationship between "I-Thou" and "We-You."

Despite the emergence of threatening situations in the world security arena in recent years, I have tried to show that dialogue can be the prevailing aspect of our thought and knowledge. Both as a political personality speaking with various political leaders of the Western and Eastern world, and now in dialogue with world religious and cultural personalities and institutions from the standpoint of an NGO, I see the horizon for the dialogue of civilizations and cultures open and believe that we can pave the way further step by step.

Of course, evaluating the possibility and the success of dialogue in highly critical political situations is not that difficult. Despite prevailing obstacles, what provides hope is the attention paid by academic, cultural, and artistic centers to the notion of dialogue among cultures and civilizations, both as a strategic idea and a practical concept in the sphere of the needs of various societies. Researches, books, and educational programs in interdisciplinary forms are examples, which I hope lightens the path for world politicians further. The present collection consists of the efforts of honored scholars of the world and Iran about dialogue of civilizations. I sincerely appreciate the efforts of Professor Fred Dallmayr and Dr. Abbas Manoochehri for the publication of this collection and wish them and their colleagues success.

Mohammad Khatami
February 2007

Preface

This is a collection of papers that were presented in two workshops in May 2002 and May 2003 in Tehran, Iran. Both workshops were organized by the Department of Political Science in the International Centre for Dialogue of Civilizations (ICDC) in Tehran. The topic of the first workshop was "Political Theory and Dialogue of Civilizations," and the theme of the second was "Political Science and Dialogue of Civilizations." The first workshop was held as an adjunct or follow-up to a larger conference held in Shiraz, Iran, in May 2002 on "Center and Periphery and Dialogue of Civilizations." The second workshop was a two-day meeting or conference organized in three sections: "Political Theory and Dialogue of Civilizations," "International Relations and Dialogue of Civilizations," and "Communication and Dialogue of Civilizations." Here the papers of both workshops have been combined in one collection. Papers were originally presented either in English or in Farsi. All papers have been translated to the other language so we have a bilingual collection, though in separate covers. Professor Dallmayr, who was present in the first workshop, has been kind enough to write an Introduction to this collection. At this point, I would like to thank our colleagues in the Department of Political Science at the ICDC for making this work possible. Both I and professor Dallmayr wish to acknowledge the support we have received from the International Centre for Dialogue of Civilizations and the Institute for Cultural Studies and Research (both in Tehran) in terms of the organization of the meetings and the translation of papers into English and Farsi respectively.

Abbas Manoochehri
Tehran, June 2006

Introduction

Fred Dallmayr

Given its basic focus, this is a timely volume. The notion of a "dialogue among civilizations," to be sure, is not entirely new. As a prominent public formula it first emerged around the turn of the millennium. It was President Khatami of Iran who first launched the idea as a public agenda in 1998. In response to the President's proposal, the General Assembly of the United Nations proceeded to designate 2001 as the "Year of Dialogue among Civilizations." As we all know, the time was not very propitious to the idea: 2001 was also the year of September 11 and of the horrendous terrorist attacks associated with that date. These attacks and their aftermath seemed to confirm and give credence to a very different global agenda or scenario: the scenario of a "clash of civilizations" erupting mainly at the fault lines between Western and Islamic civilizations and their respective cultural and geopolitical worldviews. In the opinion of many observers, the political events since September 11 have furnished incontrovertible evidence of the predestined enmity and collision between cultures animated by different goals and aspirations.

The contributors to the present volume do not share this grim perspective. In their view, the events of September 11 and their aftermath do not diminish, but rather strengthen and corroborate the need for a peaceful global counteragenda: the agenda of a "dialogue among civilizations." Their view is not based on mere wishful thinking but on professional training and sound expertise. The thesis of the looming "clash of civilizations" had been advanced by Samuel Huntington, a professional political scientist and leading student of international politics. It is fitting that the counteragenda should also be picked up and elaborated by professional political scientists and theorists specializing in the different subfields of that discipline: international relations, comparative politics, and political theory or philosophy. The volume actually goes back to two meetings held in 2002 and 2003 respectively where the dimensions and implications of the alternative agenda were discussed by practitioners of the discipline. As one should note, the first meeting was strictly in the format of a "workshop" with participants presenting short position papers for the purpose of simulating interaction and discussion. The second meeting had more the character of a regular conference with participants offering full-length papers followed by more limited discussion. Most of the papers in Part One of this volume resulted from the workshop whereas most papers in Part Two were presented at the conference.

Part One deals with the relation between political theory or philosophy and the idea of a dialogue among civilizations. My own opening position paper seeks to underscore the intimate connection between political theorizing and global dialogue. As I argue, the basic question addressed by political theory/philosophy is: How can we live together justly and ethically in a community? Indebted to the legacy of Aristotle, this formulation of the central political question stands in sharp contrast to an approach that locates the core of politics in the "friend/enemy" distinction (and which in a way militarizes all politics). Transferred to the global arena, the central question of political theory is: How can we live justly and ethically in a global community? This formulation opposes the assumption of an international anarchy of nation-states (with its built-in violence) as well as the prognosis of an inevitable "clash of civilizations."

Countering the alleged "normalcy" of warfare, my paper asks how the global community can develop just and ethical modes of interaction? In my view, the answer cannot be found in a top-down "universalism" which postulates the existence of a priori standards; nor can it be found in a complacent "relativism" (often predicated on a self-enclosed "identity politics"). Instead, just and ethical modes of interaction need to be negotiated through dialogue among all the participants, a dialogue not limited to instrumental interests, but including the articulation of ethical and religious perspectives and commitments. By way of conclusion, I suggest that such dialogue is not only a political postulate, but actually reflects our basic "human condition": the condition of speaking and dialogical creatures.

The issue of the relation between political theory and cross-cultural dialogue is taken up also by Hosseini Beheshti in his position paper. Beheshti takes his point of departure from the obvious fact of the diversity of cultures and then asks how this diversity can be reconciled with the need for global order. He considers a number of proposals, such as the ideas of an "overlapping consensus" (Rawls) and of a prudential modus vivendi (Hobbes), finding these proposals for various reasons unsatisfactory. Turning finally to dialogue, he explores such notions as "representational dialogue" and "dialogue as proceeding" (Dervin and Schaefer), defending these notions as superior to other alternatives.

Norma Moruzzi's position paper aims in a similar direction, but corroborates the superiority of dialogue through reference to concrete historical examples, especially the example of Greek intercity relations as recorded by Thucydides in his study of the Peloponnesian War. While Pericles's Funeral Oration vindicated dialogue and persuasion as superior Athenian virtues, and while the Mytilenian Debate illustrated the Athenian ambivalence on this issue, the Melian Dialogue finally demonstrated the abandonment by Athens of dialogue in favor of violence—an abandonment that foreshadowed its own defeat by Spartan force. Mostafa Younesie's position paper complements the preceding argument by drawing attention to the crucial role of "justice" as a required building block in any civilizational interaction.

Part One is rounded out by three additional papers, which explore the relation between political theory and dialogue from a variety of angles. Abbas Manoochehri adds philosophical depth to the discussion by drawing attention to the arguments of such leading thinkers as Martin Heidegger, Paul Ricoeur, Hans-Georg Gadamer, and Raimon Panikkar. The main accent of his paper is on (what he calls) "differential hermeneutics" indebted to Gadamer, Panikkar, and Jacques Derrida: a hermeneutics (or mode of interpretation) giving full recognition to the difference between cultural traditions and language games. Global reconciliation, he writes, "means listening to the voice of the other by entering the in-between realm of dialogue." Fatemei Sadeghi's paper supplements and expands this discussion by shifting the focus to some recent French thinkers, especially the work of Julia Kristeva. Among the many contributions of the French writer, the paper concentrates especially on the linguistic opposition between the "symbolic" and "semiotic" dimensions, that is, between the domain of modern rational discourses and the more dispersed or anarchical realm of existential experiences and traditions—an opposition which corresponds loosely to the distinction between culture and nature.

For Sadeghi, there is a two-fold danger: intercultural dialogue may privilege the "symbolic" or rational-logical order while repressing the "semiotic" openness of nature; on the other hand, a privileging of the "semiotic" may encourage an antimodern atavistic essentialism (including an essentialist feminism). Against both dangers, the paper recommends a symbolic/semiotic negotiation transforming dialogue into an existential encounter. The final paper in this part by Golmohammadi discusses the extent to which present-day communications and information technologies can both advance as well as restrict and obstruct civilizational dialogue—a point which underscores the tension between the technological and the lived-existential dimensions of cross-cultural interactions.

Part Two shifts the accent to the relation between civilizational dialogue and contemporary international politics. In his opening position paper, Seyed Kazem Sajjapour examines the status of such dialogue in the field of international relations. From a standard "scientific" angle, he argues, civilizational dialogue is not an empirical "theory," nor is it a concrete policy, although it functions in the mode of a "paradigm" or framework guiding future research. In his paper on the "science of international relations," Hossain Salimi presents the dominant or mainstream paradigm in the field: international "realism" with its accent on self-interest, power, and conflict. He also introduces some recent modifications, especially constructivism and globalization theory. The following paper by Homeira Moshirzadeh explores more fully the "theoretical" underpinnings of civilizational dialogue.

For Moshirzadeh, such dialogue can be linked most fruitfully with (what is called) "critical international theory," an approach that in recent decades has challenged state-centered "realism" in favor of a stronger attention to cultures and their interpretation. Faithful to its roots in Kant and the Frankfurt School, "critical international theory" emphasizes the role of discourse and discursive interaction on all levels: from epistemology to ethics or morality and public policy. Through an extensive review of recent literature, the paper provides evidence of the ongoing transformation of the field of international relations due to the work of critical theorists. Hadi Khaniki's paper further deepens the theoretical grounding of civilizational dialogue. The paper first examines a number of recent political theories: from interest-based liberalism and Habermasian critical theory to ethical communitarianism and conversationalism (Bakhtin, Charles Taylor, and others) in order next to gauge their compatibility with the focus on dialogue. Khaniki concludes by defending a "fruitful synthesis" between cross-cultural dialogue and communitarian and conversationalist theories of politics.

The remaining papers in Part Two examine important aspects of contemporary international politics where the accent on civilizational dialogue can or does make a crucial difference. Karl Schonberg focuses on the status of "universal human rights" in the contemporary globalizing context. His paper takes exception to a top-down universalism (also termed "imperialism") which would utterly set aside the significance of different cultures and traditions; at the same time, however, it refuses to endorse a contextual relativism which would permit the violation of even minimal universal standards of rights. Schonberg finds the solution to this conundrum, and accordingly the required universal standards, in the notion of human autonomy and freedom of choice, in the sense that the meaning of "rights" and the very definition of our humanity depends on "our capacity to reason and to choose our own destinies."

One of the crucial rights in modern times is that of citizenship, a topic explored by Joseph Camilleri in his paper on "Citizenship in a Globalizing World." For Camilleri, citizenship as such has a long historical pedigree — which is subjected to new stresses and strains in our present globalizing age. Following an overview of the evolution of citizenship in the West, his paper raises the question whether citizenship today can still be tied exclusively to the nation-state or whether it should not be rethought as a corollary of "civil society." Such a rethinking brings into view notions of "differentiated" and "transnational" citizenship potentially linking up the Western pedigree with non-Western traditions. Camilleri at this point offers a breathtaking overview of possible contributions in this field by the teachings of Hinduism, Buddhism, Confucianism, and Islam. The concluding paper by Fabio Petito draws our attention back to the launching of civilizational dialogue in the writings and speeches of President Mohammad Khatami. In a captivating manner, Petito also explores parallels between the Iranian President's approach and some ideas advanced by the Czech president, Vaclav Havel. He quotes in this context an inspiring passage where Havel pinpoints as the central political task of our time "the creation of a new model of coexistence among the various cultures, peoples, races, and religious spheres within a common interconnected civilization."

All the papers assembled in the present volume testify, in my view, to both the urgency and the viability of the agenda of civilizational dialogue as a guidepost and ethical paradigm for our global community. All the contributors owe a special debt of gratitude to the Centre for Dialogue in Teheran and to Professor Manoocheri for organizing the successive meetings in 2002 and 2003. The meetings have been rich occasions for dialogue and learning for all participants. We can only hope that the meetings were only opening gambits and that they will be followed by more gatherings in the future. The greatest hope of the participants, however, is that the theme of our meetings — the dialogue among civilizations — will continue to make headway in a world still grimly overshadowed by violence, warfare, and terrorism (and counter-terrorism). The volume is dedicated to the victims of bloodshed on a global scale.

Part One

CIVILIZATIONAL DIALOGUE
AND POLITICAL THEORY

Chapter One

Political Theory and Civilizational Dialogue

Fred Dallmayr

First of all, I want to thank Abbas Manoochehri for inviting me to participate in these discussions today. As I see it, our meeting deals with a crucial topic: the relation between political thought or political philosophy and the "dialogue among civilizations." The topic gains its relevance and even urgency because of the context in which we find ourselves: the context of globalization, which also includes the globalization of terror and counterterror evident in the steady deepening of so-called terror wars. In my view, it is a prominent task of political theory or political philosophy to reflect on these contemporary developments. To be sure, political theory has a long and venerable tradition, and political theorists are well advised to remember that tradition. However, unless theorizing keeps in touch with changing times and events, the legacy of political thought is likely to shrivel into museum pieces, into antiquated relics offering no lessons for the present and future. Hence, I welcome this endeavor of political theorists assembled here to address burning issues of our time.

Let me tell you a little of what I consider to be political theory in our time, a political theory or philosophy adequate to the needs of our time. First a word about political theory or philosophy. What is it? Let me start with philosophy. As I see it, philosophy is the love for wisdom: *philo—sophia*. What does that mean? It means the love for a kind of life which is lived reflectively, wisely, prudently. Hence, philosophy is a kind of reflective living; it is an awakening from the slumber of ignorance, the slumber of unreflective life and absentmindedness. Philosophy basically asks these questions: How should we live? What is the point of our living? What is the meaning of goodness and truth? These are the premier questions of philosophy. If this is so, and let me just assume that it is, then what is political theory or political philosophy? Political theory or political philosophy, as I see it, is an effort to live reflectively in a larger community. The central concern of political theory or political philosophy is always: How should we live together? This, I think, is the core of political theory and its basic questions are: How is it possible for us to live together properly, justly, wisely, and reflectively? or How can we live together without coercion, without violence, without corruption? In other words: How can we live together morally, justly, and peacefully?

Now, if this is so, if philosophy is a call for us to wake up to a reflective life, to think of how to live properly, and if it is true that political theory or political philosophy is a wake-up call for us to think about how we should live together in a community, then our question now is: How can we do this today? What can political theory, political philosophy mean in our time which is a time of globalization—a time in which societies and cultures are increasingly interpenetrating and influencing each other? Political theory in this situation needs to reflect on the question: How can we live together in the global community in a just and justifiable way—in a way which is not oppressive, not exploitative and not unjust? If that is the crucial issue, then our question is: How can we find a notion of justice, which would be acceptable to a wider community, now a global community or a cross-cultural community?

In that regard, several answers have been proposed. Some argue that we need to adopt a universal definition of justice, which is accepted by all people across the world: some kind of universal declaration of principles, moral principles. This is what is called "universalism." On the other hand, there are those who argue that we can never agree on universal standards. We have to limit ourselves to the standards that have been developed historically in a given cultural or civilizational community. This is sometimes called "relativism." Now, I am personally not in favor of a universalism, which defines a global standard from the top down, in other words, a hegemonic kind of universalism where a certain kind of culture or tradition monopolizes the definition of justice for the rest of the world. Nor am I in favor of a relativism where every culture is self-enclosed and does not care about other cultures and is unwilling to learn from other traditions and other cultures. This leads me directly to the dialogue among civilizations.

In our time, in order for political theory or political philosophy to be relevant, we have to find the right way of living together in the global community. My belief is that the right way of living together in the global community can only occur through a mutual dialogue in which all participants are willing to learn from each other. This means that political theory can no longer be purely a Western prerogative. It has to include Islamic political theory, Indian political theory, Asian political theory, African political theory,

Latin American political theory, with none of these voices being hegemonic or dominating. In this situation, each party or each voice has to listen to the others and try to inquire with others about the question: What is justice? What is the just way for us to live together in our shared world? Hence, the dialogue of civilizations is not a marginal question of political theory. It is "THE" question of political theory today.

Let me conclude. You realize that I had only fifteen minutes for this opening statement and I had to simplify everything; but these are the main points I wanted to make. Philosophy is the effort to think about our life, how we live, how we should live. Political philosophy is the attempt to reflect, to think about living in common and how we should live in common. My argument is that, in our global age, the only way to reflect about living together in a global community justly is through dialogue, through a mutual learning process, not through domination and exploitation. This idea of dialogue, for me, is architectonic. It comes from a long tradition of hermeneutics. From a certain angle, dialogue is actually the human condition. It is not merely a method of talking to one another. It is my being in the world, which makes me a being of dialogue. I do not know who I am without being in dialogue with others. This is how we are in this world. There is a very famous line by a great German poet, Hölderlin, who says that we, as humans, are dialogue. We do not make dialogue, we ARE dialogue. So, you can see how for me the dialogue of civilizations and political theory are intimately connected. They are inseparable. I hope these comments will allow our discussions to get started.

Chapter Two

Dialogue among Cultures and Political Theory

Seyed Ali Reza Hosseini Beheshti

Over the last two decades or so, pronounced cultural diversity of human societies and cultural communities has received the attention it deserves. We observe nowadays various arguments postulating the recognition of equal respect toward differences, which for a long time had been ignored or considered unimportant or arbitrary. Although to some extent such arguments involve explaining the nature of such diversity and to explore why ways of life differ, they go much further and ask how we should respond to such differences. In this respect, the argument leads to a more fundamental question: On what basis should the process of political decision making be formed so as to accommodate cultural diversity as a permanent feature of contemporary societies?

The aim of this paper is to examine whether dialogue can be employed as a means in such a process. The first section of this paper is concerned with the nature and sources of cultural diversity. It is also important to see in what way cultural diversity raises problems that concern political theory. This is the concern of the second section. Next, I shall examine ways in which dialogue can be employed to aid the formation of political decision-making processes to accommodate cultural differences. In particular, I shall suggest that interpretations of dialogue such as those offered by Brenda Dervin and David J. Schaefer which aim to transfer the burden of dialogue as a discipline from participants to procedures, may be useful when dialogue among cultures and civilizations is concerned. I do not claim that even in this respect my argument is conclusive, as my goal is to tackle the problem by shedding light on some of its different aspects for further investigation.

OUR CHANGING AND DIVERSE WORLD

Contemporary states should be viewed as inhabited not by a single society but different societies with different cultures. The existence of cultural diversity and different cultural communities are not, however, new phenomena. The problem is probably as old as human social life itself. Various sources of cultural difference can be distinguished: some differences appear as the consequence of immigration, as in the case of the British Caribbeans or Asians; others are concerned with distinct territorially concentrated groups like Canadian Aboriginals; and there are demands for the political recognition of some religious groups which wish to protect their community of faith from what they conceive as the corrupted culture of the main society, like the Amish in the United States. All of these examples involve cultural minorities. Yet there are cultures that cannot by any definition be viewed as minorities, like feminists whose arguments concern a large section of society. I shall explain some of these sources of cultural difference a little further.

The first is the result of individual or group migration. Reasons for such migrations can vary: some seek somewhere to live a better life, others would escape the despotism and suppression of their native home, while still others may be forced to leave their own lands by an aggressive occupier. In many countries, immigrants from other countries are asked to adopt the way of life of the host country. They are expected to adjust themselves in such a way that the culture of the host country is not undermined. This means that when their traditions come into conflict with the dominant culture, they should either adjust or abandon those traditions so that the culture of the majority remains preserved.

The second source of cultural difference concerns territorially concentrated minorities. Again, the origins of a minority vary from one case to another. What they have in common, however, is that they have been settled in certain region(s) of a country for a considerably long time. The French Quebecois movement is an interesting example in this respect. It has resulted in changes in the divisions of power in Canada. As a result, the province of Quebec, which is 80 percent francophone, has extensive jurisdiction over issues that are significant to the survival of the French culture, including education and language. However, such minorities, too, have been subjected to assimilation. The issues concerning the protection of the indigenous people of Canada, the Aboriginal people of Australia, and Indian Americans, are examples of this kind. It should be noticed, however, that while in these democratic societies assimilatory policies were suggested (in most cases by liberals), such proposals often were supposed to work against discrimination, and therefore, viewed as affording the members of such minorities the very fundamental freedom of association, as a right to be guaranteed to individuals in a color-blind constitution. This was the case when, for instance, in 1969 the Canadian government released a White Paper on Indian Policy which recommended an end to the special constitutional status of Indians. Accordingly, the government proposed that the reservation system, which had protected Indian communities from assimilation, should be dismantled.[1]

Assimilation, therefore, was a way of dealing with those with a different cultural identity. However, there have been occasions when cultural groups have been granted partial autonomy. For instance, when the Ottoman Turks conquered much of the Middle East, North Africa, Greece, and Eastern Europe during the fourteenth and fifteenth centuries, through the millet system they allowed Jewish and Christian minorities not only the freedom to practice their religions, but a more general freedom to govern themselves (though in purely internal matters) with their own legal codes and courts.[2]

There are some cases, however, which do not fit easily within the two categories mentioned above. Thus, when the culture of an individual or group is identified by religion, it is hard to consider it as a case of either ethnic minority (e.g., the Afro-Caribbeans in Britain) or national minority (e.g., the Canadian Indians). For instance, although the *Satanic Verses* affair in Britain mainly concerned British Muslims from an Indian background, the publication of such literature may concern any British Muslim citizen regardless of his or her ethnic background. Another case that cannot be considered in either of the two categories is the feminist argument against the male-oriented structure of contemporary societies. It seems, therefore, more adequate to speak of diversity which result from different cultural identities.

THEORIZING POLITICS FOR A PLURALIZING WORLD

Although the fact of cultural diversity has recently received recognition, it has taken place in a variety of forms as there are different views on the nature of such diversity and, consequently, different attitudes toward it: some consider it as a fact, which, though an inescapable characteristic of our societies, is not necessarily desirable. Others also accept it as fact, yet see many advantages which it can produce. Some groups consider it as a ground for demanding equal respect for their identity which they feel they had not received in the past; others intend to use it as a means to assert the value of their own culture over others. In the academic world, too, the problem has received much attention and it has been viewed from different angles and within different disciplines or in interdisciplinary studies. In political theory, for instance, the different implications which cultural diversity has brought about have resulted in strong criticism of liberalism. In response, liberal thinkers have tried to accommodate it within their theories.[3] As Tariq Modood points out, the new pluralism means that the status quo needs to be reviewed in order to give proper institutional expression and political legitimacy to the pluralism:

> Yet in order to do this we have to, not despite but because of the pluralism, rethink what we have in common and how to give that, too, an institutional and symbolic recognition and to let it have its due integrative weight.[4]

The problem may lead us to more fundamental questions concerning the force of principles like toleration in determining the kind of politics in multicultural societies. In the *Satanic Verses* affair, for instance, the demand was not concerned with whether the Muslims' way of life should be tolerated by the rest of the society, but whether and how far their demand to restrict the freedom of speech was legitimate. If the British Muslim community is to be considered as a group of citizens with a distinct cultural identity, should their demand be granted? A question that follows is: on what ground can cultural communities make their demand for equal respect? And when it comes to the politics of multicultural societies, on what ground should political decisions be made so as not to undermine the cultural identity of their different cultural communities? Can and should the state be neutral toward different cultures? If not, to what extent can the state meet the demands for cultural plurality?

In this regard, examining the modern concept of political and national identity provides a good starting point. Within the context of modern politics, as citizens of a certain state, we usually tend to think of our nationality as a singular cultural identity. Most modern nations, however, consist of disparate cultures. Such a cultural diversity is in part a result of the process of globalization. According to S. Hall, there can be three possible consequences of globalization on cultural identities: (i) that national identities are being eroded as a result of the growth of cultural homogenization; (ii) that particularistic identities such as national identity are being strengthened by the resistance to globalization; and (iii) that national identities are declining but new identities of hybridity are taking their place.[5] Hall argues further that "globalization does have that effect of contesting and dislocating the centered 'closed' identities of a national culture."[6]

To identify one's cultural identity with his or her national identity was partly due to the modern conception of human nature and partly due to the kind of rationality on which modernity relies. As for the conception of "man," the concept is changing and many interpretations are offered as more adequate and more acceptable ways of understanding the actual characteristics of man. For instance, against the modern atomistic concept of the self which views persons as rational individuals who freely choose their own way of life regardless of their attachment to the communities of which they are members, contextualist arguments underline the significance of the social matrix in the formation of the self. The self is now viewed as situated, a narrative animal, a cultural creature and possessing dialogical identity.[7] Or according to the postmodern account, the postmodern subject, in contrast to the Enlightenment subject, is seen as having no fixed, essential, or permanent identity.[8]

So far as the modern conception of man is the fruit of modern rationality, with its claims to universality and generality, it has been challenged by the critique of modernity since far from representing universal moral principles, it reflects a particular kind of human reasoning. Contrary to the modern project, which seeks to provide rational frameworks applicable to human society as such, critics have shown the difficulties that undermine achieving such universal frameworks. It has been argued that moral terms have minimal and maximal meanings, that we can standardly give thin and thick accounts of them, and that the two accounts are appropriate to different contexts and serve different purposes.[9]

Hence the argument of universality versus particularity which underlines the contradictory nature of modern politics: it has come to be a politics of universalism with the aim of equalizing rights and entitlement on the one hand; and a politics of difference which concerns the recognition of the unique identity of individuals or groups and their distinction from others, on the other.[10] Multiculturalism and widespread demands for the recognition of differences have increasingly focused on criticism of the nature of knowledge, philosophical articulation and scientific research methods. The idea of decolonizing methodologies, for instance, makes researchers aware of the force of cultural imperialism supported by institutions, vocabulary, scholarship, imagery, and doctrines.[11]

Facing the controversies mentioned above, perhaps the concept of theorizing politics is itself in need of reconceptualization.[12] Abandoning the illusionary image of political theory as a scientific discipline whose task is to articulate universally valid claims based on moral and political philosophy, we may now think of two kinds of politics and consequently of two different levels of theorizing political concepts: one in which cultural particularities are of central importance so that the distinction between different traditions of moral inquiry is at its fullest extent; and the other in which universally acceptable principles, though very thin, are required. The former forms the politics applicable within cultural communities since it is capable of securing the conditions for their self-determination as engaged in activities that constitute their conceptions of the good life; in the absence of a shared conception of the good, the latter is doubtful of value in providing any moral foundation thickly conceived for politics, yet suitable for relations between communities.[13]

We may ask then: what kind of consensus is possible in a culturally diverse world such as ours? In order to answer this question, one possible way is to think of a kind of overlapping consensus which has been suggested by John Rawls and which is valued and accepted for moral, not prudential, reasons.[14] However, since it is based on liberal conceptions and, therefore, a process that may be experienced as coercion by those who do not share such conceptions, it is open to serious challenge by non-Western cultures.

Another alternative is a modus vivendi, i.e., a prudential peace treaty among cultural communities. Divorced from thick moral arguments such as justice or freedom, it has to rely on thin principles. The most important of such principles, it may be said, is the maintenance of peace without which the very existence of human species is severely undermined. According to this view, the ultimate, and perhaps the only achievable, aim of such a political order is to maintain peace. An objection raised against this view, however, maintains that stability on the modus vivendi account is always fragile because a shift in the distribution of power would give a party an incentive to rewrite the terms of the contract so as to benefit it most.

As rightly pointed out by some critics, however, even if it is granted that a Hobessian modus vivendi model would provide no guarantee against this occurrence, it is difficult to see how any other model does provide such a guarantee.[15] Moreover, even if a modus vivendi cannot be viewed as intrinsically moral, it is a precondition of moral life. Indeed, what distinguishes a Rawlsian "overlapping consensus" from the modus vivendi model is not that the former is necessarily more stable than the latter. The difference lies in the explanation that the former can provide for the undesirability of using forceful assimilatory means in moral terms; an explanation the latter cannot provide, since it is not involved in any moral claim but prudence.

There can be other alternative models too, such as appealing to a purely political ideal in the form of the "civil association" model proposed by Michael Oakeshott, John Gray, or Chantal Mouffe,[16] which, as I have shown elsewhere,[17] fall too short to stay out of cultural disagreement. As I mentioned above, however, my intention is not to represent a comprehensive survey or an exclusive model here, but to explore some significant aspects of the problem. The brief review presented above, therefore, may sufficiently serve my purpose.

WHY DIALOGUE?

Now that the nature of existing cultural diversity in contemporary societies and its implications for political theory are outlined, it is time to turn to the status of dialogue in the formation of politics in such societies. Before proceeding further, however, two precautions are in order:

The first concerns the scope of my argument. It has been argued above that when facing the existing cultural diversity of modern societies, we may think of two kinds of politics: one which provides an adequate understanding of the relationship *within* cultural communities, the other appropriate for governing the relation *between* such communities. Here I shall be concerned only with the latter. Thus I do not wish to deal with the ongoing dialogue within every culture.

And secondly, when talking about the relationship between cultural communities, it is important to avoid a misunderstanding. Since by cultural communities I do not mean formal entities such as states, my discussion about the relations between them does not necessarily refer to international politics. Whether or not an artificial entity like the existing nation-state system, even after an extensive critical reevaluation, is capable of accommodating legitimate claims of cultural communities for autonomy, falls well beyond the purpose of the present essay, though the line of argument persuaded so far does reveal strong implications for alternative models and rethinking the concept, role and functions of governments seems to be an unavoidable task for any theory which seeks effective accommodation of cultural diversity in the real world.

Whatever model of consensus we choose to adopt (Rawlsian "overlapping consensus," Hobbesian modus vivendi, or some other models which were mentioned above), the question concerns the means through which it can be achieved, and dialogue can be considered as one such means. It can be argued that the importance of dialogue lies in the underlying acknowledgment of the existing diversity of cultures and civilizations and the right of being heard for those voices which has been ignored until very recently. Dialogue can also be considered as a means for mutual understanding. Although it may not transcend entirely certain obstacles like untranslatability and incommensurability as the consequences of deep differences between cultures, dialogue can be useful in clarifying the limits and nature of such problems.[18] Or from a more Hobbesian view, one may argue for the significance of dialogue for the maintenance of peace and order as the necessary condition of the existence of civil society. The important question, however, is to ask what kind of dialogue would be more appropriate in the dialogue among cultures.

Employment of dialogue in philosophical enquiries has a long history, perhaps as long as the history of philosophy itself. In the Western tradition, it reminds us of the Socratic way of philosophical deliberations, allowing for more systematic treatment of the contrasting the position of a person who continually presses his objection to the protagonist's case. From Plato's *Republic* in ancient Greece to contemporary Ludwig Wittgenstein's *Philosophical Investigations* and Maurice Cranston's *Political Dialogues*, the dialogue form is used to approach philosophical questions in a dialectical spirit.

While the exercise of dialogue is as old as culture and civilization itself, in recent times a profusion of practices, techniques, and definitions has arisen around the term "dialogue." Before the linguistic and hermeneutic turn, the main purpose of using the dialogue form was the discovery of truth, the construction of arguments, and the clarification of minds.[19] The hermeneutic approach, however, upholds a dialogical conception of the grounds and context of knowledge in the human sciences. Hans-Georg Gadamer and Jürgen Habermas, for instance, view the process of understanding as a dialogue between the researchers of other cultures and the subjects whose lives and actions they study.

In Gadamer's view, to understand means for two people to understand one another and understanding is primarily agreement or harmony with another person. Even where there is no direct dialogue, as Austin Harrington describes, for Gadamer "[t]radition pre-structures the self-understanding of each present age and thereby binds us into dialogue with our collective past."[20] As Fred Dallmayr points out, "[w]hat is particularly important in Gadamer's view of dialogue is its radically non-instrumental sense: dialoguing here involves not only an act of questioning but also the experience of being 'called into question'—often in unsettling and disorienting ways."[21]

Habermas's "Discourse Ethics" too is meant to settle differences trough an ongoing dialogue. "If we keep in mind the action-coordinating function that the normative validity claims play in the communicative practice of everyday life," he writes, "we see why the problems to be resolved in moral argumentation cannot be handled monologically but require a cooperative effort."[22] He distinguishes his approach from Rawls's in that whereas the latter put the moral judge into "a fictitious 'original position' where differences of power are eliminated, equal freedom for all are guaranteed, and the individual is left in a condition of ignorance with regard to the position he might occupy in a future social order,"[23] the former requires a "real" process of argumentation in which individuals concerned cooperate.[24]

Gadamer's and Habermas's dialogical approach, however, have been criticized from different aspects. It has been argued, for instance, that since for them the term "subject" of interpretation includes the thing produced and actions performed by these persons, and no verbal exchange is possible with inanimate things and actions, the majority of persons with whom dialogue might be conceivable will not be available for interrogation and, therefore, the term "dialogue" should not be understood in any literal sense.[25] Another critique maintains that "[b]y making validity claims the yardstick of proper communication, his [Habermas's] model marginalizes or excludes modes of interaction and broad domains of human experience not subsumable under argumentative reason."[26] Taylor has observed pointedly the segregating boundary, which, motivated by hypergoods, procedural ethical theories draw between moral goods. In Habermas's case,

> [T]he boundary between questions of ethics, which have to do with interpersonal justice, and those of the good life is supremely important, because it is the boundary between demands of truly universal validity and goods which will differ from culture to culture. This distinction is the only bulwark, in Habermas's eyes, against chauvinistic and ethnocentric aggression in the name of one's way of life, or tradition, or culture.[27]

I am not going to evaluate such criticisms here, because to do justice to hermeneutical ethics and in particular recent developments of Habermas's thought is beyond the purpose and limits of this paper. But even though it offers a more adequate understanding of the process of ethical argumentation within each culture, it seems to me that the failure of the communicative ethics in including a relatively large number of traditions of moral enquiry (to use MacIntyre's term) whose rationality differs from Western modes of rational enquiry (including postmetaphysical views), makes it less attractive to be used in understanding possible ways of intracultural relations. As has been mentioned above, what is required here is a common ground formed by thin moral requirements. Any form of consensus which requires something more than our common moral sense about what is good, would fail as soon as it starts to articulate such moral sense into rationally defensible moral principles.

It is for this reason that I think arguments such as Brenda Dervin and David J. Schaefer's "Beyond Rhetorical and Representational Dialogue"[28] may be more useful in this respect. The aim of their discussion is to transfer the burden of dialogue as a discipline from participants to procedures. In order to do this, they offer a criticism on the idea of innocent dialogue, i.e., that dialogue is assumed to be a process that inherently makes better communication possible and inherently makes it easier to negotiate differences between contending interests. They proceed then to classify two modes of conceptualizing dialogue: "rhetorical" and "representational"; the former positions dialogue more as means to an end, whereas the latter views it as an end in itself. Central to the rhetoric concept of dialogue is the assumed monistic concept of the truth and, accordingly, the purpose of dialogue as rhetoric is to persuade the uninformed and uninitiated as to the correctness of statements and arguments. In contrast, the aim of dialogue as representation is to include the voices of all relevant parties as it holds that there is no one truth that can govern collective

life and that diverse parties must advance their positions and then jointly negotiate and seek consensus and agreement.

Dervin and Schaefer then point out a number of contradictions as dialectical paradoxes of dialogue, such as objectivity versus subjectivity, collectivity
versus individuality, uncertainty in reality versus uncertainty in knowing, outcome versus process, thinking versus being, consensus versus resistance and
creation and innocent dialogue versus negotiation of self-interests. They proceed to state briefly their own approach which they call dialogue as procee-
during that, as they claim, can transcend such contradictions. Accordingly, the
modes of dialogue must move from attention to nouns to attention to verbs,
i.e., from the *whats* and *whos* of dialogue to the *hows*. Central to this approach
is the idea that what humans most universally share is the telling of their life
journeys and struggles.

It is still early to see the exact consequences of this approach and its pre-
cise distinctions with the two other since, as Dervin and Schaefer argue, their
theory is in its early stages of development. Yet we may begin with their useful arguments and classifications even though we arrive at different consequences. There are a number of points which make the representational model
of dialogue useful to the politics between cultural communities. First, since it
opposes the monistic concept of truth, the model acknowledges cultural plurality in a way compatible with cultural diversity as a permanent feature of
the contemporary world. Second, because the aim of this kind of dialogue is
to include the voices of all relevant parties, unlike the liberal understanding
of cultural difference, it does not suffer from excluding nonliberal cultures.
Third and most significantly, it does not presume any thick moral principle as
the basis of consensus among different cultural communities.

CONCLUSION

As I mentioned above, the politics between cultural communities cannot be
understood in terms of thick moral principles. What is required is a nonmoral
basis on which different cultures can agree. I also argued that such a morally
neutral basis is more like a Hobbesian modus vivendi than the Rawlsian overlapping consensus. We may, for instance, argue that to believe in the sanctity
of human life provides such a universally acceptable basis. We may also argue that peace and order, as the precondition of such a belief, would result in
strong commitments to the stability of the proposed modus vivendi and,
therefore, although not a moral principle in itself, could be considered as the
precondition of a life morally valuable. As argued above, since it transfers the
burden of dialogue from participants to procedures, the representational

model of dialogue may be employed to achieve such a modus vivendi among diverse cultural communities. However, whether or not the proposed model would pass all the tests is a question which is in need of further examination.

NOTES

1. For an interesting discussion on the issue see for example Will Kymlicka, *Liberalism, Community and Culture* (Oxford: Clarendon Press, 1989), in particular chapter 7.

2. For a critical account of this system see for example Kymlicka, *Multicultural Citizenship* (Oxford: Oxford University Press, 1995), 156–58.

3. J. Raz's "Multiculturalism: A Liberal Perspective," *Dissent* (Winter 1994) and Kymlicka's *Multicultural Citizenship* (Oxford: Oxford University Press, 1995) are good examples of such revisions in the liberal thought.

4. T. Modood, "Establishment, Multiculturalism and British Citizenship," *Political Quarterly* (1994), 64.

5. S. Hall, "The Question of Cultural Identity," in S. Hall, D. Held, and T. McGrew, eds., *Modernity and Its Future* (Oxford: Open University Press, 1992), 300.

6. *Ibid.*, 309.

7. I have in mind here arguments offered by Alasdair MacIntyre, Michael Walzer, and Charles Taylor, respectively.

8. S. Hall, "The Question of Cultural Identity."

9. See M. Walzer's *Thick and Thin: Moral Arguments at Home and Abroad* (Notre Dame and London: University of Notre Dame Press, 1994).

10. See C. Taylor's "The Politics of Recognition," in Amy Gutmann, ed., *Multiculturalism and "The Politics of Recognition"* (Princeton, NJ: Princeton University Press, 1992).

11. A good example of works on this view is Linda Tuhiwai Smith's *Decolonizing Methodologies* (London: Zed Books, 1999).

12. Two interesting examples of such reconceptualization of academic disciplines are Wanda Teays's *Second Thoughts: Critical Thinking from a Multicultural Perspective* (Mountain View, CA: Mayfield Publishing Company, 1996) and Brian Fay's *Contemporary Philosophy of Social Science: A Multicultural Approach* (Oxford: Blackwell, 1996).

13. I have discussed this point at greater length in my *Theoretical Foundations of Politics in Multicultural Societies* (Tehran: Bogheh, 2002) (in Persian).

14. See John Rawls's *Political Liberalism* (New York: Columbia University Press, 1992).

15. For the full argument see P. Neal, "Vulgar Liberalism," *Political Theory*, vol. 21 (November 1993), 636.

16. Michael Oakeshott, *On Human Conduct* (Oxford: Clarendon Press, 1957); John Gray, *Post-Liberalism* (London: Routledge, 1993); Chantal Mouffe, *The Return of the Political* (London and New York: Verso, 1993).

17. See my *Theoretical Foundations of Politics in Multicultural Societies*, chapter 10.

18. For a discussion on these two problems see my article "Theoretical Obstacles of Dialogue between Civilizations," in Masuod La'li, ed., *What Khatami Is Talking About?* (Tehran: Nashre Ekhlase & Nashre Azadi Andishe, 1998) (in Persian).

19. For a detailed argument on this matter see Richard McKeon's "Dialogue and Controversy in Philosophy," in Tullio Maranhao, ed., *The Interpretation of Dialogue* (Chicago: University of Chicago Press, 1990), which examines the status of dialogue within the history of the Western tradition.

20. Austin Harrington, *Hermeneutic Dialogue and Social Science* (London: Routledge, 2001), 31.

21. Fred Dallmayr, *Dialogue among Civilizations* (New York: Palgrave Macmillan, 2002), 27.

22. Jürgen Habermas, "Discourse Ethics: Notes on a Program of Philosophical Justification," in his *Moral Consciousness and Communicative Action* (Cambridge, MA: MIT Press, 1999), 66–67.

23. *Ibid.*, 71.

24. *Ibid.*, 72.

25. Harrington, *Hermeneutic Dialogue and Social Science*, 110.

26. Dallmayr, *Dialogue among Civilizations*, 43.

27. Taylor, *Sources of the Self: The Making of the Modern Identity* (Cambridge, UK: Cambridge University Press, 1989), 88.

28. Brenda Dervin and David J. Schaefer, "Beyond Rhetorical and Representational Dialogue," *Peace and Policy*, vol. 6 (2001), 29–33.

Chapter Three

Dialogue of Civilizations and Political Thought

Norma Claire Moruzzi

"Dialogue of Civilization" is a relatively new concept. It was proposed by President Khatami as an intellectual argument and a practical political alternative to Samuel Huntington's theory of a "Clash of Civilizations." Huntington's phrase emerged out of a long tradition of political thinking that presumes political interests to be unified and oppositional: politics understood as a set of monologic actors inevitably in conflict. But the presumption of a clash of civilizations further emerges out of and continues a more recent tradition that was itself an intellectual response to the modern colonial project: the proposition of a basic (and hierarchical) opposition between interests and regions defined as "civilizations." What had previously been understood to be competing or overlapping religious, imperial, and regional interests were reconceptualized as distinct civilizations whose absolute differences provided a cultural argument for the political and economic dominance of one civilization over another. Because of this problematic historical heritage, the term civilizations inevitably implies lack of common identity, and competing monologic interests, whether they are in dialogue or in clash. In order to avoid this inevitable assumption of political conflict, I want to focus here on the other half of the phrase, dialogue of civilizations, the concept of dialogue. What influence can the concept of dialogue, both between and within civilizations, have on political thinking?

In thinking about the concept of "dialogue," we realize it is not so different from the idea of speech, which is fundamental to Aristotle's conception of politics, and to the origins of what is called the Western political tradition. Aristotle emphasized that it is through speech that men govern themselves, and that it is speech that distinguishes us as human beings rather than animals. The politics of speech and self-governance that Aristotle discusses is a democratic politics. This democratic political tradition is often claimed as a Western political tradition. But we should realize that at the time of its origin, there was no particular division of the world into "West" and "East." Democracy was a Greek innovation, and Greece during the fourth, fifth, and sixth centuries B.C. had much more contact with the regions of the eastern Mediterranean and even with the Persian Empire to the east, than it did with the almost completely unknown lands of far western Europe. What we now consider the "West" had no role in the Greek innovation of democracy. It had little historical claim even to the development of the philosophical idea, which was nurtured in the "Eastern" Islamic civilizations of the Mediterranean during the period when Christian Europe had rejected the classical model of learning.

But democracy is in fact not even a Greek innovation. More specifically than that, it was a unique political experiment in one city-state, the city-state of Athens. What the Athenians called democracy would not be considered at all democratic in the modern world: the Greeks owned slaves, denied women any rights of political participation, and restricted citizenship to a small elite group of men born in Athens of recognized Athenian parentage. Nonetheless, Athenian democracy was a unique experiment in the idea and practice of self-governance, originating in one particular place and time. It is in fact so specific, and so original, that it cannot really be considered "Greek" or "Western" at all, but is rather a unique gift Athens has provided to the world. Even in its Golden Age in Athens itself, democracy was a fragile experiment, flourishing for only a very brief period and often under threat. Democracy is always fragile, and always an experiment, but it is also an experiment equally available to any people willing to try their own adaptation of the Athenian gift.

The earliest commentators on the Athenian democratic experiment recognized the fundamental relation between dialogue and democratic practice. Without real dialogue, there can be no democracy, and any serious threat to dialogue is a threat to democracy itself. One of the most profound analyses of the relation between democracy and dialogue is provided at the very beginning of the tradition of political thought, in Thucydides's history of the Peloponnesian War. Thucydides's book is still one of the most extensive and subtle explorations of the role of dialogue in democratic politics, both within the state, and between states. The rest of this presentation will explore three different examinations of dialogue and democracy in Thucydides's history, and consider the extent to which Thucydides considered the political role of dialogue indicative of the integrity of democratic practice.

Pericles's Funeral Oration is one of the most famous sections of Thucydides's history, and one of the most famous political speeches in all of history. In the Funeral Oration, Pericles, the elected leader of the Athenian city-state, provides his fellow citizens with a description of themselves that is meant to inspire them with pride in their city and a commitment to its values. He describes the democratic state, and the democratic citizen's honor and identity. Athenians value persuasion (rather than force) in politics and in public life. In their private lives, they are tolerant of individual differences. They take an interest in the good of the community, rather than being preoccupied with their individual self-interest, and they have a broad interest in the general developments of civilization: in the arts, the sciences, and the culture of learning. Against this Athenian civic model of articulate democratic identity, Pericles contrasts the values of their rivals, the Spartans: a military society that relies on force rather than speech, and military discipline over individual achievement.

Pericles's Funeral Oration describes the best aspect of the Athenian democratic identity. But shortly after it, Thucydides includes a description of a key political argument that is always referred to as the Mytilenean Debate, and identifies a critical point for Athenian democratic politics. Athens is deep in the war with Sparta, and Pericles is dead. Lesser men are competing for leadership of the city. Two generals, Diodotus and Cleon, argue over the proper response Athens should make against Mytilene, an Athenian ally that made an alliance with Sparta, and then was taken back by the Athenians. What punishment is appropriate? But the argument between the generals takes on a larger significance, about how the citizens should govern themselves and others. Diodotus argues for the politics of persuasion, and for self-interest through foresight, restraint, and cooperative relations with allies and neutral parties (the careful, multilateral policies of Pericles). But Cleon explicitly denounces the politics of speech, persuasion, and foresight, and argues for the imposition of self-interest through violence.

Diodotus wants to reincorporate the Mytilenes as a useful ally; he advises his fellow citizens to watch them, not to trust them, and to raise the tribute they must pay. To punish them excessively will only make other cities more fearful of Athens, and more desperate if they attempt to revolt, thus causing Athens more financial and military trouble in the long run. But Cleon claims the Athenians have a right to vengeance, and argues that Athens should punish Mytilene by killing all the men, and enslaving all the women and children. Furthermore, he argues that anyone arguing otherwise is betraying Athenian self-interest. Cleon, arguing against persuasion even within Athenian internal politics, wins the debate, and orders the total destruction of Mytilene. But the next day the Athenians have a change of heart, meet again and discuss the problem of Mytilene, and decide to send out a fast ship to overtake the first messenger of destruction. The city of Mytilene is saved, but so is the democratic character of the city of Athens. Although they had decided against the politics of persuasion and for the politics of force, the Athenians themselves revisited their decision, discussed it again, and changed their minds: the essence of dialogue and democracy being a willingness to discuss a problem without being silenced by a demand for imposed unity.

Within the Western, democratic political tradition itself, we can see that there have always been two competing traditions. One is represented by Pericles and Diodotus: a political practice of negotiation, dialogue, and self-interested restraint practiced within the state and in the state's relations with others. But the other tradition is represented by Cleon: the domination of a single self-interest, within the state through intimidation, and in the state's relations with others through force. The temptation to rely on violence rather than dialogue (and therefore to endanger democracy in the name of state interest) existed already in Athens. The Mytilenean Debate is a crisis point for the Athenian democracy, and indication of the fragility of democratic commitments even in the city of its origin. The Athenians reconsider the case of Mytilene, and keep their honor as Pericles had described it. But a few years later, it is gone. In a later section, always referred to as the Melian Dialogue, Thucydides describes the complete abandonment by Athens of political dialogue, and its replacement by brute force. In doing so, he also describes the Athenian betrayal of their own democratic identity and heritage: a democracy that has abandoned dialogue in its dealings with others, has also abandoned itself.

The Melian Dialogue is somewhat similar to the Mytilenean Debate but different in several significant details. Melos was a neutral city that had managed to keep its neutrality throughout the war between Athens and Sparta. It wished to remain neutral and independent, but Athens presented the Melians with the Mytilenean choice: either become a tribute city, or face death and enslavement. The Melians insisted that all they wish to do is remain as they are, free and independent, and argue that a choice between subservience and death is no choice worthy of a democratic city-state, as Athens still claims to be. Athens responds that as the dominant military power, they have the ability, and therefore the right, to set the alternatives, and that the weaker Melians simply have the choice between the alternatives presented to them. All this is argued in the form of a dialogue, but the integrity of the speech is corrupted by the explicit threat of force. The Melians realize this, and argue that Athens is betraying its own identity. The Athenians realize this too, and argue that since they have superior force, they do not need to rely on dialogue. The Melians choose to reject both of the alternatives proposed by Athens. They fight for their freedom, and lose; all the men are killed, and all the women and children enslaved.

Athens wins the military battle (although she eventually loses the Peloponnesian War), but Thucydides shows that she has lost her own struggle for democracy. Within the scope of his whole history, he demonstrates the primacy of dialogue for democratic identity. But he also chronicles the struggle within that identity for a tradition of dialogue (relying on respect, restraint, and multilateralism), as opposed to the imposition of a single will (that of a state or an individual) by force. In the Melian Dialogue, he further shows the abandonment of the practice of dialogue despite formal assertions of its political role (the Melian Dialogue is always called a dialogue, but is in reality an attempt at dialogue on one side, and a statement of superior position on the other).

Democratic politics is dialogue. Thucydides himself was a cynical but committed democrat, an Athenian patriot and general who recognized the hopes and failings of his own society, and the unexpected nobility of his opponents. His work is a warning, describing the fragility of democracy in any context, and the necessity of struggling for real dialogue within the state as well as between states. Within as well as between civilizations, the same lessons of dialogue and democracy can also be applied.

Chapter Four

Dialogue among Civilizations, Justice and Political Thought

Mostafa Younesie

INTRODUCTION

If we want to look at political thought in social and civil contextual engagement, it possibly can be examined through the matrix of civilizational dialogue and not merely through metaphysical, subjective, or abstracted ideas. I want to explore this topic in accordance with this hypothesis. Accordingly, I will present the current and prevailing state of political thought in most of the universities or academic circles in descriptive, evaluative, or pathological ways. Thereafter, I will put this presentation in a broad and contextual framework, explaining and prescribing a more or less appropriate and practical matrix for developing an attractive and healthy political theory. Since accomplishment of this task needs a proper mediator, acceptable for both parties of this discussion, I think "justice" can be an appropriate category for this mediation for both sides of this relationship. Both matrix and political thought need a basis and foundation and also the mediator has to have special qualities for the accomplishment of the tasks, which are acceptable for the civilizational dialogue and political thought.

POLITICAL THOUGHT

In a contrastive and heuristic way, the main constituent parts of the contemporary and mainstream weltanschauung of the academic conception of political thought in the modern West and the modernized East are: subjective monologue, ego-orientation, and nation-state (nationality). It is against this background or macroperspective that one of its foregrounds, i.e., political thought, must be understood. As such, we can define political thought as the disciplined reflection in the atmosphere of nation-state on the public issues or problems. All of the mentioned parts are connected to each other, making a network endowed with an internal logic. During the course of the evaluation of this descriptive narration, it is noticed that this account is very abstract, metaphysical, simple/naive and one-dimensional. I will try to focus on these two critiques.

With regard to the abstractness of this presentation we know that historically and sociologically it is possible to trace the above reading through genealogy. Thus, the above reading is not ignorant of historical and sociological facts but rather wants to go a step further. In the prevailing circumstances, we offer a kind of metatheory, metaphysics, metanarrative . . . in the era of the death of these categories and subjects,[1] which might have diverse meanings and results. It seems that there is no escape from metatheory, metanarrative, or metaphysics, if theoretical and practical messages and purposes are oriented toward a broad spectrum of audiences and different categories of people. Further, it can be said that any claim against different kinds of metatheory is simply based on a basic implicit assumption. Therefore, mainstream and prevalent political thought has been described and evaluated with regard to the theoretical and practical problems, felt more or less in the modern West and modernized East. Accordingly, our presentation is based somehow on a kind of metatheory but not a marginal, spurious, and merely intellectual kind of "meta."

So far as simplicity or naïveté of the definition is concerned, it will be argued that this simplicity in not null and void but possesses many dimensions, providing a complex ground. With the intention to reach to the fountainhead of this complex grounding, there appears a semiopaque horizon whose opacity can be reduced through analysis.

CIVILIZATIONAL DIALOGUE

The process of research begins with a special state of mind and in his search for foundation, the researcher is always guided by many assumptions. However, the discovery of this foundation in no way guarantees its correctness. Therefore, it seems possible to propose other foundation(s) with a critical and pathological view. In this context, civilizational dialogue or more properly, dialogue among civilizations can be one of them, which points in two directions. On the one hand, the proposed matrix is civilizational—a context that is civic as well as cultured—rather than individual and uncultured or nonhumanistic. On the other hand, the course of thinking and practicing in this matrix is based on a dialogical and not a subjective or monological foundation. Moreover, with regard to the above-mentioned paradigm or matrix, the constituent parts of the proposed background in a comparative and critical mode are: dialogue as a civil/agonal praxis,[2] other-orientation, and speakers of civilizations.

Dialogue is the interconnection and interaction of different speeches and reasons. There is a collective and synthetic rather than individual and analytic conception and orientation toward "logos," since synthetic logos has more interconnections with community. Furthermore, this synthesis of logos or speeches/reasons is supposed to take place in a dialectical way, i.e., a process of interactions among thesis and antithesis that will finally make a network of logos. However, these logoi are not merely verbal movements but are actions/practices in relation to other human beings not abstract entities. They interact with each other as ethical entities. Moreover, this practical dialogue takes place in both a civil process and agonistic context—not in a noncivil (nonhuman, noncommunal) and nonproblematic/smooth/easy mode. At the same time, this dialogue does not negate competition of the engaged and ethical persons or groups for their goals.

Necessarily, civil/agonistic dialogue itself has relations with real and factual others. Important here is the kind of orientation or attitude of persons or group toward the others, because there can be diverse and different stances and positions. Human beings are not void of feeling to each other[3] and it is impossible to forget, hide, or cover the special feelings: positive, negative, optimistic, pessimistic, and sympathetic. Therefore, it seems imperative to select a feeling, both proper and suitable for dialogue, which at the same time enhances and compensates for the defects of subjective monologue. This orientation must be a friendly feeling,[4] a feeling not hostile but not too intimate.

This perception leads us toward the agents or those who practice civilizational dialogue. Here the speaker category becomes very important because civilizations cannot speak for themselves and there must be living human beings to speak for or against them. There must be two orders or levels of speakers, first those chosen internally in a certain and specific civilization and secondly those speaking across civilizations. Thus, dialogue has to take place at two levels, i.e., intra- and intercivilizational levels. It can be seen finally that all these parts have specific and related meanings for themselves as well as for each other and above all have connections with other elements of our perspective/weltanschauung.

NECESSITY OF MEDIATION AND MEDIATOR

Despite background and foundation, a chief medium or mediator is needed to correct the relations among civilizations and their speakers. This medium must be justice because it establishes a correct and true relationship between components of every context.[5] Why can justice be a suitable mediator? It seems that injustices are being committed with reference to civilizational dialogue by the most prevalent political thinkers. Therefore, it is necessary, first of all, to negate this injustice and make the way clear before presenting affirmative notions or goals. If these injustices remain on the scene, dialogue will be only a rhetorical show, boast or pretension.

As a medium, therefore, justice is necessary for putting aside the injustices in the fields of politics and civil society in order to have a correct dialogue[6] and moreover a correct civilizational dialogue.[7] As a proper mediator, justice can be linkage between civilizational dialogue and political thought. It is through the mediation of justice that we can speak about the just and shared space of political thought; only then will there be a proper civilizational background that is acceptable, trustworthy, and reliable for all who are involved in dialogue.

CONCLUSION

With the actuality of this background and justice as the sublime medium, the community formed by intercivilizational dialogue will proceed theoretically and practically toward a correct and true relationship, which will safeguard peace. Given the institutionalized presence of justice in civil society and politics, we can ascertain its connection with the dialogical and civilizational background and vice versa. In a nutshell, with this background, political thought promotes intersubjective/intercivilizational praxis and communication among speakers of diverse civilizations about the just ways of collective living in the transnational atmosphere.

NOTES

1. Bernard Flynn, *Political Philosophy at the Closure of Metaphysics* (London: Humanities Press, 1992), 1.

2. Chantal Mouffe, *The Return of the Political* (London: Verso, 1993), 41–57.

3. N. Crossley, *Intersubjectivity: The Fabric of Social Becoming* (London: Sage, 1996), 9.

4. Michael D. Barber, *Guardian of Dialogue: Max Scheler's Phenomonology of Knowledge, and Philosophy of Love* (Lewisburg, PA: Bucknell University Press, 1993), 117–22.

5. G. D. Vecchio, *Justice: A Historical and Philosophical Essay* (Edinburgh: Edinburgh University Press, 1952), 1–2.

6. Tom Campbell, *Justice* (Atlantic Highlands, NJ: Humanities Press International, 1990), 99–113.

7. T. L. Pangle and P. J. Ahrendorf, *Justice among Nations: On the Moral Basis of Power and Peace* (Lawrence: University of Kansas Press, 1999).

Chapter Five

Peace and Dialogue of Civilizations: The Path of Differential Hermeneutics

Abbas Manoochehri

The logos is common to all, but people behave as if each had a private reason.

Heraclitus

Statt immer nur von einem ich-du Verhältnis zu sprechen, sollte man eher von einer du-du-Beziehung sprechen, weil ich-du immer nur von mir aus gesprochen ist, während es doch in Wirklichkeit eine gegenseitige Beziehung ist.[1]

Martin Heidegger

INTRODUCTION

The concept of peace cannot be confined to any particular discipline. Philosophy, political thought, theories of international relations, ethics, and polemology, each have dealt with the notion-question of "peace" in their own particular way. What is common among all of them, however, is that they usually deal with the notion of peace in relation to the problem of war. In this paper, after a short review of the history of thought about the issue of war and peace, nationalism and its relation to the notions of war and peace will be analyzed. In this regard, cultural nationalism and its latest political manifestation, namely the idea of "the clash of civilizations," will be examined, and then the idea of dialogical peace will be pursued.

WAR AND PEACE IN THE HISTORY OF THOUGHT

Pythagoras is the oldest thinker who is known for his idea of harmony as the characteristic of the world.[2] Herodotus and Homer too have used the two notions of *arthmios* and *eirene*, both meaning harmony. Although Heraclitus is the oldest figure referred to as regards the idea of eternal war, he actually believed that there is a "hidden order" which is "more powerful than the apparent contradiction."[3] Plato and Aristotle have also referred to the significance of peace while dealing with the question of *politeia*. According to Plato, any constitution should be oriented toward peace (*Laws*, 628 de). Aristotle too, has referred to the significance of peace in his *Politics* (1333a 21–13334a 16). Thucydides, however, considered war to be the constant interstate situation in the world. He believed that anarchy and the lack of trust dominates relationships amongst the states, while the internal hierarchical structures have intensified this situation.

Unlike the Greeks who had more of a normative view of peace, Romans held a more pragmatic view of peace. In *pacta sunt servanta*, which means: contracts should be upheld, the notion of contractual peace is implied. In the modern era, the question of peace has been dealt with in the context of various theoretical formulations. Realists like Machiavelli and Hobbes defined the world of politics as that of a "jungle" whose dominant character is "the state of war." Such a situation was considered to be due to human nature. Hence, peace could be no more than a "strategy to avoid war."[4] Liberals on the other hand, have combined the inevitability of war with the possibility of peace. Liberalism does not concentrate on the state as the main player; instead it has taken the coalition of individuals and groups as the main players. Liberal theories, therefore, explain war and peace by referring either to "human nature" (Locke), or the interplay of states in the international system (Kant). From the socialist perspective, war and peace result from the interaction of social classes, either from conflict or from concordance. Anarchists, on the other hand, have always explained war as a consequence of the existence of state and peace as a condition in which there is no state.

NATIONALISM, WAR AND PEACE

Unlike modern political thought that considers various factors as the origin of war, contemporary social and political thought considers nationalism as the origin of war. Anthony Giddens and Isaiah Berlin both refer to various causes of political conflict and war originating from the modern sense of nationhood. According to Giddens:

Nationalism can be defined as shared feelings of attachment to symbols which identify the members of a given population as belonging to the same overall community. [And] . . . the global diffusion of the nation state has been accompanied by an ever increasing accumulation of the means of waging war in the hands of nation states.[5]

Berlin has pinpointed the fact that the need to belong to a collectivity which goes back to Greeks has always been concomitant with the sense of confronting "the Other." Nationalist sense of belonging has always, he writes,

emphasized the difference between one group and its neighbors, the existence of tribal, cultural or national solidarity, and with it, a sense of difference from, often accompanied by active dislike or contempt for, groups with different customs and different real or mythical origins, and so was accepted as both accounting for and justifying national statehood.[6]

Such a sense of difference has in recent years become the foundation of notions such as "the end of history" and "the clash of civilizations." In his article, "The Clash of Civilizations?" Samuel Huntington has referred to the emergence of new cultural conflicts on the world arena. According to him, clash of civilizations is the last stage in the process of conflicts in modern history of the world. He defines "civilizations" as "cultural units" and gives six reasons for "clash" among them.

One way of reading Huntington's paper is through the textual hermeneutics proposed by Paul Ricoeur and Quentin Skinner. According to Ricoeur, a text can be read as a written discourse. A written discourse has both common and particular characteristics when compared with the spoken discourse. Ricoeur considers four "traits" constituting a speech as an event and a text as a written discourse. Regarding a text as a "fixation" of "intentional exteriorization," Ricoeur distinguishes between what is spoken in a speech and what is "said" in a text. According to him, what in effect writing fixes is not the event of speaking but the "said" of speaking, where we understand by the said of speaking that intentional exteriorization constitutive of the aim of discourse thanks to which the *sagen*, the saying, wants to become *Aus-sage*, the enunciation, the enunciated. In short what we write, what we inscribe, is the noema of the speaking. It is the meaning of the speech event, not the event as an event.[7]

By referring to the three levels of the speech act—locutionary, or "the act of saying," illocutionary, or "that which we do *in* saying," and perlocutionary, or "that which we do by saying"—Ricoeur concentrates on the third level as "the least inscribale" and yet that which "is the discourse as stimulus." Ricoeur, in his article "The Hermenuetic Function as Distanciation," describes the perlocutionary level as having "direct influence upon the emotions and the affective dispositions."[8] In his words, the perlocutionary act,

> [B]eing primarily a characteristic of oral discourse, is the least inscribable element. But the perlocutionary action is also the least discursive aspect of discourse: it is discourse qua stimulus. Here discourse operates not through the recognition of my intention by the interlocutor, but in an energetic mode, as it were, by direct influence upon the emotions and affective attitudes of the interlocutor.[9]

Ricoeur, therefore, gives the word *meaning* a very broad connotation that covers all the aspects and levels of the intentional exteriorization that, in turn, renders possible the exteriorization of discourse in writing and in the work. In a similar vain, Quentin Skinner has applied the speech-act theory to the study of texts and political ideas. By distinguishing "motives" from "intentions," he says:

> To know a writer's motives and intentions is to know the relationship in which he stands to what he has written. To know about the intentions is to know such facts as whether the writer was joking or serious or ironic or in general what speech-act he was performing. To know about motives is to know what prompted those particular speech-acts, quite apart from their character and truth status as utterances.[10]

Skinner, therefore, focuses "on the idea of the text as an object linked to its creator" and thus on what the creator of a text "may have been doing in creating it."[11] In order to do what he refers to as two "general hermeneutic rules" for the "recovery" of a writer's intentions. His first rule is to focus not just on the text to be interpreted but on the prevailing conventions governing the treatment of the issues or themes with which the text is concerned. This rule derives from the fact that any writer must standardly be engaged in an intended fact of communication.[12] Skinner considers this rule to be applied as a critical as well as a heuristic device, in order to test the plausibility of ascribing any particular intention to a writer in a particular work. And, Skinner's "second rule" is to "focus on the writer's mental world, the world of his empirical beliefs."

Huntington's text, therefore, when read as Ricoeur and Skinner have suggested, has a "world" and a "message." By reading Huntington's article "The Clash of Civilizations?" one can observe both the world and the message constituting his text. Huntington's "world" is clearly described by him in the form of "reasons" for the clash among civilizations. The first reason, in his view, is the existence of "basic" differences amongst various civilizations. The second reason is "the diminishing of the world." The third reason is the experiencing of economic modernization that has led to the social alienation of people around the world. The fourth reason is the emergence of a kind of civilizational consciousness emerging out of the dual impact of the west, namely the powerfulness of the west and the cultural particularism of non-Western societies. Huntington's fifth reason is cultural differences, which are cause for disharmony amongst cultures. The last reason is regional economic integration.[13] Huntington expresses this view of the world as that in which the fundamental source of conflict . . . will not be primarily ideological or primarily economic:

> The great divisions among humankind and the dominating source of conflict will be cultural. . . . The clash of civilizations will dominate global politics. The fault line of civilizations will be the battle line of the future.[14]

With such a view of the world, Huntington enters into a discourse in a written form and gives a message by his perlocutionary act of *ultimatum*. Huntington's message can be read all throughout his article. In a way, this message of ultimatum has permeated the article which is prestructured by his view of the world. His world is that of a threatened subject and his message is an ultimatum to the "threatening" other; his fundamental concerns is that: a West at the peak of power confronts a non-West that increasingly has the desire, the will, and the resources to shape the world in non-Western ways.[15]

Huntington then makes it clearer as to what he means by the "non-West"; according to him, as the ideological division of Europe has disappeared, the cultural division of Europe between Western Christianity, on the one hand, and Orthodox Christianity and Islam, on the other, has emerged.[16] He then expresses his thought through a speech-act of a threatening ultimatum; he says:

> The West is now at an extraordinary peak of power in relation to other civilizations. . . . The very phrase "the world community" has become the euphemistic collective noun replacing the free world to give global legitimacy to actions reflecting the interests of the United States and other Western powers.[17]

Then he adds: "The central axis of world politics in the future is likely to be, in Kishore Mahbubani's phrase, the conflict between 'the West and the Rest' and the responses of non-Western civilizations to Western power and values."[18] So, as Huntington sees it, "a new form of armed competition is thus occurring between Islamic-Confucian states and the West." Therefore, he concludes his argument with the final ultimatum:

> In the short term it is clearly in the interest of the West to promote greater cooperation and unity within its own civilization . . . ; to limit the expansion of the

military strength of Confucian and Islamic states; to moderate the reduction of
Western military capabilities and maintain military superiority in East and
Southwest Asia; to exploit differences and conflicts among Confucian and Islamic states; to support in other civilizations groups sympathetic to Western values and interests; to strengthen international institutions that reflect and legitimate Western interests and values and to promote the involvement of
non-Western states in those institutions.[19]

As such, therefore, the clash of civilizations is the *ultimate* outcome of the
existing situation as seen by Huntington. Therefore, the notion of clash is
the talk of the ultimate; the ultimate clash for the *ultimate* "result." The
thought of *ultimatum* is the metaphysics of the "ultimate" and the ultimate
is the naming by the metaphysical power-subject. Ultimatum is a speech-act
saturated with power and spoken by the subject of superiority in power relations. Therefore, the talk of clash is the ultimate word in the metaphysical
language of *will to power*. Such language of threat and ultimatum is rooted
in Hobbesian atomism and its monological epistemology. In the Hobbesian
vision everyone is threatened by others and is mediated to them by power.
Such self-understanding is the extension of an atomistic and mechanical-
empirical conception of the world. Therefore, man's self-understanding is
affected by power. Huntington's "reasons," as regards the "inevitability" of
the clash among civilizations, are actually cases of behaviorist "reasoning"
applied to the arena of intercultural relations. Indeed, the theory of the clash
of civilizations is the new-global arena as seen by the behaviorist theory of
modernization. However, unlike its previous forms of speech-acts, in which
modernization theory tended to prescribe to other (non-Western) societies
the way for "development," now it threatens other (non-Western) civilizations with extinction.

Unlike Huntington, who has associated culture (or civilization) with war,
there are theoretical arguments which clearly associate culture with peace. In
the "World Conference of Cultural Policies," held by UNESCO in Mexico
City in 1982, the notion of peace defined by Benito Juarez was upheld. According to Juarez, peace is a relationship among various people and is equal
to the respect for he cultural "other." As such, peace is attainable in the world
through the expansion of "cultural relations." A similar view has been articulated in Mitchel's "cultural diplomacy." According to him, cultural language can be in the service of a friendly diplomacy. The relationship between culture and peace has been dealt with in Freud's notion of "cultural
evolution." The question, however, is how such a relationship between culture and peace can be actualized. Differential hermeneutics is a possible answer to this question.

"DIFFERENTIAL HERMENEUTICS"

According to hermeneutic philosophy, understanding (*verstehen*) is prestructured in the world in which we live with *others*. From the hermeneutic perspective these prestructures make up one's being. The problem, however, is our alienation from what has made us and is making us. It is like an alien that is ignored. Hermeneutics tend toward familiarization of what has remained alien. Such familiarization is the result of *Andersverstehen*, "understanding differently." This understanding is not just consensus or repeating something after the other, but amounts (in Fred Dallmayr's words) to "a willingness to enter the border zone or interstices between self and other."[20] In fact this understanding can be attained only at "the risk of self-critique and self-decentering."[21] The result of this understanding, in Gadamer's view, is the intertwining of difference and identity: Difference exists within identity; otherwise, identity would not be identity. As such, hermeneutics is (to quote Dallmayr again): "[A] process of reciprocal questioning at the intersection between self and other, between familiarity and strangeness."[22]

Liberation from alienation is therefore possible through the familiarization of the alien which is a—part (both a part and apart) from/of us. The sphere of this familiarization is, however, "in-between." As Gadamer puts it: "The true locus of hermeneutics is in-between."[23] This process of familiarization can take place on the cultural level through a process of "double injunction" referred to by Derrida.[24] Derrida, on the one hand, rejects "cultural assimilation" and, on the other hand, warns of "cultural narcissism." Difference, hence, is kernel to a hermeneutics of cultural identity. For Derrida, "what is proper to a culture is to not be identical to itself."[25] This differential hermeneutics of self-identity is possible through the sphere of "in-between." To quote Bernhard Waldenfels: "Life-world is surely given, it is given to me and to us, but in such a way that it is cogiven with whatsoever may be given at all." The cogivenness of the life-world is, however, not confined to the intracultural level:

> A part from [the] intracultural articulation of the life-world, we have to take into consideration intercultural worlds varying historically and geographically.[26]

In other words, the life-world is inclusive of distances both within and between cultures. A similar view is presented by Wim Van Brinsbergen by the notion of "intercultural philosophy." According to him the intercultural philosopher is primarily

> a mediator, striving towards an empirically underpinned and practically applicable theory of cultural mediation. . . . Interculturality always presupposes a

medium which cannot be relegated to any of the cultural orientations which are being mediated within it; this opens up a immense space for manoeuvring. On the other hand an empirical orientation means that we limited ourselves in this space, not only by explicit and intersubjective procedures, but also by a critical awareness of our own epistemology and of its globally available alternatives. In this context there are enormous challenges and potentials for intercultural philosophy.[27]

Van Brinsbergen then invokes dialogue in relation to intercultural philosophy and asserts that

The dialogue is not only one of the oldest philosophical genres, it is also a form of communication which has established itself in the modern, and especially the postmodern, world as the most ideal form: with assumptions of equal contributions from both sides, equal initiative, equal rights, for the participants in the dialogue. One tends to assume that, from a pluralistic perceptive, the dialogue offers the best possible conditions for revealing the relevant aspects of a matter, perhaps even revealing truth itself. The word dialogue is often mentioned in the same breath as the word intercultural.[28]

Such inclusiveness can be conceived and understood as a "diatopical hermeneutics," which in Raimundo Panikkar's word is:

[T]he required method of interpretation when the distance to overcome, needed for any understanding, is not just a distance within one single culture or a temporal one, but rather the distance between two (or more) cultures, which have independently developed in different spaces (topoi) their own modes of philosophizing and ways of reaching intelligibility along with their proper categories.[29]

So, unlike Huntington's global atomism, which leads to clash on a global level, hermeneutics begins with the differential cobeing as the ontology of human-being-in-the world, an ontology which is extended to the global level. In a way, here we can think of an "ontological difference" between being-antagonistic and cobeing. This conception of human being, however, is itself rooted in Herder's conception of humanness which is not geoculturally confined. As Dallmayr states, this conception "constitutes a bulwark against the relentless standardization of the world."[30] Standardization of self-understanding is in accord with Cartesian ethnosubjectivism coupled with Hobbesian atomism and conjoined with realpolitik, in which: "Whatever exceeds the confines of the sovereign cogito must either be appropriated/assimilated, or else be excluded and controlled."[31] What is lacking in such perspective, is the possibility of experiencing "reason's exposure to what is unfamiliar or alien."

In contrast to such a vision, and in accordance with the "hermeneutics of difference" in Gadamer's thought:

> [I]t is completely mistaken to infer that reason is fragmented because there are various languages. Just the opposite is the case. Precisely through our finitude, the particularity of our being which is evident even in the variety of language the infinite dialogue is opened in the direction of the truth that we are.[32]

Indeed, such Heideggerian perspective seeks the common root of the harmony of languages through an intercivilizational perspective. This perspective is succinctly described by J. L. Mehta in these terms:

> [H]aving climbed back to the source from which Western metaphysical thought has sprung up, [Heidegger] not only finds in this source a wellspring hidden in itself much that has remained the unthought through sustaining foundation of Western philosophy, but, taking the step back, leaps from this point into a region which is above the opposition of East and West, beyond the clash of traditions and the conflict of religions. This region of all regions, suspended in itself, is itself above all regional loyalties and the Babel of conflicting tongues.[33]

According to Heidegger, then, thinking can lead to the unconcealment (*aletheia*, "*Unverborgenheit*") of our being-human, now buried under an antagonistic self-assertion which has permeated the life-world (*Lebenswelt*) both within and between cultural-civilizational spheres of our existence, an existence which restricts the possibilities of our selfhood. We, therefore, can be what we, as authentic selfs, are, only through the realization of the existential link (*Bezug*) which is now buried (*verborgen*) by instrumentalization of language at all levels.[34]

Such "link" can in fact insure a more peaceful world for human existence. In Gadamer's words:

> [T]he future survival of humankind may depend on our readiness . . . to pause in front of the other's otherness—the otherness of nature as well as that of historically grown cultures of peoples and states. In this way we may learn to experience otherness and human others as the "other of ourselves" in order to partake in one another.[35]

One can therefore, in agreement with Fred Dallmayr, say that any dialogue needs to be "both intra- and intercivilizational," so that linkages can be established "across both historical and geographical boundaries."[36] Such dialogue can facilitate true "diminishing of the world" by closing the distances which seem inevitable from a monological perspective. This is when the globe becomes truly globalized. This would help us to follow the "path" toward what

Dallmayr calls "grassroots globalization or globalization from below," which means: "the attempt to forge or build up the global city through the interaction of cultures and peoples from around the world."[37]

CONCLUSION

Whereas ultimatum, as a form of monological speaking, is a concealing speech-act, ultimatum in a cultural monologue is double concealment. Because it re-conceals what is already concealed. Reconciliation, however, can unconceal what is concealed. Reconciliation means hearing differentially, which means listening to the voice of the other by entering the in-between of the "dialogue." Cultural dialogue makes global reconciliation possible; therefore, what is distant comes to the nearness (*nahe*). By bridging the distance between civilizational selfhood and otherness, global "gathering" is experienced. Such bridging is possible through dialogue. So, unlike monologue and ultimatum, which is destructive distancing, dialogue is constructive gathering.

NOTES

1. "Instead of always speaking only from I-Thou view point, one should speak from a Thou-Thou one. For, I-Thou is always spoken only from my perspective, whereas in reality it is a mutual relationship." (From *Zollikoner Seminare*)

2. It is also well known that he has been influenced in this regard by the thought current in Asia minor, where he lived and studied for a long time before he returned to Greece.

3. See A. V. Hartmann and B. Heuser, *War and Peace and World Orders in European History* (London: Routledge, 2001), 63–65.

4. M. W. Doyle, *Ways of War and Peace* (New York: Horton, 1997), 105.

5. Anthony Giddens, *Sociology* (London: Macmillan, 1986), 155.

6. Isaiah Berlin, *Against the Currents* (London: Penguin, 1982), 338.

7. Paul Ricoeur, *From Text to Action: Essays in Hermeneutics*, vol. 2 (Evanston, IL: Northwestern University Press, 1991), 146.

8. Ricoeur, 147.

9. Ricoeur, 79–80.

10. Quentin Skinner, "Motives, Intentions and Interpretation of Text," in James Tully, ed., *Meaning and Context: Quentin Skinner and His Critics* (Princeton, NJ: Princeton University Press, 1988), 73.

11. Skinner, 78.

12. Skinner, 77.

13. Samuel Huntington, "The Clash of Civilizations?" *Foreign Affairs*, vol. 72 (Summer 1993), 22–29.

14. Huntington, 22.

15. Huntington, 26.

16. Huntington, 30.

17. Huntington, 39.

18. Huntington, 41.

19. Huntington, 49.

20. See Fred Dallmayr, *Beyond Orientalism: Essays on Cross-Cultural Encounter* (Albany: State University of New York Press, 1996), 47.

21. Dallmayr, 47.

22. Dallmayr, "Borders or Horizons? Gadamer and Habermas Revisited," *Chicago-Kent Law Review*, vol. 76 (2000), 831.

23. Hans-Georg Gadamer, *Philosophical Hermeneutics*, trans. D. Linge (Berkley: University of California Press, 1971), 295–307.

24. Dallmayr, *Beyond Orientalism*, 57.

25. *Beyond Orientalism*, 58.

26. Bernhard Waldenfels, "Homeworld and Alienworld," *Phenomenological Studies*, vol. 12 (1998), 75.

27. William M. J. van Brinsbergen, "Cultures Do Not Exist" (homepage).

28. van Brinsbergen, "Cultures Do Not Exist."

29. Raimundo Panikkar, "What Is Comparative Philosophy Comparing?" in Gerald J. Larson and Eliot Deutsch, eds., *Interpreting across Boundaries: New Essays in Comparative Philosophy* (Princeton, NJ: Princeton University Press, 1988), 130.

30. Dallmayr, *Beyond Orientalism*, 55.

31. Dallmayr, "Borders or Horizons?," 829.

32. Gadamer, 16.

33. J. L. Mehta, *Martin Heidegger: The Way and the Vision* (Honolulu: University of Hawaii Press, 1976), 463.

34. Martin Heidegger, *Poetry, Language and Thought*, trans. A. Hofstadter (New York: Harper and Row, 1971), 165–83.

35. Gadamer, *Das Erbe Europas: Beiträge* (Frankfurt-Main: Suhrkamp, 1989), 31–34.

36. Dallmayr, "A Gadamerian Perspective on Civilizational Dialogue," *Global Dialogue*, vol. 6 (Winter 2001), 72.

37. Dallmayr, "Globalization from Below," *International Politics*, No. 36 (September 1999), 330.

Chapter Six

Dialogue of Civilization from a Feminist Perspective

Fateme Sadeghi

This article is an attempt to clarify some aspects of interactions among civilizations from a feminist point of view. Questions that this article tries to answer are: If we consider the "symbolic" order of modern societies, on one hand, and "semiotic" anarchy (in Kristevian terms) of other societies, on the other, is there any possibility to establish a dialogue among these cultures on the basis of mutual understanding? Or would that be an agonal dialogue which, as Lyotard puts it, "falls in the domain of agonistics" of power? And finally, how would a nonagonal dialogue be possible without reduction of any culture into another?

There are considerable similarities between feminist theories and Edward Said's opinion in his *Orientalism* (1978).[1] Said notes that not only is the colonial subjectivity a male one, but in fact "Orientalism" itself is a patriarchal discipline which looks upon its objects from a gender-oriented perspective. From this point of view, the oriental object has been regarded as an erotic, slumberous, mystic, and anomalous one. Also, these traits are traditionally attributed to women in the East as well as the West. On the other side of this binary opposition, stands the active, clear, rational (Western) subject. According to Said, this vision that is a common feature among scholars and novelists like Flaubert manifests the inseparability of the limitations of (human) science and fiction.

An important aspect of Orientalism seems to be the identification of the East with feminine, nonlogic, archaic, and anarchic, on the one hand, and the West with the masculine, logic, and progressive, on the other hand. This has had certain effects on mutual relationships between the East and the West. It leads to domination and power relations, in which one side tries to overcome the other. Said criticizes the domineering character of West-East relations as it appears in orientalist discourses. He, however, does not point

41

to the common features regarding the oppressed groups including women and femininity in both the East and the West.

Julia Kristeva in her *Revolution in Poetic Language* (1974) and "Women's Time" (1978),[2] analyzes the relation of the nonmodern and modern as a relation of feminine and masculine, with the former representing the "semiotic" and the latter the "symbolic." Without trapping herself in the *aporia* of essentialism as in orientalist perspective, she outlines the nonreductionist ways of interactions between the two. From her point of view, these relations are multidimensional, where every participant bears simultaneously a dominating/dominated role, and where the relations between the West/the East, metropolice colony, developed/developing are similar to gender relations.

The obstacles of a cultural interaction based on a mutual understanding might be considered from three aspects: temporal opposition, lingual oppositions, and the (sociopsychological) problem of repression. The first two problems are concerned with the cultural oppositions of civilizations as fixed and essential identities. The third problem is concerned with the repression of inner diversities and oppositions. It is concerned with the fact that certain civilizations are oppressing their inner diversities as anarchical, centrifugal to their existence.

TEMPORAL OPPOSITION

As a fundamental element of civilizations and cultures the concept of "time" constitutes one of the oppositions in cultural connections. It seems that different concepts of time in various cultures and overemphasis of one of these as the "civilization time," play an important role in any interaction. Referring to Nietzsche, Kristeva identifies two main concepts of time: first, the "cursive time" as linear, masculine; and second, the "monumental time " as cyclic, and biofamilial or somatic. The two concepts of time manifest themselves in the ways of life, especially in the rhythm of everyday life and natural and cultural ceremonies.

In the cultures based on cursive and paternal time, the emphasis is put on the rashness in everyday life, in cultural ceremonies like national autonomy, independence, revolution, and war, which are mainly historical and social. In the monumental, cyclic, somatic, and maternal time, however, the emphasis is placed on the ceremonies based on natural and seasonal change and equinox such as Iranian Noruz, Pentecost, Easter, carnivals, fashions, etc. Therefore, it seems that female subjectivity provides a specific measure that essentially retains repetition and eternity from among the multiple modalities of time known through the history of civilizations. On the one hand, there are cycles, gestations, and the eternal recurrence of a biological rhythm, which conforms to that of nature. On the other hand, and perhaps as a consequence, there is the massive presence of monumental temporality, without cleavage or escape, which has little to do with linear time.[3] As such, it seems that there is a similarity between this concept of time as suitable for the female subjectivity and the concept of time in archaic civilizations, since in both of them, time is an accurate, a cyclic, and a monumental concept.

Two concepts of time are not limited to certain cultures such as the West, but coexisted in different civilizations. A good example would be the idea of resurrection in Western and Eastern cultures, which is rooted in matriarchal mythologies and refers to the revitalization of plants and human beings by the help of the Earth-Mother. In the idea of resurrection, human time is similar to natural and earthly time, and consists of repetitions of eternal life and death. Basically, the emphasis on monumental and natural time in premodern cultures is actually in contrast with linear and historical time of modern cultures. The differences between the two are being regarded in a way that the Oriental cultures are essentially different. Also, they are considered as societies for a long time in a "mythological slumber."[4] This seems to be one of the main obstacles to mutual understanding.

Further examination (especially from Kristevian point of view) would reveal not only the value of the two concepts, but also the interdependency of different concepts of time as the representation of the psychological and cultural growth of human individual and societies. The cursive time, according to Kristeva, is "a project, teleology, linear and prospective" concept; it is the "time as departure, progression and arrival. In other words, it is the time of history," the "obsessional" paternal, or civilization time.[5] For, it is established on the basis of repression of the Oedipal desires (in developing this concept, Kristeva uses Lacanian psychology, while connecting it to the social transformations of modernity as a process of transformation of social psychology). The cursive time is the time of language and sentences consisting of starts and ends, nouns, verbs, descriptions, and as expressing certain ideas and meanings.

The monumental time, in contrast, belonging to the pre-Oedipal phase, and as a maternal and cyclic time based on natural and bodily developments has a close relationship with instinctual desires. As such, the monumental time is in fact developed on the basis of earth and place; it has originated in agricultural civilizations in whose mythologies earth and women possess sacred positions. Then, "when evoking the destiny of women, one thinks more of the *space* generating and forming the human species than of *time*, becoming or history." According to Kristeva, this concept is what Plato in *Timaeus* designated as the *aporia* of *chora* (place), referring to the atomists of the time.

They contrasted metaphysics and God as abstract, unearthly ideas with the nourishing space and material origin of the universe.[6] Time in this meaning is rather a space-time whose rhythm is determined by nature. On the basis of this very interpretation, Luce Irigaray compares the idea of the Platonic cave and coming out of it with the exiting from the mother's womb to achieve lightness, virility, mental perfection, and *episteme*. According to Irigaray, this process became possible only through negating the maternal and feminine.[7] The same idea plays an essential role in Machiavelli's political theory as well as Cartesian philosophy. For Machiavelli "virtue" is actually a capacity of seducing Moira, the goddess of fate as a woman. In Cartesian philosophy the rational subject has been established in contrast with the somatic.

More than anything, Kristeva's interpretation of time shows the inseparability of the two kinds of times and the importance and relevance of both concepts in the development of civilizations and cultures as well as their rituals and customs. In cultural interactions, especially in the authoritative kind, these two concepts of time could be regarded as problematic. However, there is no binary opposition. The two concepts of time originated with each other without necessarily being phases in the cultural, rational development of the soul (e.g., as in Hegel's philosophy). They indeed are coexisting, interdependent and nonfixed identities. From this point of view, civilizational and maternal time is not rigidly fixed. Fixation is rooted in the repressive character of our language, which eliminates and ignores the complexity of meanings and phenomena. This happens even when we speak of differences and praise diversities. But even in the symbolic order, namely the order of father and logocentrism, as Derrida and Lacan put it, we can think of diversities not as oppositional, but as intertwined and complex. However, on the basis of colonial relations, it is the linear time which is mostly relevant. On the basis of this concept of time, Eastern cultures and civilizations are regarded as retrogressive, backward looking, undeveloped, etc., whereas Western ones as progressive, forward looking and developed. In such an interpretation, the incommensurable qualities of civilizations come to be annulled. Rather, they are reduced to the commensurable qualities.

Eastern civilizations, hence, are regarded as incapable of adapting themselves to the linear times, while the West and modern civilizations are regarded as the innovators of the linear time, which is cultural rather than natural. The East has been considered as having been caught in the naturally mythological slumber and as needing to be awakened by the West. This is the difference of concepts of time, which is reflected in the progress of one culture and the backwardness of the other. Obviously this kind of thinking is rooted in the idea of domination of both nature and women as Bacon formulated it at the dawn of modernity.

LINGUISTIC OPPOSITION

All logical and nonlogical interactions including dialogue of civilizations make use of and are developed in language. Different linguistic understanding consists of different subjectivities, meanings, and language foundations. The word "language" here is used in a broad meaning, that is, a system of thoughts and practices, associated with every culture or "discourse," in Foucault's terminology.

Intercivilizational and intercultural dialogues face the very problem of discursive and language differences. As in the case of time, language opposition concerns and has close relationship with the (nonessential) difference of masculine and feminine language, or at least implies cultural conflicts. Needless to say, as in the case of time, no essentialist theory, either feminist or other, can contribute to theorization of a relational concept like "civilizational dialogue."

According to Kristeva, inspired by Bakhtin, language itself is characterized as multiple rather than double. Bakhtin insisted on the polyphonic character of language, including different kinds of texts, speakers, and listeners. Considering the broad meaning of language, Kristeva argues for the complexity of language and suggests "polylogue" instead. She distinguishes between two related and overlapping forms of language, which are "semiotic" and "symbolic." Also, for Kristeva, the language analysis is always political. For, the speaking subject is a political or politicized subject. Therefore, the political process of signifying can be either semiotic, feminine, and almost anarchic, or symbolic, masculine, and systematic. In the first case, language is destabilizing and centrifugal against power relations, and in the second it is stabilizing and center-oriented.

The symbolic mode of language is a language of transparency, power, and conformity, the language of sociability. As Lacan puts it, it is the language of the father, of being involved in social life and of leaving behind the dependency on the mother, which a child has to learn in the process of upbringing. Therefore, the symbolic mode of language accords with patriarchal cultures, from which general moral principles have been abstracted. It is the language of science, taxonomy, grammar, newspapers, social rules, and authority. The semiotic mode of language, on the contrary, is the language of nature, which is connected to bodily female and maternal experiences. It is rooted in the pre-Oedipal phase of infant development. The term "semiotic" does not deal with signs. Rather it deals with the expressive language of art, music, and non-systematic experiences, such as babies' babble, before entering into the system of speaking like adults. "Semiotic" can be regarded as closer to "somatic." The semiotic mode of language, like female time, is dependent on *chora*, the nourishing, feeding, and maternal matrix.

At a first glance, it seems that these modes of language have nothing to do with each other, since they are independent and each of them, especially the symbolic one, is formed as a result of repression and sublimation. While the semiotic is repressed by the symbolic in the process of socialization, however, the subject is always *both* symbolic and semiotic.[8] And whereas the symbolic order is governed by the law of father, the semiotic is derived from chora and is rooted in childhood and infantile experiences. Indeed, as Kristeva following Lacan argues, "the speaking subject is always a split subject divided between unconscious and conscious motivations," between nature and culture. "Since physiological processes of speaking (the breath we have to take, the way tongues move around teeth, the way we sit, stand or hold a pen in order to speak or write) are derived from the body, speech itself constrained by nature."[9]

Given the two modes of language, each representing one side of the oppositions in the civilizational and cultural conflicts, Kristeva's comments can be useful in conceptualizing different modes of interaction. From this point of view, it seems that in a conflict, the semiotic which is represented by the archaic, premodern cultures is always against the symbolic, which is represented by modern cultures to form an essential, fixed binary opposition. Such an idea is expressed by Huntington, for instance, as the "clash of civilizations" or by some essentialist feminists as "eternal femininity" against masculinity. Such an interpretation is not limited to Western intellectuals. Iranian and Islamic philosophers like Avicenna and Sohrawardi have similar ideas (though according to them, and contrary to the Western intellectuals, the Orient has been reread positively and the Occident negatively). Avicenna interpreted the "Orient " (*sharq*) as the domain of light, sense, and familiarity and the "Occident" (*qharb*) as the land of darkness, reason, nostalgia, homesickness, exile, using the close meanings of words of *qharb* and *qhorbat* in the Arabic language. As such, *Ishraq* (Illumination) in Sohrawardi's philosophy refers to this very idea on the basis of which he named some of his treatises as *Al-Qessato al-Qhorbat al-Qharbia* (*The Story of the Occidental Homesickness*) and *hekmato al-eshraq* (*Philosophy of Illumination*).[10] However, this idea did not cause them to maintain a kind of similarity between femininity and Illumination, similar to Nietzsche's identification of woman with *Wahrheit* in *Beyond Good and Evil*. Regarding the Oriental pole as something more masculine than feminine, they are inspired by Plato whose philosophy has mostly guided Islamic philosophers. According to Nietzsche and Kristeva, the human being is "a being always in process and becoming," which can be applied to human historical and language products as well. Nevertheless, the semiotic and female part of civilizations, either in the Orient or in the Occident, is always oppressed and doomed to silence.

The idea of dialogue of civilizations implies a critique of the oppressive character of the world system as a symbolic order, which defines itself as a Western rational masculinized entity contra the Eastern sensual feminized Other. Therefore, the world system as a symbolic mode of language has been characterized as a binary opposition, which suppresses the semiotic and female as unnecessary and excessive while dispossessing it. Civilizations as texts are polyphonic rather than monophonic. So are the Western and Eastern civilizations. Therefore, survival of each civilization is dependent to its polyphonic character.

THE PROBLEM OF REPRESSION

This problem partly concerns the general psychological character of every civilization, which in Freud's account, is established on the basis of repression. Also, according to Kristeva, it is based upon the repression of chaotic *jouissance,* that is, female desire. It means that in the process of being civilized the rational masculinized (not masculine necessarily) subject has been celebrated and the feminized (not feminine necessarily) irrational object has been repressed.

Therefore, although opposing the Western culture and its suppression of differences and diversities, the very notion of dialogue still seems not very encouraging regarding the internally centrifugal semiotic discourses. It seems that even suppressed cultures and civilizations can be in turn internally oppressive by imposing silence on inner diversities. Indeed, this is where the idea of dialogue of civilizations and the critical attitudes within different civilizations and cultures are distinguished from each other. If a dia/polylogical approach is accepted not only among civilizational levels, but also among different kinds of attitudes within a certain culture, then this very idea will include different perspectives and lifestyles within a certain culture. Without recognizing the internal diversities among different groups within a society, dia/polylogue among different cultures would be reductionist, and a set of ideas and practices would be imposed on different attitudes. In other words, without enhancing more democratic interests among different levels of the societies, intercultural dialogue would not be of much use. For, in that case both sides will enter into the domineering symbolic language and repress the semiotic. This does not mean that an intercivilizational dialogue should be cancelled. Rather, what is needed is an emphasis on the interdependency of internal and external as well as the necessity of facilitating more capacities for the oppressed groups within a culture and civilization, while searching new ways of peaceful interactions among them.

This idea challenges certain kinds of Orientalist relations, and the domination of the symbolic, linear, and masculine over what has been considered semiotic, monumental, and feminine. If any kind of dia/polylogue among civilizations leads to the domination of the symbolic over the semiotic, to a monophonic kind of interaction, and to the oppression of the nonformal and nonlogical voices, it will be an agonistic battle over interests and power without leading to an instructive interaction. Furthermore, it is in part a problem of considering essential entities as being required for abstract generalizations in any kind of thinking. In that case, a presupposed abstract idea extends itself to the actual process of living. It means that on the basis of an abstract generalization, a certain practice is being shaped and is projected onto reality. The idea of dialogue like the "clash of civilizations" suffers from this very problem. Both of them presuppose a pregiven cultural entity. In both cases certain kinds of practices are supposed to represent certain identities and are projected onto the multiple realities. Such thinking oppresses the multiplicity of human lives. A good example would be the emphasis on veiling and traditional family values as the abstract symbols of being a good Muslim.

CONCLUSION

The first two oppositions, that is, the temporal and lingual oppositions, are concerned with the external and intercivilization relations, whereas the third one, that is the problem of repression of internal diversities, is concerned with set-backs of the internal interactions within a given civilization and culture. Accordingly, in the first and second oppositions, the idea of "dialogue" can be strongly critical of the current rules of the world system. It criticizes the essentialist as well as agonistic views dominant in the contemporary world politics. As such it deconstructs the presumption of eternal animosity of cultural identities and binary oppositions. This is also criticized by critical poststructuralists including the feminist theorists. The third view of dialogue, however, seems to be less critical of the preexisting structures of exclusion and seclusion within every civilization. Here the idea of "civilization" as an essentialist substance, either in the idea of "dialogue" or "conflict," is itself reinforcing the subjective and abstract notion of civilization and rejects the flexibility of cultures.

Therefore, without focusing on the Oedipal and symbolic modes of interaction in the idea of dialogue, which some philosophers like Michele Le Doeuff believe to be patriarchal in itself,[11] not much headway can be made in changing the symbolic and patriarchal order of political science. As previously mentioned, such a conception presupposes civilizations as fixed identities. This implies a kind of cultural relativism where power relations might be ignored. It might be similar in the case of existing patriarchal characteristics of any given culture. In this sense, the idea of dialogue by itself seems hardly able to remove the power relations that are embedded in the notion of "nature as a resource of culture" and "human being as a source of power." For this reason, its critical capabilities must be oriented toward finding new approaches to culture and nature as well as human relationships.

NOTES

1. See Edward W. Said, *Orientalism* (Harmondsworth: Penguin Books, 1978).

2. See Julia Kristeva, *Revolution in Poetic Language* (New York: Columbia: University Press, 1984), and "Women's Time" (1978) in Ann Garry and Marilyn Pearsall, eds., *Women, Knowledge, Reality* (New York: Routledge, 1996).

3. Kristeva, "Women's Time," 64.

4. Fred Dallmayr, *Beyond Orientalism* (Albany: State University of New York Press, 1996), 158.

5. Kristeva, "Women's Time," 65.

6. "Women's Time," 63.

7. Eric Matthews, *French Philosophy* (Oxford: Oxford University Press, 1996), 191.

8. Kristeva, *Revolution in Poetic Language*, 24.

9. Ruth Robbins, *Literary Feminisms* (London: Macmillan, 2000), 127.

10. See Majid Fakhry, *A History of Islamic Philosophy* (London: Longman, 1983).

11. Michelle Le Doeuff, "Women in Philosophy," in Mary Evans, ed., *Feminism*, vol. 4 (New York: Routledge, 2001), 109–35.

Chapter Seven

Dialogue in the Virtual World: The Impact of Communications and Information Technologies on the Dialogue among Civilizations

Ahmad Golmohammadi

INTRODUCTION

Pivotal communication and information are among the prominent features of modern life. Today, the dizzying pace of advancement in communications and information technologies, especially the Internet, is a fact that cannot be averted, while the cost of communication continues to drop at an unimaginable rate. It appears that in this battle "time" will eventually be forced into an unconditional surrender, or in the words of Harvey face inescapable "destruction." The same fate is also awaiting "space" which is shrinking at an unprecedented rate. Communications technologies, through their tinkering with time and space, are giving birth to a small and compact world. This digital world is housed within instruments of few-centimeter dimensions, such as mobile handsets, or those of slightly larger size, such as monitors or digital television sets. The lightening pace of developments in the field of communications has given rise to another characteristic of today's world, pivotal information. What is flowing through vast communication networks is a massive amount of information, which is mounting by the second. This furious process of production, distribution, and utilization of information has turned today's world into an information-centered world.

COMMUNICATIONS AND INFORMATION TECHNOLOGIES

These communications and information technologies have impacted various aspects of individual and social life through different means, a prominent example of which is the creation of the virtual and digital space (cyberspace). Though the extent of these influences varies from one society to the next, it

51

is safe to say that no society has been left untouched by these technologies. Today, culture, economy, politics, and other aspects of social life have, more or less, been affected by communications and information technologies. These varied and extensive influences have given rise to a vast body of research, which has focused on the various consequences of these types of technologies. In the closing years of the twentiethth and the early years of the twenty-first century, the effects of communication and information technologies came to take center stage in the works of economists, sociologists, cultural scholars, and other researchers in the field of social sciences, who are still grappling with the various aspects of this phenomenon and its ramifications.

In the meantime, the political and cultural impacts of these technologies, especially the Internet, have come to assume added interest. The researchers and those active in the field are attempting to find answers to the questions relating to the influence of communication and information technologies on democracy, government, gender, ethnicity, identity, and other prevailing factors of political life. In other words, they are trying to determine what possibilities and limitations are brought about by the use of these technologies as regards a sounder political life—especially when it comes to changing the factors that tend to limit or distort "verbal communication" and level of adherence to democratic rules and human rights.

The question whose answer is the focus of the present paper, in fact, relates to one of the indices of a sound political and social life and how it is impacted by communications and information technologies: how do communication and information technologies affect the possibility and conditions of dialogue and thus the dialogue among cultures? Do these technologies provide a suitable ground for dialogue (of cultures) or do they impose a set of obstacles and limitations on it?

A preliminary response to the above question is that these communications and information technologies constrain and distort dialogue and thus the dialogue of cultures. In fact, the factor that gives order to the data and guides the lines of reasoning of the present discussion is the theory that communications and information technologies, owing to their creation of a general domain with certain characteristics, limit and distort the dialogue of cultures.

However, the theory's negative view of these technologies' detrimental influence on the dialogue among cultures should not lead to a denial of their positive aspects. It goes without saying that communications and information technologies have the potential of creating opportunities for dialogue and thus dialogue among cultures, which has become an issue of serious discussion. For instance, it is safe to say that the Internet, through providing unprecedented possibilities for free reproduction, real-time dissemination, and fundamental decentralization, has, more than in any other time, facilitated dialogue and dialogue among cultures. However, in the present study, in spite of our acknowledgment of the positive aspects of the Internet and the related technologies, we will only focus on their negative and limiting effects, since knowledge is the prerequisite of any effort in their alleviation.

Before we enter into the discussion of the link between communications and information technologies and the dialogue of cultures we need to clarify the key concepts of the above theory. These concepts include communications and information technologies, the virtual public domain (cyberspace), dialogue, and the dialogue of cultures. Though the number and the scopes of meaning of these terms are rather limited and there exists little disagreement with regard to their connotations and applications, any attempt at providing a more accurate definition and delimitation of them would contribute to a deeper understanding of the subject and would guard against possible misconceptions.

As is implied by the term itself, from a simple and nontechnical perspective, communications and information technologies refer to the tools and methods which facilitate a mediated communication between two or more people. Though there exist a wide range of these tools and methods, in the present discussion we will only focus on their most widespread and effective types, i.e., telephone, fax, and, most important of all, the Internet.

Cyberspace, derived from the Greek word *kyber* (to guide), means a "guidable space" and was coined by William Gibson in his novel *Neuromancer* (1984). In *Neuromancer* cyberspace refers to a guidable digital space of computer networks accessible to users, or to a visual, colored, electronic space within which individuals conduct their information exchange.[1] In other words, cyberspace is an imaginary space created by communications and information technologies. The space thus created is an expansive one, readily accessible to any individual or group equipped with requisite conditions and tools. Therefore, this space is, in reality, a type of public sphere to which Habermas refers to as a domain for dialogue that is free from coercion and is based on a practical agreement. In the present discussion cyberspace is considered as a public sphere, of the virtual type rather than the real type. Thus, entering it and conducting a dialogue within its boundaries call for different methods and conditions than those of a real public sphere.

It should also be borne in mind that by the dialogue of cultures we have in view its broadest possible connotation. If dialogue is to be considered as any exchange of meaning or meaningful signs, the dialogue of cultures would imply any type of exchange or transaction of cultural elements belonging to various cultures with (1) a deep cognizance of cultural diversity or the existence of multiple, varied cultures; (2) the capacity to be open to criticism; (3) and willingness to coexist and mingle with other cultures. In other words, only those transactions and exchanges qualify as cultural dialogues, which contribute to openness to cultural criticism and to cultural integration and coexistence.

DIALOGUE OF CULTURES

After these preliminary remarks it is now time to elaborate the link between these two variables and to see in what manner communications and information technologies distort and circumscribe the dialogue of cultures. As was indicated at the beginning of our discussion, the present paper intends to prove that this link and this limiting and distorting character arises from the virtual public sphere created by these communications and information technologies. In spite of its expansive scope for the flow and exchange of a vast array of cultural signs, this virtual public sphere does at the same time act to constrain and warp.

This limiting and distorting effect arises from the nature, structure, and qualities of the virtual public sphere. The public sphere is characterized by a structure and qualities that limit the possibility of its entrance and distort dialogue within its confines. Though this sphere has the potential of serving as a domain for exchanges that would raise the awareness of individuals and groups with regard to cultural diversity and make them more open to criticism and cultural criticism, and contribute to a broader context of coexistence and cultural integration, there are aspects of this public sphere relating to its structure and nature that tend to weaken that potential. The identification of these constraining qualities and the elaboration of their limiting and distorting mechanisms is the main concern of the present paper.

In general, these qualities or limiting factors with negative effects on the dialogue of cultures may be divided into two groups. The first are those that limit access to the public sphere and prevent the individual and groups hailing from various cultures, or other representatives of these cultures, from gaining entrance to the cyberspace or public sphere. The second category includes those factors that in one way or another prevent the exchanges and dialogues that lead to cultural awareness and integration as well as to openness to criticism within the framework of the public sphere, or those factors that disrupt the process of such exchanges. The first set of factors relate to the prerequisites of dialogue, while the second group affects the process of dialogue itself. Here, we will discuss both categories.

As was mentioned above, the first set of factors are those that in one way or another reduce the possibility for the representatives of various cultures having access to the virtual public sphere. In other words, these types of factors stand in the way of existing cultures' equal access to the public sphere and prevent some from ever being heard at all. This restriction, in turn, is given rise by two factors.

The first factor pertains to the requisite facilities and equipment for entering the virtual public sphere and participating in cultural dialogue. Though entrance to the actual public sphere is also, to a considerable degree, dependent on access to facilities and means—which however are of a less sophisticated nature—whose uneven distribution adversely affects participation and dialogue in the actual public sphere, the efficacy of such facilities becomes more pronounced when it comes to the public sphere of the virtual kind, for here the tools are considerably more sophisticated and expensive. For instance, without a computer and a telephone line with Internet access it is impossible to enter cyberspace in order to take part in the extensive process of cultural exchange.

Though cyberspace is usually viewed as a space open to all who wish to enter it, in reality it is not as accessible as it may seem at first sight, since the requisite tools are unevenly distributed. This lopsided distribution is due to geographical, economic, political (subnational, national, regional, and international), and social divisions. The process of formation and reproduction, and the effects of this inequality are extremely complex. Nonetheless, it is safe to say that today the required tools for accessing the virtual public sphere are unequally distributed among the people of various geographical areas, countries, cultures, social strata, and genders.[2] This has caused some researchers to speak of cyberspace as having an elitist nature. In the words of D. J. Hess: "Cyberspace is a kind of space that belongs to the elite and is a playground for the rich."[3]

The second factor is the requisite skills for entering the virtual public sphere. In case of a fairly equitable distribution of the required tools and facilities for entering the virtual public sphere, access would still depend on the ability to utilize such means. The more inequitable the distribution of these skills the more uneven the participation in the virtual public sphere will be.

Though the same factor can be extended to the public sphere, its effects are much more pronounced in the case of the virtual public sphere. While it is true that widespread efforts are underway to simplify access to communications and information technologies, including the necessary tools and skills for entering the virtual public sphere, today the (effective) use of these tools calls for a certain level of competency. It is also a fact that the use of communications and information technologies has become as simple as using one's native language, but a minimum level of knowledge remains indispensable for accessing the virtual public sphere through these technologies.

The distribution of these requisite tools is also inequitable, a fact that arises not only because of cultural barriers but also because of class and gender as well as national and political inequalities.[4] In many instances noncultural inequalities are matched by cultural inequalities or serve to accentuate the latter. Thus, as a rule, the level of competency among individuals and groups is much higher in Western cultures (European and American) than among those of other cultures.[5]

Therefore, it is a fact that the distribution of requisite skills for entering the virtual public sphere is just as uneven as is that of the necessary tools and facilities. These factors are restrictive in that they, in one way or another, hamper equal access to the public sphere for representatives of various cultures. Under such circumstances the virtual public sphere, which is an immensely vast domain capable of encompassing the symbols and representatives of a wide spectrum of cultures transforms into a space monopolized by a handful of cultures where many cultures become marginalized or excluded altogether.

A VIRTUAL PUBLIC SPHERE?

It goes without saying that such restriction also serves to hinder dialogue among cultures. Were we to consider the exchange of cultural symbols as a key element of dialogue—since it serves to raise the level of awareness with regard to the diversity of the existing cultures—it would soon become obvious that the virtual public sphere would be a less than satisfactory medium for such cultural exchanges, owing to its restrictive characteristics in terms of providing equal access to all cultures. In other words, in the virtual public sphere the presence and symbols of some cultures are much more prominent than those of others, a fact that has an adverse effect on the awareness of cultural diversity and, in turn, on dialogue among cultures.

The second set of factors which characterize the virtual public sphere and which have a less than salutary effect on the dialogue of cultures have to do with the nature of dialogue which takes place within this particular sphere. While the negative effects of the first set of factors pertain to the fact that they restrict access for various cultures, the adverse consequences of the second group arise from the fact that they tend to limit and distort dialogue itself. The first group of factors limits the facilities and conditions of entrance to the virtual public sphere and participation in dialogue, but the constrictive and distorting effects of the second set of factors come to fore in the process of the dialogue itself. Now we need to determine these factors and the mechanism through which they limit and distort dialogue.

The first factor belonging to the second group of limiting and distorting factors may be termed aversion to diversity. In spite of the fact that various cultures are not equally represented in the cyberspace or virtual public sphere, it is safe to say that cyberspace does, to a certain extent, embrace the elements and symbols of a wide range of cultures. Although the virtual public sphere falls short of being a true representative of all existing cultures, it does represent a fairly reasonable number of them. However, the fact remains that this limited and minimal diversity is insufficient as far as prodding individuals into engaging in cultural dialogue, especially in terms of becoming aware of the true diversity of various cultures.

Research indicates that some difficulties relating to the virtual public sphere, especially those of the processing of information, prevent access to the new and different areas of virtual space. Thus, many contend that though it is easier to find friends in the virtual world it nonetheless is more difficult to meet different people. In such a world people normally go straight to where they can find discussions that are to their liking and thus get to meet people who share their interests and sensibilities.[6]

Therefore, cyberspace, similar to the real world, is not a place where you would "enter into an amazing network of people, places, and new thoughts and ideas." There, an individual "does not encounter people of various societies and modes of life" owing to the existence of a multitude of individuals and guises. In such a space there may exist diversity, however, this much is clear that the ordinary man will not come in touch with that diversity, since with one brain, one job, one partner, one family, and one life no one will find the opportunity to enter the diverse world.[7] In this way, the virtual public sphere constricts and distorts the dialogue among cultures, for it fails to provide a suitable ground for the exchange of cultural signs that lead to an enhanced knowledge of cultural diversity.

Another factor that confines and distorts the virtual public sphere and thus the dialogue among cultures is the presence of a kind of anxiety that attends the digital communications or dialogue within the virtual world. In other words, in order for a real dialogue of cultures to take place—a dialogue attended by an awareness of cultural diversity, cultural criticism and openness to such critique, and cultural integration—there should not only be a full-fledged exchange of signs, but there should also be the opportunity for thoughtful reflection about these signs, a condition hardly met by the virtual public sphere.[8]

At first glance, cyberspace appears to be a suitable place for a comprehensive exchange of cultural signs and their contemplation. However, the reality is quite different. It may be the case that in cyberspace communication links are never broken, but this in itself is no guarantee for an inclusive exchange of cultural signs. More important is the fact that though there is no technical factor compelling individuals into quick and simultaneous reaction, the truth is that digital communication, especially via the Internet, gives rise to a sort of anxiety. In other words, the Internet provides the opportunity for real-time communication and thus urges us to respond immediately.[9]

The anxiety and simultaneity associated with the virtual public sphere makes it an unsuitable medium for dialogue and therefore one that restricts and distorts dialogue among cultures. Dialogue among cultures consists of an exchange of cultural signs accompanied by cultural criticism and openness. However, if the above sense of anxiety and compulsion to immediate reaction preclude the possibility of contemplation of such cultural signs such a dialogue would barely result in cultural criticism and openness.

Communication within the virtual public sphere is not only characterized by simultaneity, speed, and anxiety but is marked by an inordinate amount of freedom which is responsible for some of the restriction and distortion associated with this public sphere. Though freedom is an indispensable aspect of any wholesome and constructive dialogue, the freedom in cyberspace is of the unbridled type, i.e., the freedom to ignore others and to turn a deaf ear to what they have to say.

This type of freedom is the consequence of a set of technical and other characteristics of the virtual public sphere that may be referred to using labels such as anonymity, the relative impossibility to trace, and thus immunity from legal prosecution. Today, the technical and nontechnical aspects of the structure of virtual public sphere provide the users with the opportunity to escape the scrutiny of various monitoring systems. For instance, one may use the Internet in such a manner that it would be extremely difficult or costly to track one down. This renders the virtual public sphere into a vast domain where one can roam incognito and express his heart's desire without having to take into account its legal ramifications.

It goes without saying that such anonymity, impossibility to trace, and immunity from prosecution impact negatively on dialogue and dialogue among cultures. They provide the grounds for the transformation of the virtual public sphere into a domain for the expression of extremist views and aspirations. Within such a domain the freedom of expression loses its true meaning and the commitment to this lofty value comes under threat. In other words, the freedom of expression in the virtual public sphere becomes the freedom to speak, i.e., to say whatever, without any obligation to listen.

But dialogue is made up of the two constituent elements of speaking and listening, both of which play an equally significant role. If the individuals or cultures existing within the virtual public sphere have the ability or choose not to hear each other out then dialogue would be of no consequence. Under such circumstances the presence within the virtual public sphere of the signs of various cultures will do little to contribute to an enhancement of knowledge regarding the diversity of cultures or to the development of cultural criticism, openness, or integration. In sum, this characteristic of the virtual public sphere, i.e., unlimited and unaccountable freedom, is another factor that restricts and distorts dialogue among cultures.

The above factors and characteristics, which may be expanded beyond what was discussed in the present paper,[10] are among the major factors and characteristics which limit and distort dialogue and the dialogue of cultures within the virtual public sphere or cyberspace, since they, in various forms and degrees, prevent the exchange of signs from various cultures, an exchange with the potential of contributing to an awareness of cultural diversity, criticism and openness, and integration.

Some of these factors and characteristics, e.g., the uneven distribution of facilities and conditions for entry to the virtual public sphere, preclude various cultures from having an equal degree of presence, a fact that restricts and distorts the knowledge of the number and scope of various cultures. Another group of factors create a situation where individuals become unable or unwilling to encounter other cultures within a virtual world of limited cultural diversity. And finally, there are factors that distort the nature of dialogue itself by transforming it into a unidirectional flow incapable of providing cultural awareness, criticism, openness, or integration.

The thrust of all these considerations underscores the central claim advanced in the present paper: that communications and information technologies, through their creation of a virtual public sphere, constrict and distort dialogue and, by extension, the dialogue among cultures, a fact that, however, should not result in ignoring the numerous contributions made by these technologies.

NOTES

1. See M. Dodge and R. Kitchin, *Mapping Cyberspace* (London: Routledge, 2000), 1.
2. B. D. Loader, ed., *The Cyberspace Divided* (London: Routledge, 1998), 35–56.
3. D. J. Hess, *Science and Technology in a Multicultural World* (New York: Columbia University Press, 1995), 116.
4. A. G. Wilhelm, *Democracy in the Digital Age* (New York: Routledge, 2000), 6–7.
5. P. C. Clement, *The State of the Net* (New York: McGraw-Hill, 1998).
6. H. Rheingold, "The Virtual Community," *Unte Reader* (March–April 1995), 62.
7. M. Kadi, "Welcome to Cyberia," *Unte Reader* (March–April 1995), 59.

8. J. M. Streck, "Pulling the Plug on Electronic Town Meetings," in R. Toulouse and T. Luke, eds., *The Politics of Cyberspace* (London: Routledge, 1998), 44.

9. C. Stoll, *Silicone Snake Oil* (New York: Doubleday, 1995), 167.

10. See C. Calhoun, eds., *Habermas and the Public Sphere* (Cambridge, MA: MIT Press, 1992); and C. Dunlop and R. Kling, eds., *Computerization and Controversy* (New York: Academic Press, 1991).

Part Two

INTERNATIONAL RELATIONS THEORY AND CIVILIZATIONAL DIALOGUE

Chapter Eight

Dialogue of Civilizations and International Relations

Seyed Kazem Sajjadpour

I would like to begin by thanking my colleagues in the Centre for Civilizational Dialogue, especially Dr. Manoochehri for organizing this discussion on the relationship between Political Science and Civilizational Dialogue. At this gathering, I think my job should be to elaborate how international relations theories can be useful and relevant to the study of civilizational dialogue. Although I am not an expert on this subject, I will try my best to focus on this topic, mostly by raising three questions: How is the study of international relations theories relevant to the study of civilizational dialogue? Why is the constructive theory useful for the study of civilizational dialogue? And what are the future prospects of constructivism and civilizational dialogue? Before going to the main topic I must apologize for my English as the translation of some technical words into Persian might be difficult; but I think in an international event like this, English would be a better channel and medium to express myself.

Regarding my first question of how the study of international relations theories is relevant to the study of civilizational dialogue, I believe that we have a "dual difficulty of structural ambiguity," a concept that I call also a "creative ambiguity." Let me explain first what the function of a theory is. A theory, in international relations as well as in social sciences, has three basic functions based on the positivist and behaviorist approaches, namely, to describe, to explain, and to predict the social phenomenon and issues related to the social life. However, we are aware of the fact that these are traditional functions of theory, which are under attack.

Positivism itself is under attack because it cannot produce the proper answers even by using different theories, especially when it comes to prediction. Furthermore, the attacks are more acute when we look at the arguments of postmodernism and other critical arguments that all these theories have built-in presumptions, hence are unable to explain the reality and are designed for especial interests. Since they are designed for special purposes, they reflect certain tendencies rather than the objective examination of truth and reality. Therefore, when we look at the above three traditional functions and their challenges, we may say that the functions of a theory are ambiguous. Instead of choosing a specific definition, we may come to the conclusion that theory is, to be sure, interesting and useful, only its definition is subject to interpretation. However, the definition of a particular theory depends on which school you start with and what orientation you have. I think it is fair to conclude now that there are many definitions of a theory and that theory by itself is ambiguous. But we must underline the gain that it is useful. We should reduce our expectation that theories have to predict everything and analyze all dimensions. I think all theories regardless of their orientations, backgrounds, and interests can be useful in understanding realities of international relations, keeping in mind that we are not escaping from the ambiguity dimension.

Now, it seems proper to say something about the concept of civilizational dialogue. I find that this concept is ambiguous too. Some questions may be raised in this regard: (a) Is it a theory? My answer will be "no," although it has some elements of a theory. (b) Is it a policy? My response will be, of course, it might be, but it is not a classical policy. (c) Is it an intellectual policy with a lot of novelty? Is it a paradigm? Is it a concept? My answer will be positive but one should be aware about the concept and rationality behind this. (d) Is it an idea? Is it a subject? I would say "yes." Is it a process? I would say: may be.

How does this theory or idea relate to practice? When we look at this dimension, we find a list of at least nine different definitions of civilizational dialogue and probable answers to all of these questions would be "yes or no," "may be" and "can be." In other words, they do not have a definite answer. Thus I can conclude that they are ambiguous. Regardless of all the ambiguities in this concept or notion, I think at least two dimensions are clear. First, the goal and the end of civilizational dialogue: it is a goal-oriented process or concept which is to prevent clash. The second dimension is that, for the first time in international relations which are traditionally dominated by state actors or powers, we have a new level of analysis, i.e., civilizational level which is interesting, regardless of all the difficulties in defining civilizations and their boundaries.

I would conclude the first question simply by saying that the concepts of theory and civilizational dialogue have ambiguities, which make them, in a way, a good subject for political science and international relations. Because of the ambiguities along with its utilities, it can lead us to creativity and to strive for one important goal: to prevent clashes. However, the ambiguities can be subjected to different interpretations and conceptualizations. Thus, with due attention to this dual ambiguity, but being creative, let me go to the second question: How is constructive theory useful to the study of civilizational dialogue?

I believe that constructivist theories can be used to explain, expand, and operationalize civilizational dialogue better than others in international relations theory. Before going into details to this specific question, I would like to underline the fact that all international relations theories without exceptions are state-centric and none of them can be exempted from being state-centric. At the same time I should say something about "anarchy" which is the assumption of international relations theories according to realists: states should manage anarchy. When we shift from realism to critical theories, the idea is that anarchy is what states make. Therefore, states are still the main subject. Regardless of the fact that civilizational dialogue is not completely state-centric, we know that it is also not without being somehow related to states. Civilizations and states have mutual relationships, although this has not been clearly defined. Concluding this point I would suggest that you will face difficulty in applying all international relations theories to the study of civilizational dialogue because in one way or the other, they are very focused on states. Constructivism can be helpful partially if not completely in this process. The main focus of realism is power, pure or naked. But if anarchy is what the states make, states can make civilizational dialogue too.

Constructivism is about how states create, make, or construct anarchy in order to get benefits. There are three elements of constructivism which can be used in our analysis: *Flexibility:* constructivism is flexible because it is not structural, deterministic, and fatalistic. There is a degree of flexibility when you use the constructivist theories, which is very useful and can be applied by states or nonstate actors to play, to construct and to change. *Subjectivity:* civilizational dialogue is about subjectivity. It forms another dimension of constructive theory, which is about ideas, about thinking, and about how to go beyond the objectivity and rigid realities. I think constructivist theories also talk about making situations and agents that can have some paradigms, notions, and views and can construct and impose them on reality. *Identity:* it is a third dimension, which is useful in constructivist theory and is crucial in civilizational dialogue. Regardless of ambiguity, civilizational dialogue is about civilizational identity. This is based on a cooperative dimension of civilizational identity and not necessarily conflict. We can also use different instruments of civilizations to construct a new global identity. President Khatami, I believe, was talking about the creation and construction of a global identity, which has elements of civilization, culture, and so on. This global identity can be constructed and can be used for peaceful goals and ends.

Thus, I think constructivism can be helpful at least partially in the study of international relations and partially in civilizational dialogue by stressing the role of agents more strongly than other theories. Of course, these agents in normal constructivist theory are still states, but we should go beyond states and look at the role of different agents. If we use constructivism in international relations for expanding the conceptual horizon of civilizational dialogue, we must be attentive to the role of agents.

Regarding the third and final question—what is the prospect for the future?— my colleagues have already mentioned the context in which different theories have evolved. I think all international relations theories and concepts are the by-products of their time, such as "realism" was the by-product of World War II, "liberalism" was the by-product of interdependence of the seventies, and "constructivism" a by-product of the cold war. "Civilizational dialogue" also emerged in the context of clashes, which have ethnic and cultural backgrounds. Therefore, I believe that the context is very important for the study of international relations theory. To know this in today's context I would put forward the example of the new administration in the United States, which claims that they have a new set of theories in international relations.

Here I must mention that the Bush administration is the most militarized administration in U.S. history. Its orientation can be seen in terms of the budget it has allocated which is more than a billion dollar a day for military affairs. The U.S. administration has been challenging the basic norms of international law and dominating all the discussions in international relations. If we read the journals of American political theories these days, we find a return to realism, in its very stark form, for instance, to the use of military force, regardless of global resistance and opposition. I read a quotation from Richard Perle's recent writing where he challenges all the peace activists: *"We liberated the totality of Iraqi people."* I am not going to discuss the Iraqi issue but I am highlighting it because I am sure there is a return of power politics in a very old-fashioned way and even a direct colonial presence.

Thus, in this situation where is the role of international relations theory and civilizational dialogue? I imagine that this return to realism would have its backlashes and cannot be the paramount notion of international relations. It may change regimes militarily but not socially or culturally. That is why I think a very interesting division has started. You may see very clearly the new needs in the world, i.e., the need for not using force, the need for dialogue, and for construction of new identities. Finally, the civilizational dialogue after a short span of this realist militarism will emerge, of course with modifications and I hope with more clarity.

So, to conclude, I think international relations theory, especially constructivist theories can be used for expanding our conceptual horizon of civilizational dialogue regardless of all the ambiguities; the horizon seems better in the future than what it is today.

Chapter Nine

The Evolution in the Conflictual Foundation of the Science of International Relations

Hossein Salimi

Some questions in the field of political thought defy ultimate answers. Attempts at their resolution remain unconvincing and thus they continue to be posed afresh with ever-increasing urgency. The following is one such question: Does the possibility of arriving at a shared understanding of politics and of the political world exist? Put differently: Is it possible for those from varied geographical and political backgrounds to reach a common understanding of politics and the political process through the employment of uniform methods? Do certain assumptions derived from the circumstances of time and place underlie the mental outlook of the students of politics? To what extent do the assumptions of thinkers about the nature of man and politics affect their ideas? And finally, are not the conflictual foundations of the science of international relations an indication of a particular epistemological approach?

Obviously, providing responses to all these questions exceeds the limited scope of a single article. Nonetheless, the mere statement of them draws our attention to the fact that, at the threshold of the twenty-first century, the notion of the dialogue of civilizations has entered the mainstream parlance of international relations at a time when new ways of thinking about international affairs are supplanting the traditional and classical modes of understanding of these topics. In fact, it may be claimed that the classical approach in the field of politics and international relations, which manifests itself in the form of "realism," is founded upon a particular answer to the question posed here. This happens at a time when new approaches in the area of political science provide a wide range of answers to the question of understanding and perception. In this article, we aim to prove that the classical approach to international relations, which falls within the realist paradigm, is based on the following epistemological principles:

1. The political reality is external to the mind and is susceptible to perception by all through the employment of scientific methods; and the discipline resulting from this scientific endeavor is similar for all its practitions.
2. According to the classical approach, man is a self-oriented creature pursuing its own interests and security, and the basis of political relations is that of conflict, disagreement, and war. But in new and different approaches the foundation of the relations between societies may be based on an exchange of meanings rather than on the conflict of interests. This is a major development taking place in the field of political thought and action and one with the potential of creating the intellectual background for the wider reception of the idea of dialogue of civilizations within the emerging intellectual milieu.

Here, we will make an attempt at searching for these notions through various theories of international relations.

CLASSICAL REALISM AND THE UNDERSTANDING OF POLITICS

The two principal notions underlying the present paper may be found in the views of the majority of realist thinkers in the field of politics, i.e., belief in the external nature of reality and the possibility of its common understanding, and the self-oriented and interest-seeking nature of humans and their innate confrontation and perpetual conflict over interests.

If we take Thucydides as the pioneer of the realist approach in ancient Greece, we would find these two notions reflected in his renowned *History of the Peloponnesian War*. Thucydides was of the view that there exists an underlying rule in relations among states, one that is commonly accessible to all humans. He makes explicit mention of an enduring law in the dealings among governments that is founded upon the notion of struggle for power and interests. To him, speaking of justice and equitable arrangements in the relations between states is meaningless, since the weaker states are cognizant of the necessity to cave in to the demands of their more powerful rivals and the latter are well aware of their dominant position. Implied in this view of the Geek historian is the idea that these relations are essentially conflictual and interest-centered and, therefore, it is impossible to arrive at a realistic and true assessment of the political relations among the nations without taking cognizance of this overarching principle. Of course, there are those who consider Thucydides's views as merely hinting at a realist outlook that, they claim, only dates from the modern period when the science of international relations began to make its first appearance in the thoughts of Thomas Hobbes.

Hobbes holds a mechanistic view of man and society, which to him are like so many modern man-made machines and instruments. This outlook is clearly evidenced in the opening pages of his *Leviathan*:

> For what is the heart but a spring, and the nerves but so many strings, and the joints but so many wheels, giving motion to the whole body, such as was intended by the artificer. Art goes yet further, imitating that rational and most excellent work of nature, man. For by art is created that great Leviathan called a commonwealth or state, which is but an artificial man; though, of greater stature and strength than the natural, for whose protection and defense it was intended, and in which the sovereignty is an artificial soul, as giving life and motion to the whole body.[1]

By way of this analogy, Hobbes attempts to equate social products with natural products and to prove the former just as susceptible to being produced and just as capable of becoming the subject of objective understanding as the latter. According to Hobbes, social and historical phenomena are similar to those of nature, in that they can be objectively understood, an understanding that can then be extended to others who would come to an equal understanding of them. In other words, to Hobbes the external reality of natural phenomena is the same as that of human actions, a fact that may be extended to their analysis. As noted by Hobbes:

> The register of knowledge of fact is called history. Whereof there be two sorts: one called natural history, which is the history of such facts, or effects of nature as have no dependence on man's will; such as are the histories of metals, plants, animals, regions, and the like. The other is civil history, which is the history of the voluntary actions of men in commonwealths.[2]

Thus, in Hobbes's opinion, humans are equal in terms of the possibility of having equal access to knowledge, with one proviso:

> No discourse whatsoever can end in absolute knowledge of fact, past or to come. For, as for the knowledge of fact, it is originally sense and ever after memory. And for the knowledge of consequence—which I have said before, is called science—it is not absolute, but conditional.[3]

The knowledge arrived at by man is conditional, but it is objective and capable of expansion and communication to others. According to Hobbes, this type of knowledge leads to an approach that is based on self-interest and conflict among men. This founder of the realist approach to the nature of man and his essence considers human nature as directed toward self-preservation and an ever-wider search after the fulfillment of desires. He devotes a great deal of his discussion to the meaning of man and his thinking. However, eventually he arrives at the conclusion that, "I put for as general inclination of all mankind a perpetual and restless desire of power after power, that ceases only in death."[4] And this is why according to him,

> the final cause, end, or design of men, (who naturally love liberty, and dominion over others) is getting themselves out from that miserable condition of war, which is necessarily consequent (as has been shown) to the natural passions of men, when there is no visible power to keep them in awe, and tie them by fear of punishment to the performance of their covenants, and observation of these laws of nature.[5]

Also he writes: "In the nature of man, we find three principal causes of quarrel. First, competition, secondly, diffidence, thirdly, glory. Hereby it is manifest that during the time men live without a common power to keep them all in awe, they are in that condition which is called war, and such a war as is of every man against every man."[6] Hobbes considers this conflictual and belligerent condition also to dominate the relations between nations. He notes:

> Every sovereign is possessed of the same right in ensuring the security of his subjects as does every individual in protecting his body and soul, and this is the same law that shows the people with no civil government how to behave toward one another.[7]

This brief overview indicates how in Hobbes's outlook the possibility of gaining the knowledge of reality, struggle after self-interest and self-preservation, and the conflictual foundation of political behavior have become intertwined in order to create the foundations of realism. The Hobbesian man is one whose essence is made up of a desire for security and maximization of personal gains. He is capable of a knowledge of reality that is in line with a common understanding of social facts and, therefore, his political behavior, in the domestic as well as in the international area, is based on the notion of confrontation with others. Though, at the outset, in order to protect his life and his interests, he is forced into cooperation and coordination with others, this, nonetheless, is not indicative of the true nature of his political behavior. This is especially true in the international sphere where, owing to the absence of a dominant power, conflict and war constitute the essence of the behavior of governments toward one another.

Many scholars consider E. H. Carr as the originator of the modern realist paradigm in the post–World War II period and as the founder of the classical and modern method of the scientific approach to international studies. A close look at Carr's ideas would indicate the presence of key Hobbesian elements in his outlook, i.e., the possibility of an objective and communicable knowledge of political facts, and the conflictual outlook to the analysis of the political behavior of men and governments.

In his widely acclaimed *Twenty Years Crisis*, Carr claims that the ideas of weakness that gave rise to global wars were those that, instead of being attempts at a communicable understanding of political realities, were flights of arcane and unattainable dreams. They failed to take into account the external reality as well as the desire after power and the conflictual nature of international relations. According to Carr, the days of utopian ideas and search after quixotic ideals in international relations are long gone and it is time for a realism aimed at an understanding of the laws governing the existing realities of the political world. Carr provides the following definition of realism:

> In the field of thought, realism places emphasis on the acceptance of reality and on the analysis of its reasons, roots, and consequences. The realist tendency is about limiting the scope of idealistic intentions and objectives. In the field of action, realism places emphasis on the irresistible existing forces as well as the inescapable characteristics of the existing tendencies. It considers the highest rationality and outlook, the rationality and outlook that adapt the individual to these forces and tendencies and leads to their acceptance.[8]

To Carr, the unequal distribution of power is the most critical issue in the international system, and a true understanding of the root of conflict and war hinges on gaining an objective picture of the mode of distribution of this power. Owing to the fact that war and conflict are the most important and fundamental bases of relations among states, their true understanding is essential to the comprehension of the foundation and realities of international relations. According to Carr, those who try to ignore the conflictual nature of international relations, which is the very reality of the situation, are in fact among the privileged and powerful class who are intent on justifying their privileges and prerogatives through the use of terms such as "interests." In this connection, he notes:

> The "doctrine" of compromise and coordination with regard to the interests is the natural assumption of the dominant, privileged class. The members of this class are in possession of the prevailing view in the society and, therefore, naturally, present their interests and position in terms of an epistemology.[9]

Thus, compromise and coordination between interests is a myth concocted by the powerful as a means of justifying their power and interests. However, the reality of international relations is something altogether different and that is an incessant struggle for more power. The apprehensible "reality" according to Carr is nothing but "struggle for power." That is how "realism" has culminated in a "conflictual" approach in classical realism. This is the framework within which the objective understanding of reality results in a denial of ideals and the essential value of conceptions such as compromise between interests and desires. The same outlook may be detected in the thought of Hans J. Morgenthau.

Morgenthau also views political science as a science of discovering realities; not just the realities that are external facts fathomable by human intelligence, but inescapable realities which we are compelled to recognize and harmonize with or to ignore at the cost of plunging into fanciful thinking and idealism. As regards objectivism, Morgenthau's writings indicate that he considers political realities and their conflictual essence as part of human nature. He notes:

> Political realism believes that politics, like society, is susceptible to objective laws with roots in human nature. To improve the conditions of the society it is necessary first to comprehend the laws governing the functioning of the societies. The functioning of these laws falls outside of our control, therefore, man's struggle against them results only in his ruin. Realism also draws a distinction between reality and belief. In other words, it is possible to distinguish between objective realities corroborated by evidence and elucidated by argumentation and that which is mere mental judgment separated from external reality and shaped by bias or baseless thoughts.[10]

Through these remarks Morgenthau explicitly puts forth his objectivism. This objectivism and affirmation of the definitiveness of the scientific analyses of realists in the field of politics leads to the adoption of an approach by Morgenthau that is based on power and conflict. Like E. H. Carr, Morgenthau also considers international politics as an arena for the struggle of countries for ever-increasing power and profit. According to Morgenthau:

> International politics, like other fields of politics, is a struggle for the attainment and preservation of power. Whatever the ultimate goals of international politics, power remains an immediate objective. Statesmen and nations may be in search of freedom, security, welfare, or pure power. They may define their goals based on religious, philosophical, economic, or social ideals. They may be hopeful that their ideal is to become a reality through its own internal force, divine dispensation, or the natural evolution of human affairs. They may facilitate its realization through non-political instruments such as cooperation with other nations or

international organizations. However, whenever they want to achieve their goals through international politics, they must engage in an ever-arduous struggle for the attainment and preservation of power.[11]

The intimate link between the conflict-based approach and the realist methodology is so evident in Morgenthau's thought that it calls for no further elaboration. This outlook is even espoused by the most renowned neorealists. Kenneth Waltz, perhaps the most famous realist political thinker of our time, is one such individual. Though Waltz raises many objections to the traditional realism of the likes of Morgenthau and Carr, he, nonetheless, is of the opinion that an understanding of the reality and objectivity of global politics is possible through the employment of modern tools. Of course, he attempts at arriving at a deeper understanding of reality and objectivity by using newer concepts such as structure and system. In other words, his route and mode of understanding is different. According to Waltz, any method not making use of such concepts as "structure" and "system" runs the risk of debilitating into reductionism and atomism, which exclude the possibility of a true understanding of the foundations of global politics. This, however, is not the point under discussion here. The conclusion of immediate concern is that Waltz also considers an understanding of reality to be possible, a fact upon which he founds his realism.

Waltz is of the opinion that the apprehension of political reality is possible through the use of concepts such as system. He attempts to place the international political environment and situation within the framework of a system. Being convinced of the fact that the arena of international relations is one of incessant struggle and competition for power among governments, he considers the domination of a supreme power or a universal government as impossible, a fact that renders the atmosphere of international politics into a scene of anarchy. In an anarchic environment there can be no supreme sovereignty, though it is possible for a particular system to gain sovereignty whose main axes are made up of two or more pivotal powers. Stability and equilibrium in an environment of anarchy are reached and maintained within bi- or multipolar systems. That is the reason behind Waltz's idea that the struggle for power—and power itself—is only a means and not an end. The ultimate objective is survival and security. The self-preservation and security of a national government is the most important goal in the international arena, a factor that impels governments to position themselves with respect to the international system and the existing poles of power. It is for this reason that the mere fact of direct access to instruments of power as well as direct involvement in conflicts and wars loose their pure importance for Waltz, who replaces them with a new concept. Through the maintenance of their position vis-à-vis the global system, governments can ensure their security and interests.

This approach to international politics is an attempt at moving away from a confrontational environment of a war of all against all, though it does not constitute a full-fledged departure, since it continues to posit the global environment as one characterized by hostility and war. This assumption causes Waltz to consider notions such as mutual dependence as meaningless and as sources of distortion of the reality of international politics as well as misconceptions and deviations impeding the emergence of the necessary conditions for the realization of international peace. To him, in global politics, mutual dependence and coordination based on cooperation are nothing but mere chimeras. Nonetheless he holds that conflictual competition among governments, within the power structures of the global poles of power, has the potential of giving rise to particular forms of cooperation oriented toward security and interests.[12]

This brief overview has underlined the fact that in the tradition of theoretical realism the conflictual approach is the dominant outlook, which through the employment of classical epistemological concepts presents conflict and war as an inescapable fact of human nature as well as the underlying principle of global politics. Here, it should be borne in mind that the conflict-based approach is not exclusive to the realists. The Hegelian outlook that, in the nineteenth century, evolved into a powerful tradition with regard to the politico-philosophical understanding of the world, was also underpinned by this conflictual interpretation. It is noteworthy that Hegel also held the view that "whatever is real is rational." Though, in Hegel's view, the process of the self-realization of the mind and the soul differs from that of the attainment of reality, nonetheless, what is important for our present discussion is his belief in the identity of reality and rationality. This may account for his belief that conflict and contradiction are essential to the human nature and society and that war is the element that contributes to the flourishing and the advancement of society and history. The same Hegelian idea lies at the basis of the Marxist view that considers the comprehension of the external realities of society as necessary to the true understanding of the real nature of human societies; an outlook that transforms the notion of an incessant class struggle into the guiding principle of the Marxist political philosophy. Though it is not the objective of the present paper to elaborate the Hegelian development of this idea and its Marxist ramifications, it nonetheless, appeared as interesting to highlight the concomitance of the two notions of the "claim to an understanding of reality" and the "conflicual approach" in the views of the followers of Hegel and Marx.

THE EVOLUTION IN THE CONFLICTUAL FOUNDATION OF UNDERSTANDING OF INTERNATIONAL RELATIONS

A look at the mainstream of the literature on international relations in the course of the final two decades of the twentieth century would indicate that the realists' mechanistic, objectivist, and conflictual approach is in the process of a gradual transformation; one that appears to be conducive to the emergence of the requisite intellectual background for the reception of ideas such as the dialogue of civilizations. Two new principles are to be detected in these nascent outlooks:

1. Political reality, like political mentality, is relative and subject to change, and there exist many completely different ways for its comprehension and interpretation. Political reality is not rigid and independent of the minds and ideas and it may not be viewed as a physical object capable of definitive understanding.
2. It is true that the strongest human instinct is directed toward a desire for ensuring security and interests; nonetheless, the creation of symbols and meanings is part of man's essence and that which distinguishes him from other animals. Thus, the political life of men may not be fully accounted for based on the notion of an incessant search after security and power. Men are capable of giving birth to new meanings and of fashioning their surroundings according to their ideals and desires.

To illustrate these characteristics, which are deemed as the signs of a patent transformation in the theories of international relations, I have chosen three thinkers from three distinct intellectual traditions, whose ideas I will briefly elaborate in the following pages.

Alexander Wendt

Alexander Wendt, a leading proponent of constructivism, is heavily critical of mechanistic outlooks in social sciences and international relations. He considers the existence of man to hinge upon his ability to give birth to meaning. Man creates meanings and, thus, is capable of changing them. Wendt's point of departure is an epistemological turnabout with regard to politics and political reality; thus, his thought is considered to have effected a fundamental transformation in the realist approach to global politics. To Wendt, human and social phenomena are not machines and are not susceptible to dissection and analysis in the same manner as mechanical phenomena. Accorded equal status as that which is at the basis of social and political understanding is human "consciousness." Wendt considers the political outlooks and social sciences of every period to be deeply influenced by the contemporary theories in physics and mechanics. For instance, he believes the theories of classical realism and traditional political perspectives to have been shaped by the Newtonian mechanics; hence the tendency to treat human behavior and phenomena as objects and machines capable of being subjected to mechanical analysis.

Wendt makes an attempt at putting forth new theories that receive their inspiration from quantum mechanics, a tendency that lies behind his notion of "quantum mind." He derives ideas from quantum physics and the theories of Heisenberg to prove that the human mind like subatomic particles is active and unlike mechanical phenomena is not constrained by deterministic, mechanical laws. In this connection, he notes: "I am of the opinion that man and society are truly quantum phenomena. It is possible to establish a bridge between the universe of particles in quantum physics and the universe of particles in social science through the theory of quantum consciousness."[13] According to Wendt, the dominant view in social sciences, which considers human relations to be governed by a set of inescapable and deterministic laws, has its roots in the prevailing mechanistic outlook in empirical science. One subscribes to this view only if one looks upon social affairs as objects or as components of a machine. Just as in the case of objects that are subject to deterministic, mechanical laws, there exist similar laws with regard to social phenomena that are capable of elaboration. Those who ascribe objectivity to social affairs are, in reality, the adherents of classical mechanics, since they consider them on a par with objects; and this is the underlying assumption of the scientist discourse in the contemporary social and political sciences.

In Wendt's view, the importance of human consciousness, thought and ability in the shaping of what transpires in society and politics is so that it may not be treated as a mere physical object. Therefore, the contemporary mode of scientific approach to social and political issues is in need of a fundamental reassessment. The starting point in Wendt's reevaluation is his new approach to the status of man and his consciousness. However, he does not stop there and extends his quantum-based epistemological approach to the sphere of politics. At the same time, Wendt remains a realist; thus, he continues to view governments as the principal actors in the field of international relations: "Governments are the internalized form of mentalities in foreign politics."[14] Based on this view, in the field of global politics, the consciousness-based mentality of modern man has manifested itself in the form of governments, which have transformed into the essence of this aspect of human life. According to Wendt, "governments continue to remain at the center of the international system, and to be critical of international politics for its government centeredness is tantamount to being critical of the forest for its tree centeredness."[15]

Thus, Wendt continues to give pride of place to government as the pivot and quintessence of international politics. However, to him, government is not like a rigid physical object. Government is the manifestation and the result of human mentality, consciousness, and will. In Wendt's view, the notion of conflict-based relations is not essential to governments. In other words, it is impossible to define an immutable essence for a government. Therefore, it is perceivable for global politics to gravitate toward a nonconflictual situation of cooperation and coordination. To Wendt, man is not doomed to a conflictual search for security and interests, since the world of politics and the circumstances of international politics are the creation of man and his conscious mentality. The continuous advancement of this mentality toward an ever closer coordination creates the possibility for the achievement of a state of cooperation.

Roland Robertson and Martin Albrow

Ever since the 1980s, the theories of globalization have contributed to the emergence of a popular new trend in the understanding of global politics. At times, the epistemological foundations of this outlook are in stark contrast to those of classical realism as well as to the prevailing views in international relations. Roland Robertson, a leading proponent of this outlook, believes that globalization more than implying a new set of circumstances in the world is an indication of a transformation and displacement in man's outlook and consciousness as well as in the essence of society.[16] Robertson, like Martin Albrow, is of the opinion that the understanding of the new global identities and phenomena is no longer possible through the employment of the tools provided by classical social sciences. As noted by Albrow, sociologists and specialists in classical social sciences must be criticized for their reductionist views with regard to historical conditions and mode of political analysis.[17] Therefore, in their view, the type of outlook that assigns centrality to the government and interests and considers conflict as the prevailing state of international relations is to be fundamentally brought under question.

The notion of culture looms large in Robertson's elaboration of the process of globalization. To him, culture is the most important aspect of man's life and the manifestation of his existential essence in the societal arena, since culture is derived from meaning and meaning is the preeminent characteristic of man and the element that most distinguishes him from animals. According to Robertson, as was proclaimed by Henri de Saint-Simon, the formation of social sciences is impossible without the establishment of a union and brotherhood among men, and vice versa. The majority of classical sociologists are after the elaboration of the notion of society, a society that is placed within the context of a national government. The foundation of understanding society and human relations in the arena of society is the set of demarcations that separate a government from others. Social, economic, and, even cultural phenomena in classical social sciences are defined within these boundaries and are only comprehensible within them. In other words, in the current situation of social sciences, the assumption exists that the phenomena are to be defined within the framework of the society and societies within the framework of national boundaries. However, according to Robertson and Albrow, in the global age, the essence and scope of social and human phenomena have undergone transformation. Albrow contends that today reality is in a state of constant flux.[18]

Under such circumstances one is not to ascribe an immutable and objectified reality to the phenomena of the world. In other words, in today's world constant conflict over interests is no longer the dominant principle in international relations. In fact, we have entered upon a new era in which human needs and identities have become closely intertwined. The modern world is a world of uncertainty and instability. It is thus a world in which cultural interactions are brought into prominence as the global dimension of human existence. Man's humanity and his meaning-generating nature find universal manifestation through the aid of new communication and information technologies. Culture is a realm of interaction rather than conflict, of dialogue and mutual influence rather than war and hostility. If cultures in the age of conflict were pretexts for hostility among national governments, in the global age they are grounds for understanding and friendship among various individuals and social groups. It is thus that in the views of such thinkers as Robertson and Albrow the conflictual foundations of international relations are in the process of transformation.

Francis Fukuyama

Fukuyama's theories have been subjected to vehement criticism in the scientific and political circles in Iran. His idea of the "end of history" has been heavily censured as implying the ultimate victory of the liberal democratic political model and its indisputable global domination. The same critical outlook may be found throughout the world. However, there appears to be a point in Fukuyama's theory that has been glossed over by many of his critics and that has a relevance to our present discussion. In many of his books and articles, Fukuyama underlines the fact that the ideological grounds for incessant war and conflict are gradually fading from our world. In other words, he believes that the conflictual essence of history is undergoing transformation. Fukuyama makes reference to Hegel who considered conflict and war as the essence of motion and history, a perpetual contradiction that is manifested in the contradiction among ideas and is the essence of the dialectical movement of history. In fact, it is the constant contradiction within this dialectical movement that gives rise to history.

Thus, Hegel does not view conflict qua conflict, and even war, as negative. In fact, at times, he goes as far as considering the avoidance of war as a cause of historical stagnation and characterizes conflict as a source of dynamism and progress. Fukuyama is also interested in this aspect of the subject. He contends that if the essence of history were to be viewed in its Hegelian context, i.e., as conflict and contradiction, especially as contradiction among ideas, then at the present juncture in history the contradiction has been resolved. Hegel also was of the view that at a particular point in time history-generating contradictions will come to an end, a time when rationality will have reached its perfection and when its potentials will have been actualized.[19] Fukuyama believes that today, in spite of the existence of minor and newsworthy contradictions, the fundamental and history-generating contradiction between the two main ideologies of liberal democracy and communism has come to an end and after the collapse of communism there exists no comprehensive model with the potential to stand up to the liberal democratic model. Whether there is any truth to Fukuyama's contention about the ultimate victory of liberal democracy is of no relevance to the present discussion; however, the significant point here is that according to him the conflictual essence of history has been transformed and that major global events are no longer based on this incessant conflict. The prevailing of the liberal democratic discourse in the world of politics and international relations causes a fundamental transformation in the essence of the relations among nations.

CONCLUSION

This brief analysis has indicated that the classical approach to international relations was dominated by a conflictual discourse founded on an objectivist epistemology. In the realist paradigm, conflict aimed at security and increased interests was viewed more as an immutable principle and foundation and this was the mainstream idea in theories of international relations. However, in the last two decades of the twentieth century, there appeared theories that did not view conflict and war as the essence of international relations. There are those among objectivists, proponents of globalization and the followers of Hegel that are of the opinion that the foundation of international relations has undergone change and that conflict and war are gradually giving way to cooperation and coordination. It appears that this paradigm shift is taking place in the field of international relations and is laying the groundwork for the acceptance of initiatives such as the dialogue of civilizations. Though in recent years we have witnessed devastating military conflicts in the field of international politics, these events have not been representative of the essence of the global politics. The theoretical outlook and the prevailing ideas regarding global issues are undergoing a slow transformation, a transformation that is paving the way to the adoption of ideas that represent coordination and cooperation among nations, cultures, and civilizations.

NOTES

1. Thomas Hobbes, *Leviathan* (London: Penguin, 1969), 71.
2. Ibid., 129.
3. Ibid., 114.
4. Ibid., 138.
5. Ibid., 189.
6. Ibid., 158.
7. Ibid., 315.
8. E. H. Carr, *The Twenty Years' Crisis: An Introduction to the Study of International Relations* (London: Macmillan, 1939), 11.
9. Ibid., 102.
10. Hans J. Morgenthau, *Politics among Nations: The Struggle for Power and Peace* (New York: Alfred A. Knopf, 1985), 5.
11. Ibid., 45.
12. Kenneth Waltz, *The Theory of International Politics* (New York: Addison Wesely, 1979), 100–50.
13. Alexander Wendt, *Social Theory of International Politics* (Cambridge, UK: Cambridge University Press, 1999), 1.
14. Ibid., 9.
15. Ibid.
16. Roland Robertson, *Globalization, Social Theory and Global Culture* (London: Sage, 1992), 25.
17. Martin Albrow, *Global Age* (Cambridge, UK: Polity Press, 1996), 20.
18. Ibid., 85.
19. See Francis Fukuyama, *The End of History and the Last Man* (New York: Free Press, 1996).

Chapter Ten

Dialogue of Civilizations: Objective Grounds and Theoretical Guidelines

Hadi Khaniki

Though the idea of dialogue among civilizations owes a great deal of its popularity to a wide array of factors in the arena of international politics, one should not lose sight of the fact that theoretical developments emanating from the academia have also played a substantial role in the widespread acceptance of this notion. The elaboration of this idea and its discussion in academic circles derives from its relevance to the above factors. Therefore, an appreciation of the true place of the idea of dialogue among civilizations directly hinges on an examination of its theoretical underpinnings. In this part of the article we will cast a brief glance at the theoretical background of this idea. This is not merely to examine what has brought acceptance to this concept, but to search for new interpretive horizons for elaborating the notion of dialogue of civilizations.

Were the idea of dialogue among civilizations to be viewed as a framework for giving order to the international community then—through recourse to the wide spectrum of modern political philosophical theories—three approaches may be employed in gaining an understanding of the international order, each of which is receptive in a particular way to the idea of dialogue among civilizations and each of which sheds special light on the notion of civilizational dialogue.

DIALOGUE AND THE LIBERAL IDEA BASED ON AN INTEREST-ORIENTED CONTRACT

The liberal idea based on an interest-oriented compact does not imply the notion of dialogue in its connotation and rather than being dialogical is a vehicle for the elaboration and justification of "conflict." The philosophical foundation of this approach is based on an independent individual whose will and desire is his very essence and whose rationality is in the service of advancing his aspirations. An individual afflicted with an insecure condition, under natural circumstances, enters into dialogue with other individuals with a view to establishing a compact that would bring into order the social life of the community. However, this dialogue is solely aimed at aligning the civil order in such a way as to maximize individual profit within the framework of collective security.

Hobbes is the ultimate instance of this approach. His idea applies to individuals in crisis who under natural circumstances surrender to a Leviathan so as to escape from destructive crises. This acquiescence in the outcome of a free rational decision is not the upshot of a dialogue or a consensus resulting from a dialogical process. Thus, the Hobbesian model is incapable of embracing the notion of dialogue. That may be the reason why the twentieth-century philosophers of dialogue have knowingly or otherwise distanced themselves from Hobbes's interpretation of power. According to his model of society individuals come to accept a set of rules for social life out of a particular "interest." Here, no dialogue takes place between individuals and societies and any such dialogue has to be carried out through the medium of a center, e.g., a government or an international organization.

Locke's version of the society, in spite of all its differences as regards its focus of individual freedoms, bears many affinities to Hobbes. In Locke individuals and groups are in more direct contact with one another. Here individuals and societies resemble the participants in a major and all-out contest whose sole objective is to compete with each other, a competition that is entirely based on interest, but which may go beyond that.

HABERMAS, THE NEO-KANTIAN PHILOSOPHER OF DIALOGUE

The wide-ranging aspects of Habermas's thought that span the fields of philosophy, politics, and sociology have placed him in the center stage of international intellectual developments in the past few decades. Through his formulation of a galaxy of concepts—e.g., the life-world, public/private spheres and human interests—he has provided suitable intellectual frameworks for discussions about social and international dialogue.

The "life-world" is central to Habermas's philosophy. This notion, derived from the phenomenological tradition of German philosophy, at times has been used as a means of proving the impossibility of dialogue. However, in Habermas it is successfully used as an instrument for presenting dialogue as a possible and indeed necessary undertaking. For Habermas the life-world is a substratum that embraces the entire spectrum of communicative actions. In other words, it is a horizon within which move our various communicative and intellectual actions.[1] The life-world is a background of common notions, which make possible symbolic and ordinary interactions. Its scope encompasses the general field of education as well as citizenship in its political connotation, emerged over time. The more principled and concrete the structure of the life-world the more it is capable of facilitating understanding and cooperation. From a historical-analytic point of view the process of rationalization of the life-world may be viewed as positive. However, from the period of the Enlightenment onward, when societies came to undergo economic and technological transformations and the social system or order began to appear alongside the life-world, the possibility of communicative action and dialogue began to diminish. Habermas dubs this process the "colonization of the life-world."[2]

In his recent work Habermas, taking into account the economic and technological developments arising from the ever-widening process of globalization, attempts to supply a different perspective on the possibility of social cohesion within the life-world. To Habermas the rationalization of the life-world has many enemies. The rising complexity of Western societies and the spilling over of system into the public domain has inadvertently supplanted communicative actions with mediums such as wealth and power. In the East also identity challenges, such as fundamentalist orientations, pose a threat to "discourse ethics." In such a milieu Habermas strongly affirms patterns of dialogue between the West and other cultures and underscores the possibility of global legitimacy through human rights. He vehemently distances himself from any method or group that seeks to tackle global issues through "monologue" and whole-heartedly embraces the notion of a "dialogical life-world."

For Habermas it is insufficient for each individual to decide for his own whether he is inclined to accept or reject a particular norm. Here, what is called for is a true process debate. Under such conditions, Habermas relinquishes the effort to justify a particular set of ethical responsibilities. The philosopher is unable to accurately foresee the outcome of ethical debates. The thoughts and ideologies that have boasted such claims have ended up in catastrophic consequences for humanity. One must keep in view lessons learned from such disasters. Top-down attempts at social engineering in the form of immutable programs place hurdles in the way of communicative interaction. Therefore, what sets apart democracy from its ideological rivals is its belief in a dialogical life-world which is none other than a process of collective learning.[3]

Through his notion of the "logic of dialogue" Habermas has painted a new picture of dialogue in social and political realms. His emphasis on the concept of "dialogue" betrays his orientation toward Gadamer and other hermeneutic philosophers, while his reference to the term "logic" is indicative of his advocacy of analytical philosophy as well as his principal preoccupation with the age of "rationality." Habermas's emphasis on Gadamer's notion of the "fusion of the horizons of meaning" as well as the primacy he assigns to "communicative action" over against "strategic action" and "public sphere" over against "power" and "private sphere" project bright prospects for a merging of dialogical life-worlds. Given Habermas's dialogical orientation, one may safely attempt a synthesis of the theoretical aspects of his philosophical, political, and sociological views and the idea of dialogue of civilizations. Cases in point are Habermas's theories of communicative action in communications and his theory of "ideal speech situation" in political sciences that can serve as suitable theoretical underpinnings for the idea of dialogue of civilizations.

What today is being discussed within the framework of dialogue among civilizations at the international level implies approaches and methodologies that in the main coincide with Habermas's views and their elaborations over the years. In his theory of communicative action Habermas, at the same time that he hangs onto the desire for freedom, which is also implied in the works of Marx, is not inclined to affirm the revolutionary or positivistic means for attainment to such an ideal. Habermas accepts the notion that capitalism has been responsible for giving rise to a class society and that administrative or goal-oriented rationality has come to impose an increasing level of control over people's lives. However, he is of the contention that "the automatic system whose commands, at times, ignore the constituent elements of the very same commands,"[4] should not be taken as synonymous with the world of everyday living, i.e., the world of consciousness and communicative action.

The substance of the world of everyday living is made of the desire for freedom, whose true apprehension is only thwarted by a distorted use of reason and speech. Therefore our responsibility is to formulate theories that would make possible the universal validity of this point.[5] This particular interpretation of Habermas within broader horizons under the title of dialogue of civilizations implies many close parallels. "Communicative rationality" is central to the theory of communicative action. A communicative rationality according to Habermas comes into being in the process of unhampered dialogue and thus bears affinities to the notion of dialogue among civilizations. Communicative rationality is essential to man's use of language.[6] Here, the process of perception and understanding is aimed at arriving at an agreement that is compatible with the conditions of a rational consensus on the content of a speech. To Habermas the "use of language with a view to achieving agreement is the principal method of language utilization."[7]

DIALOGUE AND THE NONLIBERAL IDEA BASED ON POLITICAL SOLIDARITY

The nonliberal idea based on political solidarity takes the group—as the main social unit—rather than the individual as its point of departure. Here, the individual lives within a social and cultural situation as well as a network of preexisting beliefs. Thus, this type of individual is not in conformity with Kant's independent and self-subsistent version. In addition, here, collective traditions and biases are viewed as an inseparable part of an individual's identity, without which he loses his individuality. Thus, in this approach dialogue is not carried out between two individuals. Instead, it takes place among cultural and social networks and horizons, in addition to being informed by ethical dimensions (Hans-Georg Gadamer, Mikhail Bakhtin, Alasdair MacIntyre).

Gadamer

Through reference to concepts such as "tradition" and "horizon" Gadamer parts company with the rational approach based on the liberal individual and his dialogical idea gravitates more toward the view adopted by the communitarians. In Gadamer's view, hermeneutics is a symbol of the integration of human experiences throughout the world, since every experience inevitably has to be understood. In this understanding and action, or hermeneutic experience, human language plays a key role. Language is not concealed behind the experiences but is the very domain within which every experience takes place. To Gadamer understanding in its essence is not a mere act of recognition, i.e. it is not epistemological. In fact, understanding is what sheds light on our ontological place in the universe as hermeneutical beings. According to Gadamer, understanding is not denoted by the commonly used German term "*verstehen*"—a favorite of Kant and Hegel—but is implied by "*Verständigung*," i.e., a common understanding with others. It is only through encounter and dialogue with texts, views, outlooks, and interpretations of other individuals and lifestyles that we gain the ability to appraise our presuppositions and to perfect our views.

This underscores the maxim that "understanding more than anything is agreement." Understanding is founded upon dialogue. By dialogue Gadamer refers to free discussion unhampered by any conditions imposed by hermeneutists. Gadamer's hermeneutics, with its central notion of dialogue, opens up new paths for democratic interpretations. This type of approach eventually leads to the affirmation that "I am not the sole person in possession of the truth," i.e., my interpretation of any "text," "action," or "event" only encompasses part of the reality. This interpretation is based on my prejudgment, just as another's interpretation is based on his prejudgment. Every interpretation is achieved through dialogue and is placed within the interpretative horizon via the same medium. Even this very broad horizon falls short of encompassing the whole truth, for it is an instance of the history of effects.[8]

To Gadamer understanding comes into being through a "fusion of horizons" in which neither side is ignored. Here, the comprehension of a text is not arrived at through empathy or putting oneself in the position of the author. It is rather gained by viewing the text through the prism of one's own criteria. The fusion of horizons implies a going beyond the horizons of the participants. Thus, in Gadamer's view "through an understanding of the text we come to self-knowledge." Today's horizon can only come together through previous horizons. Indeed, tradition rises through the constant fusion of horizons.[9]

Therefore, the structure of "hermeneutic experience" or the "historically influenced consciousness" is built upon the dialectic of question and answer or "conversation and dialogue." This conversation and dialogue that facilitates a fusion of horizons has a "linguistic" nature. In fact, our very essence is derived from conversation and dialogue, and understanding is formed through language. Language is not something that is in our possession. In other words, it is a self-subsistent phenomenon. Every conversation is formed, or in better terms created, through a common language. This is the prerequisite for any conversation. In Gadamar the notion of language is irrevocably tied to understanding and thought.

Hermeneutics, like dialogue, is a circle confined within the dialectic of question and answer. Hermeneutics is an authentic life situation with a historical origin and is transpired through the medium of language. Thus, it may be labeled conversation, even when it applies to cases of interpretation of texts. Dialogue is the basis of mutual understanding. Thus, the seminal characteristic of any dialogue is receptive listening and respect for the other point of view, not as a means of understanding the personality of the interlocutor but with the goal of absorbing the idea under discussion. It is essential to assign truth to the other party's claim in order to arrive at mutual understanding. In this manner, instead of attributing the other side's views to his personality we come to view them as belonging to a particular school of thought. Hermeneutic dialogue as opposed to mechanical dialogue, if we may be allowed to coin such a phrase, is a search for a common language. This search, as in the case of a real conversation, more than an attempt at providing the required instruments for achieving mutual understanding is itself an act of understanding and agreement.

Bakhtin

Through his emphasis on the me/other relationship as the point of departure in his philosophy and ontology, as well as in the formulation of notions such as conversation, Bakhtin departs from the liberal individualistic approach at the same time that he maintains a safe distance from communitarian tendencies. What is central to Bakhtin is the type of relationship among humans. In fact, he constructs the various elements of his philosophy upon the notions of dialogue and communication. "Outside-ness," "other-ness," and "looking from without" as aspects of understanding are among the seminal manifestations of Bakhtin's dialogical approach to philosophy. At a time when positivists and Romantics were at loggerheads over subjective and objective knowledge— where the former insisted on objective and scientific criteria as the only basis for complete knowledge while the latter stressed empathy, especially in the area of cultural and human sciences—Bakhtin's ideas opened up a new horizon and brought about a major development in the field of human sciences.

In the realm of culture outside-viewing is a crucial factor in understanding. Culture only manifests itself through the eyes of the other, the alien culture. . . . A meaning only exhibits its depth when it comes into contact and confronts the other, the alien meaning: they enter into a dialogue which transports them above the obstructive and one-sided aspects of their meaning and culture. We pose new questions to the alien culture—ones that have never been put to it, previously—through which we seek answers to our own questions. And the alien culture replies by manifesting novel aspects and angles of meaning. . . . Such a dialogical confrontation does not lead to integration or merging together. Each hangs on to its unity and opened-up integrity, and both enrich one another.[10]

Thus, in Bakhtin's view knowledge involves some sort of dialogue. Knowledge is neither gained through self-denial and Romantic empathy, nor through a negation of the other and empirical viewpoint. Any knowledge of the other calls for a dialogue, one that is carried out from a particular epistemological and ontological perspective. It is impossible to gain knowledge of the other from nowhere and from top-down. Knowledge of the other necessitates the establishment of a link between the knower and the object of its knowledge, a dialogical relationship. In fact, Bakhtin's emphasis on man's retransition from a knowing rationality to a dialogical rationality has opened up new vistas in contemporary literature.

In his *Toward a Philosophy of the Act* (1993) Bakhtin introduces the notion of the individual's special and unrepeatable participation in existence: each one of my acts or words is specific to this very point in time and space, a response to another's act and word, which is, of course, in expectation of a response, as well. I must participate for I exist.[11] Any "act" is a fulfillment of my obligation to existence, is an actualization of presence among others, and I have no option but to "actively participate in existence." In this work, Kantian ethics is subjected to criticism because of its abstract and ahistorical nature.[12] In contrast to Kant, Hegel's philosophical system takes into account the element of history, especially in the context of the fecund notion of dialectic. However, Bakhtin prefers the "logic of dialogue" (dialogic) to dialectic, since the dialectic of thesis and antithesis can exist within the consciousness of a single individual and does not imply an other, as well as the fact that dialectical synthesis calls for an integration and merging of consciousnesses, an event not found in everyday life.

If rationality is one impetus behind the expansion and development of communicative action and a dialogue based on free exchange of ideas, the other impetus is surely supplied by the existence of a polyphonic and dialogical culture, a requirement underlined by Bakhtin under the rubric of "heterology." Through the introduction of this notion Bakhtin intends to bring to fore a collection of social voices and individual expressions. In other words, "heterology" is a negation of what Bakhtin terms monology. It is a belief in the production of meanings that stem from mutual social actions and reactions, or dialogue.

Bakhtin makes an attempt at projecting on the old figure of Dostoyevsky himself the idea of man's retransition from a knowing rationality to a dialogical rationality. If Gogol takes care to provide a meticulous depiction of his humble clerk, Dostoyevsky, on his part, places a mirror in front of his underground notetaker, a human mirror that reflects him in a different light so that he would begin to look at himself from a different perspective. Thus, by removing himself from the center of the plot and assigning a more pronounced role to the consciousness of his protagonist, Dostoyevsky manages to carry out a "small Copernican revolution." Dostoyevsky's small Copernican revolution displaced the ideology of the author from the center and, in its stead, scattered a panoply of voices and their relationships across the horizon of the text. The presence of a wide array of consciousnesses in the text together with the author's effort not to justify or give prominence to a particular thought at the cost of suppressing others create the condition for the confrontation and interaction of ideas on a level playing field.

The criterion set by Bakhtin by which to appraise the authenticity of a dialogue is the freedom of participants in questioning one another. Bakhtin ably proves that the most inductive condition for the incubation, birth, and development of an idea is "where various thoughts come into contact with one another."[13] "An idea only comes to life, assumes definitive form, undergoes development, finds expression, and gives birth to other ideas when it establishes a dialogical relationship with other ideas."[14] Thus, both the birth and the subsequent life of an idea take place among a "collectivity," i.e., it has an "interpersonal" and "intermental" quality. "In a monological world an idea cannot be refuted, just as it cannot be proven."[15] Bakhtin looks at culture and civilization through the same prism. To him a culture can only grasp its identity in an encounter with an alien culture. Without an "other" culture or civilization it is impossible to think about the "self" or "identity."

MacIntyre and Communitarianism

Epistemological skepticism about the notion of the individual as an essence independent from social existence—a key foundation of liberalism—is among the major achievements of the communitarians and a crucial step forward in the path to dialogue. According to this school of philosophers the individual continues to perceive himself within the structure of collective action and within an intermental and collective system of meanings. Based on this view our point of departure in social matters is not the individual or individual rationality but is the collective mind and its implied system of meanings. The system of meanings is to communitarian approaches what rationality is to liberal philosophies. This has close affinities to the foundations and approaches of the idea of dialogue of civilizations—as well as to the dialogical reality of today's world. These have been given further impetus by contemporary developments in the fields of technology and politics.

Instead of formulating new principles from the standpoint of an objective and universal perspective, the communitarians are of the contention that people should remain faithful to their own traditions and engage in the interpretation of the world of meanings they share in. The main points being driven home by communitarianism are that (1) the liberal notion of the "self," with its individualistic orientation, fails to do justice to our true self-realization of this concept; (2) liberalism is not sufficiently cognizant of the negative consequences of neglecting the social commitments arising from the subtle orientations of liberal societies; (3) liberalism is not, and cannot be, a suitable political guide for all societies and cultures; and (4) political ethics must be such that the people would be able to align their lives with the interests of the societies to which they accord identity.

Cultures occupy a central place in the communitarian tradition, a significance that arises from their function as instruments for elaboration of ethical values. Of course, communitarianism does not imply ethical relativism, nor does it deny validity to universalism. It, however, views commonly held ethical values as too flimsy to be of any considerable utility in politics. Alasdair MacIntyre, Charles Taylor, and Michael Sandel are prominent communitarian theorists who have elaborated these issues from their own particular point of view.[16]

In McIntyre's view all rationality occurs within a particular mind-set and is an ordered temporal tradition based on a distinct notion of good:[17]

> The prerequisite for rationality is a dialogue between traditions, which necessitates the learning of a second first language, dialogue, and conflict. The possibility must be admitted of an individual's tradition having come into possession of more suitable sources for an understanding of the world through foregone epistemological and traditional crises. Thus, clinging to a particular tradition does not imply the negation of other traditions, nor does it signify intolerance. . . . In spite of this, the possibility of criticism exists within traditions, let alone between them.[18]

In any event, what stands out in MacIntyre's thought is his belief with regard to the problematic nature of modern ethics and the rise of ethical disagreements in our time. According to MacIntyre we live in an emotional culture where ethical judgments are viewed as nothing but expressions of personal feelings or points of view. In such a culture the "self" is considered as bereft of any necessary social identity.[19]

Communitarians' devotion to a particular tradition or to a common notion of good does not preclude them from engaging in dialogue with other traditions, being forced into adopting a policy of intolerance, or having to disavow democratic values. Within the framework of a policy of cultural diversity, with its corollary view of ethical diversity, it is possible to affirm the communitarian approach as a key to resolving the paradox of establishing within cultural societies a policy based on a common good.[20]

As regards the confrontation between idealism and materialism, the communitarians tend to adopt the middle ground of mutual dependence. Therefore, in contrast to deterministic cultural and economic theories of social development, the communitarian approach accords a more prominent position to the human factor. However, from a communitarian perspective, culture and the cultural structures of reality have a meaning condition and situation. Claims to a particular type of human nature, cultural identity, and lost communitarian feeling have played a vital role in the communitarian freedom movements. Contrary to what is attempted in the liberal, communist, and totalitarian freedom projects, freedom cannot be gained through hoarding of economic resources, class struggle, or imposition of national will. It is rather considered mainly as a psychological and internal process which is externally manifested in social peace and cooperation with a view to the attainment of common objectives.

Liberalism, socialism, and communitarianism are the three predominant faces of democratic movements whose characteristics define the outlines of the history of the past two centuries. Totalitarian tendencies, which range from fascism to Nazism and from Stalinism to Maoism, and its Third-World offshoots, have all displayed complex reactions to the disruptive and chaotic democratic processes in the form of high-handed administrative policies justified under such rubrics as racial superiority, workers' solidarity, national security, or Puritanism. Therefore, capitalist, communist, and communitarian ideologies all have the potential, under the right circumstances, to morph into totalitarianism. The means of averting such eventuality is strengthening dialogical aspects that in turn can shore up the elements, which can guarantee democratic tendencies within communitarian movements and strategies. Issues embedded in the idea of dialogue among civilizations are deeply amenable to being placed within communitarian contexts.

GENESIS AND DEVELOPMENT OF THE IDEA OF DIALOGUE AMONG CIVILIZATIONS

The fast pace of developments in the field of communications, especially the rise and expansion of the network society and its consequent evolution into the digital society, has transformed the discourse generated in the international arena. An effective method of gauging the extent of these developments is to analyze the discourse employed in the deliberation of issues at various international institutions. For instance, an analysis of discourses generated at the United Nations Educational, Scientific and Cultural Organization (UNESCO) in the past three decades would yield a fairly accurate reading of the changes taking place in this area. Based on such an undertaking, the impacts of the merging communications era may be grouped into three chronological discourse patterns.

The First Paradigmatic Model

The first paradigmatic pattern, which made its appearance on the scene toward the end of the cold war, may be viewed within the context of the cold-War discourse gap and UNESCO's reaction to it. The main issues are to distinguish the dominant forms of consciousness in academic institutions, especially in the field of social sciences, to determine the seminal ideologies of the period under discussion, and finally to outline the link between them and the above paradigmatic pattern.

A closer look at the speech grounds of the first discourse would bring into sharper focus the antecedent nature of the political speech pattern as compared to various types of academic speech. The more we progress toward the close of the 1970s the more the resultant atmosphere of the Vietnam War comes to dominate the prevailing patterns of discourse at academic institutions. In the 1970s American universities witnessed the rise of the post-behaviorist movement, a movement that in spite of its close affinities to its progenitor poses serious criticisms, which characterize it as a distinct approach. Post-behaviorists came to question the systemic American behaviorism for its employment of general and natural scientifically based methods of examination of human issues, with its inordinate emphasis on statistical and mathematical procedures, and considered it as bereft of ethical content. What they prescribed was a heavy dose of the human values of freedom and equality bolstered by a belief in the diversity of mankind.[21] The upshot of this analytical approach was a heightened awareness of man, culture, and cultural values.

In the European sphere also the prevailing themes in the intellectual and academic circles continue to be determined by the leftists who through recourse to Marxist theories attempt to portray European fascism as a natural outgrowth of capitalism as well as to set forth an account of Marxist teachings distinct from their Russian versions, an interpretation of Marxism that places particular emphasis on cultural aspects and an elaboration of the notion of power based on the above principles. The criticisms leveled by the School of Frankfurt against relationships in the modern society and the domination of patterns of mass production together with the French structuralist interpretations of cultural structures oriented toward the reproduction of relationships of power are stark examples of departures from the previous positivistic and science-oriented approaches.

It is noteworthy that even in the sphere of political discourse the first discourse order is in harmony with the consensus existing in the discourse discrepancies between the right and the left. Although we continue to witness disagreement among the leftist and rightist camps about the nature of the capitalist system and its future prospects, the confrontation has lost its air of idealism and acrimony which characterized it in the pre-1990 era. Westerners came to abandon their single-track conception of development based on hard economic underpinnings and started to admit the need for social welfare realized through effective government interference in the economic, social, and cultural arena. The same reorientation took place in the Third-World countries as regards an acknowledgment of the cultural dimension as an indispensable element of development complementing the economic aspect.

This is at a time when in the Eastern bloc the crises of socialist societies have forced a need for taking stock of the achievements of Western capitalist societies. This is clearly reflected in the discussions of reform in the Russian society during the various stages of its recent history. Therefore, though on the face of it the first paradigmatic order is critical of the global capitalist system and is more in tune with the leftist justice-oriented tradition, it nonetheless appears to be a discourse structure that is closer to the common denominator of discourse and academic challenges in spite of their diversity and inherent conflicts.

The Second Paradigmatic Model

The second paradigmatic model relates to the conditions that resulted from the fall of the Soviet Union. The demolition of the Berlin Wall was the symbol of the collapse and the loss of authority of a body of teachings, which shored up that political system. In other words, the destruction of the Berlin Wall also spelled doom for communist discussions of changing macropolitical structures through revolution, the idealist models of social and political order, the central role of the ideal of justice and giving prominence to the conditions of the productive and disenfranchised classes, while it marked the rise of individualistic ideas, personal freedom, diversity, and the notion of limited government. The appearance of these ideas as fundamental concepts was a sign of overoptimism in the triumph of liberal values and the demise of critical concepts. This optimism was also fueled by the euphoria over the collapse of the communist bloc, which gave rise to such theories as that of the end of history.

The reign of liberal terminologies and ideas that accorded a pivotal role to the individual and his freedom came to influence discussions in intellectual and academic circles. In Europe, the publication in 1984 of Habermas's *The Theory of Communicative Action* may be viewed as the seminal intellectual event of the decade. The book, which brought about the so-called linguistic turn in the field of social and human sciences, placed the subject of language and communications within the focus of understanding human phenomena. However, Habermas's model of this communication was still based on the Kantian idea of an independent and self-subsistent individual. Habermas's account is an attempt to elaborate the formation of intersubjective reason as well as the mode of realization of ethical and social issues. Thus, Habermasian model for communication and dialogue may be considered as the focal point of the second paradigm.

The Third Paradigmatic Model

The third paradigm model applies to the particular conditions of the decade of 1990s that was marked by ethnic strife throughout the world, one of whose major flashpoints was the conflict in the Balkans. These international developments came to dash the hopes that were inspired by the fall of the former Soviet Union. It appeared that the future was to be plagued by ethnic wars, which would drag into the scene major powers, a situation that would result in the disruption of the cold war equilibrium of powers and bring about an uncertain and intractable course of events.

Though in the 1990s the field of political discourse continued to witness the appearance of liberal discourses on such themes as individual freedom, human rights, democracy, civil society, and the need for political competition and collaboration, the intellectual circles remained occupied with the incipient issue of the disequilibrium which had come about as a consequence of collapse of the Soviet Union. The major topic of this decade was how to strike a balance between ethics and politics that would be different from the one envisaged in the Marxist ideal, i.e., to provide a discourse that would distance itself from the atomistic idea of man and that would make possible the conception of a relationship between man and his social, cultural, and political environments. In other words, a theoretical possibility based on which to define man with a view to his social and political inclinations. In spite of the fact that under such circumstances dialogue would remain the defining characteristic of social communication, it would nonetheless be of a different type than its liberal versions and be based on new foundations that in academic circles are referred to as communitarianism.

Dialogue of Civilizations and Communitarian Theories

Instead of taking its starting point from the liberal atomistic individual, the communitarian approach begins with social relations. The focal point of communitarianism is not the establishment of relationship to atomistic individuals, but is to lay the ethical foundations of individual relationships and social choices based on cultural identities that constitute and express the individual. At the international level, communitarian principles are aimed at setting global consensus as the initial point of human efforts as well as searching for a language which based on this global communication would bring about the possibility of establishing an ethical system at the international level. In such a context more attention should be accorded to the views of Alasdair MacIntyre and Charles Taylor.

Here, the sources of division are to be sought elsewhere: the idea of the clash of civilizations is founded on a liberal outlook, taking its roots from the works of Hobbes and Locke, which hark back to an era when interstate warfare was fueled by national self-interest. The initiator of the idea of the clash of civilizations has in fact transformed the protagonists from national to international actors. Its antithesis of dialogue of civilizations, without basing itself on a liberal foundation, holds that it is to their benefit if the actors opted for a dialogical rather than a confrontational approach.

The idea of the dialogue among civilizations, out of theoretical necessities, has distanced itself from the theoretical foundations of the clash of civilizations, and any elaboration of it has to focus on the factors leading to this theoretical rift. The shift in its theoretical foundations to a communitarian philosophical model is more than anything an indication of the fact that the theory of dialogue of civilizations though unconnected with postmodernist views is nonetheless in the same camp owing to its critical outlook on modernism. Through cutting off the individual from his spatial and temporal surroundings and its belief in transcultural foundations of reality, modernist philosophy aims at bringing about a centralized model of international order. The concept of development which was at the core of international discourse in the one or two decades following the close of World War II is a stark case of this centralist view of the international system.

This turn toward a dialogical model is prompted by the understanding that the centralist outlook is no longer viable as a means of ordering global relations. Giving order to the international system hinges on the realization of the necessity for a reconsideration of centralist foundations. Such a prospective world order will have to go through the path of a dialogue between various civilizational zones, a reality that would only come about when the world is truly viewed as a mosaic of distinct civilizations. Within such a structure truth can only be had through an cross-cultural consensus and in a summary manner, a consensus whose subsistence would exclusively depend on that particular cross-cultural aspect.

The idea of dialogue among civilizations that may be founded on communitarian principles and a network order calls for a more horizontal perspective of the world order. This, however, is not to imply that this ordering model is bereft of any hierarchy. For then the idea of dialogue among civilizations would be but a fictional model incapable of meeting the requirements of creating a balance of power at the global level. The communitarian interpretation of the dialogue of civilizations far from being a utopian and whimsical idea is fully capable of implementation in the real world.

It goes without saying that through providing grounds for the notions of validity and truth based on cultural and civilizational spheres, communitarians undercut the existing hierarchical mode of relationship between various civilizational zones. At the same time, the communitarian model provides an innovative model of establishing a balance of power at the global level. It should be borne in mind that the communitarian version is not dismissive of hierarchical models of power structure. It is the system of meanings that objectively re-creates and legitimates power at the social level, and thus is the principal determinant of power relations and organization.

Communitarians merely speak of the aspects of re-creation of identities in a social communication network, identities that while being fragile overlap at several points. However, the fact should not be lost sight of that these identities re-create models for the ordering and organizing of power. When we speak about the idea of dialogue among civilizations within a communitarian context we are not trying to imply that civilizations are the only global communities and players on the world stage. This idea before anything directs the mind toward the most ubiquitous communication network at the global level, a network which according to communitarians is itself a community at the universal human and global level. Based on this view, the world stage is a common living environment characterized by requirements which call for their own values and organizational norms. Before attention is focused on the multiple civilizational spheres and their respective re-created identities, it should be directed to the highest human community that is in need of a fresh normative order.

The dialogue among various civilizational spheres is an example of models that distinguish among the participants in the generation of this normative order. Undoubtedly, with the emergence of this normative order and the rise of ethical and valuational models which would come to regulate behavior at the global level, a new power structure would supplant the previous one, a structure that given the nature of power would of necessity be hierarchical and that would give rise to a new model for communication between the center and the periphery at the global level.

A true understanding of the significance of this point has to do with the fact that the idea of dialogue of civilizations should not be viewed as being outside of the network of power relations. In terms of the existing power struggles this idea serves as a discourse of the prevailing order at the same time that it attempts to usher in a new arrangement for the emerging global balances of power.

Attention to the above point is important from another perspective: if we were to view the communitarian-oriented idea of dialogue of civilizations as being outside of the sphere of power struggles, we might get the impression that the objective is to establish global normative values within an atmosphere free from such conflicts. Within such context the same criticisms directed at the abstract nature of Habermas's ideal discourse might well be leveled against our model. Today, the dialogue of civilizations is being carried out within the framework of ongoing conflicts throughout the world. Thus, we should not sit in wait for an impartial referee who would logically pass judgment on discourses of order. A dialogical idea based on a communitarian outlook, owing to its cognitive logic, is incapable of trusting in such judgment, regardless of the fact that such judgment is impossible to occur within a realistic approach. Instead of pinning its hopes on an impartial referee this approach makes an attempt at bringing into the dialogical scene the entire spectrum of cultural resources and personalities of a particular civilizational sphere.

The communitarian approach forces the policymaker of the dialogue in a particular civilizational sphere to abandon the idea of a single-track mind-set, no matter how solid and rational it may appear, for a strategy that marshals the broadest array of cultural resources of a civilization, something that has not been the case in modern memory. In the modern era we have come to witness an ever-sharper delineation of traditional and cultural borders. Now it is time to bring the thrust of all these various spheres to bear on the process of dialogue among civilizations as a major contributing factor in the formulation of a normative order for the entire world.

As is evidenced in the empirical observations of the present research, to base the idea of dialogue of civilizations on a communitarian approach is to imply that though civilizations are the most prominent elements in the process of global dialogue they are not by any means the sole participants. Previously, we referred to the most universal form of human community and its order and normative language. Toady, the ever-increasing developments in communications technology have laid the groundwork for the formation of digital communities. These digital communities, with web logs as their indigenous examples, are a type of representatives of trans- or intercivilizational communities that have the potential of both disrupting and enriching the process of civilizational dialogue. The communitarian-oriented idea of civilizational dialogue has to inevitably take into account these types of communities and include them in the global network of dialogue with a view to boosting the positive aspects of their participation.

The communitarian-oriented idea of civilizational dialogue also calls for a reorganization of domains that are controlled by nation-states. Today, the prevalent perception is that the most common form of human community is in the process of creating a new model for establishing order and is aiming to formulate the required language, value system, and norms. And this global space calls upon all nation-states to try to bring about the optimal living conditions in tomorrow's world. Therefore, it is incumbent upon every nation-state to distance itself from the single-track mind-set of its cultural surrounding and redefine itself within an ever wider context of intellectual perspectives and systems of meaning. Such an eventuality inevitably requires an overhaul of political structures, since an emphasis on varied cultural arrangements calls for multisubjective models of legitimization of political structure. These are a set of interconnected requirements which are better understood within the context of a communitarian-oriented dialogue of civilizations.

NOTES

1. Jürgen Habermas, *The Theory of Communicate Action, Volume 2: The Critique of Functionalist Reason*, trans. Thomas McCarthy (Boston: Beacon Press, 1987), 120.

2. M. T. Gezelsophla, "In the Life-World of Dialogue," *Dialogue Report*, vol. 26 (April 2002), 4–5 (in Persian).

3. Gezelsophla, 4–5.

4. Habermas, 333.

5. John Lechte, *Fifty Key Contemporary Thinkers: From Structuralism to Postmodernity* (London: Routledge, 1994), Persian trans., 291.

6. M. H. Lessnoff, *Political Philosophers of the Twentieth Century* (Oxford: Blackwell, 1999), Persian trans., 446.

7. Habermas, 288.

8. Babak Ahmadi, *Structuralism and Hermeneutics* (Tehran: Gameno, 2001), 98 (in Persian).

9. Vahid Bozorgi, *New Perspectives in International Relations* (Tehran: Nay, 1998), 138 (in Persian).

10. Mikhail M. Bakhtin, "Response to a Question from the Novy Mir Editorial Staff," in M. M. Bakhtin, *Toward a Philosophy of the Act*, trans. Vadim Liapunov and Michael Holquist (Austin: University of Texas Press, 1993), 7.

11. Bakhtin, *Toward a Philosophy of the Act*, 60.

12. Bakhtin, ibid., 25–27.

13. Bakhtin, *Problems of Dostoevsky's Poetics*, ed. and trans. Caryl Emerson (Manchester, UK: Manchester University Press, 1984), 81.

14. Bakhtin, *Problems of Dostoevsky's Poetics*, 88.

15. Bakhtin, ibid., 80.

16. Alireza H. Beheshti, *Theoretical Foundations of Politics in Multicultural Societies* (Tehran: Bogh'eh, 2001).

17. Beheshti, *Theoretical Foundations*, 76.

18. Beheshti, ibid., 80.

19. Beheshti, ibid., 92.

21. Beheshti, ibid., 299.

21. S. P. Varma, *Modern Political Theory* (Delhi: Vani Educational Books, 1983), 19.

Chapter Eleven

Critical International Theory and Dialogue of Civilizations

Homeira Moshirzadeh

INTRODUCTION

What we usually understand by the term "dialogue" in international relations (IR) is in the context of diplomacy and what it mostly implies—negotiation. It is said that diplomacy consists of three activities: representation, reporting (i.e., collecting and conveying information), and negotiation. Negotiation aims at reaching an agreement between two or more countries over issues "in which they have partly overlapping, but also competing interests." It most often involves "narrowing the gap between initial positions."[1] This means that negotiations are state-centric, i.e., they are not only carried out and managed by official representatives of the states, but also they are centered on what states see as their national interests. Secondly they are essentially oriented toward a change in initial positions of the parties involved with the goal of reducing tensions and/or managing conflicts.

The idea of dialogue of civilizations as introduced by the Iranian president Khatami resembles conventional diplomatic negotiations in certain aspects. It means, however, something far more than, and different from, diplomatic negotiations. It is obvious that it is not state-centric. It sees interactions among civilizations—not necessarily, merely, or even primarily among states—as its point of departure. It also seems to be based on an antirealistic, antipower-politic perception of the world in another respect, i.e., it does not see violence at the international level inevitable. As it was primarily a reaction toward Samuel Huntington's theory of "clash of civilizations,"[2] it could be seen as a kind of mechanism for preventing violence in international relations based on a logic different from that of Huntington: there is nothing intrinsic to civilizations to make them confront each other violently; instead they may enter into dialogues with each other in order to reach mutual understandings, overcome stereotypical portrayals, see their similarities, and accept their differences without treating differences as a source of distrust and/or opposition or even as a necessarily negative phenomenon. The non-state-centrist approach also means to see other international actors including various groups and individuals as legitimate. Unlike states, civilizations have no official representatives; so the dialogues can be conducted at different levels and by various individuals and groups. It also assumes that it may lead to a less unjust world; hence its justice seeking character.

In this vein dialogue of civilizations can be seen as a non-statist, dialogical, multiculturalist, justice-oriented approach to IR. It is not, however, limited to IR as one of the social arenas in which human beings interact. It is also relevant to what we know as the field of study in which these interactions are described, interpreted, and explained, that is, IR as a discipline. Dialogue of civilizations can be seen as the basis for a less ethno-centrist IR by introducing new diversity to the field through alternative epistemologies, different ontologies, and various understandings of the subject matter of this field.

The main argument of this article is that, considering the characteristics of the idea of dialogue of civilizations, it has certain similarities, and can make major contributions to IR critical theory.[3] Critical international theory can be seen as a theoretical framework into which the idea of dialogue among civilizations can be absorbed and conceptualized.

Steans and Pettiford point to five assumptions in international critical theory.

1. "Human nature" is not something fixed or essential, but is shaped by social conditions in certain periods;
2. Individuals (subjects) can be classified in certain collectivities with particular concrete interests;
3. There are no "facts" about the world; our own values affect our interpretations and explanations of the world;
4. Knowledge is ultimately linked to human interests in emancipation; and
5. All human beings, despite their differences have a common interest in emancipation. Therefore critical theory is a universal doctrine.[4]

At the first glance these may not seem to be necessarily consistent with or related to the idea of dialogue of civilizations. However, the main characteristics of critical international theory that make it an appropriate framework for this idea include its emphasis on communicative action and hence on dialogue; its critical approach to the existing international order; its critical approach to knowledge in the field; and the way in which it sees the possibilities for change in the international system.

Dialogue of civilizations, as I understand it, can be seen as a kind of public debate at the international level that can be somehow characterized as the "international public sphere." It is thus an intervention or a kind of practice in this sphere with certain implications for the field of IR. Hence it is both a demand as well as a mechanism for change in international interactions and a potential foundation for change in international theory.

I will first examine dialogue of civilizations as an international public debate in light of Jürgen Habermas's theory of communicative action. Then I will discuss its implications for critical theory in IR under four topics. I will first examine the ontological implications of dialogue of civilizations for IR theory. Then I will point to epistemological aspects. The next section will be devoted to normative aspects of critical theory and dialogue of civilizations. The last section will deal with dialogue of civilizations as the terrain in which new intersubjective meanings and hence new international relations can emerge. In each section the relationship it might have with the themes of critical theory will be elaborated.

DIALOGUE OF CIVILIZATIONS AS INTERNATIONAL PUBLIC DEBATE

Dialogue of civilizations can be seen as a public debate at the international level. It presupposes at least an embryonic international public sphere in which dialogue between various parties can be shaped. The debate is supposed to be open to everyone and can be over any public subject of interest. It is assumed that this opens the way for mutual understanding and even might lead to a consensus-based agreement. According to Tajik, it is based on communicative reason and ethics; a kind of rationality that emphasizes intersubjective understanding and the human right to free choice; a rationality that promises a society free from dominance, insecurity, and distrust.[5] It seems that there are similarities with Habermas's theory of communicative action as well as his notion of public debate. Thus it is useful to examine the ideas expressed by Habermas in this regard.[6]

Public sphere as discussed by Habermas is the arena of public free debate about various issues of interest in society.[7] He writes:

> By the "public sphere" we mean first of all a realm of our social life in which
> something approaching public opinion can be formed. . . . Citizens . . . confer in

an unrestricted fashion . . . about matters of general interest. . . . The expression "public opinion" refers to the tasks of criticism and control, which a public body of citizens informally practices. . . .[8]

Public sphere is where individuals gather in order to participate in open debates. Although he has examined its bourgeois version in eighteenth and nineteenth century Europe, what is most important to him are its characteristics that shape the foundations for a true democracy. The principles of equality and accessibility form the basis of participation and democratic control. What he has in mind is the revival of this sphere in the contemporary (domestic) society. He implicitly sees this possibly without any recourse to violent subversion of the existing social order.[9]

Later Habermas[10] discusses the idea of communicative action in which he sees the debate, discourse, and dialogue free from any dominance and linguistic pathologies, oriented toward intersubjective understanding and consensus, the kind of practice most appropriate in the public sphere. This is what he calls "ideal speech situation" in which disagreements and conflicts are rationally resolved through a mode of communication which is completely free of compulsion and in which only the force of better argument would prevail. He sees language as providing means for creating consensus and agreement between speaking and acting subjects. The parties to the dialogue have surely different experiences, disagreements, and even conflicting ideas; they must, however, be able to resolve disagreements through "discourse," i.e., a special form of interaction in which action is suspended so as to mutually question the basic assumptions and commitments. In this situation only the force of better argument will prevail.

The mutual obligation to create such a situation is covered by what he calls "communicative ethics." It is through communicative interaction that speaking and acting subjects reach understanding and are bound together. According to Habermas,

As the medium for achieving understanding, speech acts serve: (a) to establish and renew interpersonal relations, whereby a speaker takes up a relation to something in the world of legitimate (social) orders; (b) to represent (or presuppose) states and events, whereby the speaker takes up a relation to something in the world of existing states of affairs; (c) to manifest experiences—that is to represent oneself—whereby the speaker takes up a relationship to something in the subjective world to which he has privileged access.

Communicative action is thus an action oriented toward *understanding* and not success over an opponent with competing interests, i.e., what may be reached through strategic action[11]—and what is usually seen as the most prominent form of interaction at the international level. The same idea was expressed by Khatami at the University of Florence where he insisted that "speaking and listening is a bilateral—or multilateral—effort aimed at reaching truth and understanding."[12]

Thus dialogue or, as Habermas prefers, discourse, is one of the key components of critical theory. It is not only the basis of democracy and the formation of a discourse ethics, it is also deemed as the basis of truth (as it is for Khatami in the statement referred to above) and objectivity, hence its epistemological implications. He sees the knowing subject as both social and dynamic, he emphasizes that knowledge is socially constituted. There is no knower without a culture, and all knowledge is mediated by social experience.[13] Theories and theoretical discourse are "an intersubjective linguistic process requiring a community of inquirers." Although "the aim of such theoretical discourse is 'true statements' . . . the criteria for testing and evaluating such truth claims are those intersubjective norms accepted by a free, unconstrained community of inquirers."[14] Thus he rejects the correspondence theory of truth and at the same time avoids relativism by resorting to what might be called a community-based understanding of objectivity and truth. But what is true in other social interactions holds true here as well: an ideal speech situation in which all inquirers are free and where it is only the power of argument that prevails.

Here again one can see how Khatami rejects the two epistemological positions that Habermas has been critical of, i.e., skepticism and a monopolized understanding of truth. He says, the idea of "dialogue is far from [what is envisaged by] either the skeptical thinkers or those who think they have the whole truth in their own hands."[15]

Habermas also criticizes what he sees as the dominance of technical interest in knowledge that leads to positivist empirical-analytical science. This is what one can see in his discussion on knowledge interests. There are three knowledge interests that constitute three kinds of human knowledge: technical interest leads to what we usually understand as positivist or empirical-analytical science; practical or communicative interest leads to hermeneutic science; and emancipatory interest leads to critical knowledge. Although he does not denounce the first type of knowledge, he is against its "monopolistic tendencies" in constituting human knowledge.[16] Khatami's critical approach to the dominant technical notion of knowledge that "leads to power instead of constraining power" also sounds similar to that of Habermas: he sees science manipulated by "individuals and groups whose single guiding principle is 'benefit' and 'utility.'"[17]

This idea has had certain significant implications for critical international theory in the form of sharp criticism of the dominant theoretical discourses in IR that are presented in neutral dressing but further certain interests. If we accept that IR is dominated by hegemonic discourses or theories serving specific interests and is not free from power relations,[18] and even see the whole discipline as a "hegemonic discipline," as Steve Smith puts it, dialogue at various levels, especially at an intercultural level, may be seen as a means toward shaping new understandings of world politics and even, when conducted by critical scholars of international relations, may result in new versions of international critical theory or at least gives the opportunity to marginal forces to have their voices in the field.[19]

Thus one can see that dialogue of civilizations as a public debate at a global level may affect both IR, and the way in which we understand it. In the following sections I will discuss some of its implications at both levels.

DIALOGUE OF CIVILIZATIONS AND CRITICAL THEORY: ONTOLOGICAL IMPLICATIONS

Ontologically, critical theorists challenge rationalist perceptions of human nature and action, emphasize the constructedness of actors' identities, and underline the importance of identity in the creation and formation of interests and actions.[20] Actors are seen socially constituted and their identities and interests as products of intersubjective social structures. This means that neither the actors' identities nor the nature of their interactions and relations are fixed. Furthermore, unlike mainstream theories, critical theory is not confined to the study of states and the state system but its focus is on the relations of power and domination in general.[21] Robert Cox in his discussions about social forces in world systems gives ontological priority to *social* actors and not governmental ones.[22] This means that not only do state actors not have fixed identities, but also that other actors may play roles in the international arena.

If, as critical theorists argue, states are on the one hand socially constructed, and on the other hand, their egotism is not something to be taken for granted but "a socially produced and historically contingent feature,"[23] it means that they are not necessarily the sole center of loyalty, they are not the single significant international actor, their characteristics as states are not immutable, and finally they may give way to other forms of community desirably less exclusive in nature. Cox emphasizes that notions such as modern state, diplomacy, international institutions, etc., are indeed intersubjective meanings that "perpetuate habits and expectations of behavior." But they are "historically conditional" and are therefore mutable.[24]

When civilizations are introduced as possible "actors" in the international system, it means that first of all the monopoly of state actors is denied. More important is the fact that since civilizations, unlike states, cannot have formal, official, monopolized sets of representatives, everyone and every group can be engaged in social action in the international system through participating in dialogues. Furthermore, civilizations, unlike other identities such as states, do not have fixed boundaries and cannot exert inclusionary and exclusionary practices such as those enforced by states. It seems that belonging to civilizations is more fluid in the sense that one may feel that she belongs to various civilizations and/or might choose one for another. Civilizations can be divided and categorized in many various ways. History, race, religion, geographical proximity, general worldviews, level of socioeconomic improvement, etc., can be and have been used as the basic criteria for distinguishing various civilizations. We may refer to one single civilization of humankind or to dozens of small civilizations sometimes within one single state. The last and not the least point is that since civilizations are not monolithic entities but are based on internal differences, they cannot be seen as something fixed, unchangeable, or representable by any single voice.

Thus although civilizations can be seen as sources of identities as states do, they are different from states in that they are not based on clear boundaries. In the words of Tajik, "civilizations signify identities . . . but civilizational identities are always . . . blurred." They generally consist of intertwined sets of identities. They are not fixed geographies or spaces. They are "spaces and arenas in which human beings define their own and others' identities; narrate their destiny and history; depict their utopias." Nevertheless these are "all intermingled."[25] Civilizations can be conceived of as arenas in which identities are continuously constructed and reconstructed, "we" and "others" are defined and redefined. Since the most significant identities in modern world politics, i.e., state identities, are shaped in the same arena, one may suggest that any kind of identity changes in broader or narrower spaces in civilizational contexts may affect state identities as well. The same changes can lead to a change in the sense of community at different levels. This has significant consequences for IR and its understanding. We may think of various levels of civilization, various levels of identity, various levels of dialogue, and mutual understanding among them leading to still new levels.

This will be the opposite of monolithic understanding leading to types of stereotyping so familiar in IR. Although as Hermann rightly suggests, the prevention of stereotyping is much easier than its removal,[26] we might see the elimination of stereotypes gradually in the long run through multilevel dialogues. In other words, this ontological shift may open the way for understanding the possibilities for change to which I will refer to below.

It has been suggested that "one of the important contributions of critical international theory was to widen the object domain of international relations to include epistemological issues."[27] As Price and Reus-Smit argue, critical theorists question positivist approaches, and their attempts in formulating true, objective, and empirically verifiable statements about the natural and social world.[28] They have always criticized social sciences in general and international relations in particular for being confined to what Jurgen Habermas calls "technical knowledge interest," or as Cox puts it, to "problem solving" theorizing.[29] What is missed in this latter approach to knowledge is the difference between the social world as a construction of time and place and the natural objective world, the control of which is seen as the goal of technical knowledge. This knowledge does not include the self-reflection component in social inquiry. Critical theorists suggest that the researcher should act in a dialectic way and regard his own research as a part of a dialectical totality.[30] The two other human knowledge interests, practical and emancipation/autonomy interests, are regarded as more relevant to the social domain.[31]

This is an epistemological challenge against the dominant positivist understanding of knowledge with all its monopolistic claims in this area. One of its main implications is the rejection of value-free knowledge and the emphasis on reflection on both what exists and what should exist.[32] Critical theorists realize that the actor and the observer cannot be separated and that they are themselves involved in "the reproduction, constitution and fixing of the social entities they observe.[33]

Critical theorists in international relations have been critical of positivist international relations because of its conservatism and lack of understanding of the possibilities for change in social life in general and international relations in particular. As Linklater says, international political theory should contain awareness of the possibility for intervening in the social world in order to modify its nature.[34] The limitations to change, however, are recognized:

> Critical theory allows for a normative choice in favor of a social and political order different from the prevailing order, but it limits the range of choice to alternative orders which are feasible transformations of the existing world. Critical theory thus contains an element of utopianism in the sense that it can represent a coherent picture of an alternative order, but its utopianism is constrained by its comprehension of historical processes. It must reject improbable alternatives just as it rejects the primacy of existing order.[35]

Rejecting the positivist monopoly of knowledge means the rejection of the so-called correspondence theory of truth, i.e., the claim that there is an association between the knowledge claims acquired on the basis of certain methodological requirements and the "reality out there." This means that no knowledge claim can be regarded as absolute and is therefore contextual. This is true about the critical theory itself. According to Cox, "critical theory is conscious of its own relativity."[36] Yet critical theorists' emphasis is more on the historical transformation of knowledge on the basis of the change in situations in the course of time. As Cox says, "the framework for action changes over time and a principal goal of critical theory is to understand these changes."[37]

There seems to be less emphasis on the role of cultural differences in shaping various knowledge claims even about the same historical situations (contemporary or historical). It seems that critical theorists like their postmodern counterparts are ready to reject "disciplinary closure."[38] When one expects dialogue of civilizations to lead to a pluralist concept of knowledge, it means that the emphasis is more on the ways in which intercultural dialogues can produce a more colorful context for knowledge claims—even if all are "critical" in the general sense of being oriented toward fair change, or in a more limited sense of being oriented toward emancipation. If critical theory is critical of exclusionary practices, one of the domains in which such practices can be seen is inside disciplines such as international relations and the critical theorists (together with others such as poststructuralists, feminists, etc.) oppose such exclusions. However, one may see exclusionary practices inside critical theory against which there should be some critical challenge. This is what can be avoided by intercultural dialogues that can lead to various versions of critical theory in international relations.

It should be added that although they see the relativity of knowledge, critical theorists are not for the Feyerabend belief that "anything goes."[39] In other words, they are not "radical antifoundationalists" and accept a kind of "minimal foundationalism." This means they acknowledge the contingent nature of all knowledge and the relationship between knowledge and power; yet they believe that there are consensus-based criteria for distinguishing plausible and unjustifiable interpretations of social life and minimum ethical principles.[40] Of course many, including Brown, see critical theorists' attempt to rebuild "foundations" as unsuccessful so far.[41] But one may say that a discourse-based notion of objectivity and truth (for which the dialogue of civilizations may be seen the as most comprehensive or inclusive expression) may shape such a foundation—though not a solid or fix one.

This means acknowledging the possibility of difference without hierarchy, "an equality that recognizes and celebrates difference."[42] This is exactly what the contemporary IR almost lacks. As Brown's discussion about Tzvetan Todorov's study of the encounter between the Westerners and American native Indians suggests, the usual way of encountering "others" has been either to see others' differences as inferiority or to assert equality by the elimination of difference. These, however, can give way to a third approach in which others' difference is recognized and even celebrated and "dialogism" can work as the main mechanism for it to be realized.[43] If this is recognized at the epistemological level, we might see the emergence of the legitimacy of new theoretical voices from the more marginalized section of IR community.

CHALLENGING THE EXISTING ORDER

Normative IR theory is considered as the body of work that emphasizes the moral dimension of IR and the ethical nature of the relations between communities/states both in terms of traditional concerns such as violence and war and the new demands for international distributive justice.[44] Brown's emphasis is on "justice" as the main concern of normative international theories as a variant of political theory in general.[45] Critical theory both criticizes the existing system and the kind of social relations which prevail and seeks to change the international system and this shapes the "normative interest of critical international theory."[46] If this is taken to be its normative aspect, it necessarily means to have value commitments. It was noted that it does not accept the possibility (and even condemns) the notion of neutrality of knowledge claims and does not claim to be value free itself. It seeks the formation of theories that are explicitly committed to revealing and removing dominance structures.[47] These theorists seek to

> liberate humanity from the "oppressive" structures of world politics and world economics controlled by hegemonic powers. . . . They seek to unmask the global domination of the rich North over the poor South. . . . Critical theorists are openly political: they advocate and promote their progressive . . . ideology of emancipation.[48]

Ashley defines "emancipation" as the securing of "freedom from the unacknowledged constraints, relations of domination, and conditions of distorted communication and understanding that deny the humans the capacity to make their own future through full will and consciousness."[49] As Devetak points out, emancipation implies a quest for autonomy, i.e., to be self-determining. It also implies a quest for security for human beings in general, a security that is not confined to states but extended to include all human social relations and all communities. "It cannot be purchased at the expense of others, whether states or people."[50] On the other hand, Cox points to the unjust distributive implications of the existing international institutions and the ways in which they benefit advanced capitalist countries, help them exploit other countries, and promote their dominance in world affairs.[51]

Critical international theory sees justice, freedom, and human security as its main ethical objectives. One may find some parallels here with Khatami's critical approach to IR. On various occasions he has criticized what he sees as unjust manifestations of the existing international system: domination, the ever-growing gap between the rich and the poor, the heritage of colonial era, ethnocentrism, tyranny, violence, lack of security for individuals and societies, etc.[52] He looks for a world in which "peace is realized" through dialogue, "justice and dialogue" are the basis of international conduct, "human beings and their rights are respected," "civil society on the basis of human rights in all countries and in the whole world is established," "democracy . . . is realized in the international arena," "human right to self-determination" is acknowledged, and finally a "moral community" in which the resort to violence is denounced as the foundation upon which a "world society" is established, a kind of "international tax" as a redistributive device is envisaged, and "various interactive cultures and civilizations protect their own identities and constitute a human . . . world."[53]

This sounds similar to what Andrew Linklater offers as his emancipatory vision of global politics in a new framework that is based on:

1. the construction of a global and political system which goes beyond the state and affords protection to all human subjects;
2. the decline of self=interest and competitiveness [which allegedly sustains the states and fosters international conflict and ultimately war];
3. the rise and spread of human generosity that transcends state boundaries and extends to people everywhere;
4. the consequent development of a humanity of mankind to which all people owe their primary loyalty. (Quoted in Jackson and Sorensen 1997: 100).[54]

For Linklater the state as a form of moral and political community is historically and socially constructed. It is seen as a means for exclusion and inclusion on the basis of some processes of rationalization.[55] This, however, is not something fixed and can be changed into a broader concept of community at a world scale. What Linklater sees as a political task is "to strike a just balance between the universal and particular in the practical application of any mode of inclusion and exclusion."[56] Linklater expects the "possibility of realizing the moral life in an international system of states."[57] Thus Linklater's "normative commitment" is concerned with the formation of a new international community in which the cultural differences are respected, material inequalities are reduced, and advances in universality are made.[58]

On the other hand, Robert Cox, while discussing the internal contradictions of the existing world order, suggests that social movements can employ these to promote effective challenges against it and create a fair world order.[59] These are, according to Stephen Gill, counterhegemonic forces that challenge dominant political and institutional arrangements. There is, however, an urgent need for a counterhegemonic discourse as an alternative set of values, concepts, and concerns.[60] Cox sees the formation of counterhegemony as an unlikely development in the international system.[61] He does not, however, dismiss it altogether. Although his emphasis is on domestic developments as a starting point leading to changes in the international system and not the other way around,[62] he does not deny the fact that transnational links may strengthen the social forces involved in the process of counterhegemony formation, most notably critical intellectuals. They are the sources of delegitimation of hegemonic orders by revealing the inconsistencies in dominant ideologies and offering alternative visions of social order.[63] These counterhegemonic forces are to challenge the existing social orders and to create a new just order.

But how can alternative world orders emerge? How can they be formed in a less particularistic and exclusionary way? How can a "just" world order be defined? How can a new world order be both more universalistic and at the same time more attentive to differences? Even before all these, how can counterhegemonic forces overcome the possibility of internal hegemony among themselves and how can they guarantee that various voices will be given equal chances to be heard? This is what will be discussed in the next section.

A NEW WORLD ORDER BASED ON NEW SUBJECTIVITIES?

From a sociological point of view, one may see how "present structures are not natural and permanent but have a history and are likely to be succeeded by different arrangements in the future."[64] Of course not all sociological approaches have such a capacity, but one may find almost all constructivist approaches with their emphasis on the role of identities, meanings, intersubjective understandings, social practices, etc., in the constitution of the international world as helpful. All these see transformation in world politics possible. Thus we do not have to conceive of the realistic world of power politics as immutable but we may see how actors in the course of their practices may change their identities, interests, etc.

One of these sociological approaches is communicative action theory of Habermas. As Thomas Risse points out, the critical theory of Habermas on communicative action can deal with empirical questions in world politics. It enhances our understanding of the ways in which actors constitute shared knowledge of situations and reach agreements about the "rules of the game"; it also implies seeking optimal solutions for common problems and reaching consensus on a shared normative framework.[65] Although Risse employs this at interstate level, he sees the possibility or even the necessity for applying it to non-state actors as well. Critical theorists accept that "no way of life can be used as a standard, and no single culture or state could legitimately lay the normative foundations for such an order." Cox wants to see "alternative intersubjective worlds" coexist without one becoming dominant or absorbing the others.[66] And Linklater sees sociological approaches emphasizing the historicity of identities and finds them capable of being "unlearned in more dialogic communities."[67]

As the quoted phrase by Cox as well as other critical theorists' similar statements about the possibility of change in the international system on the basis of change in intersubjectivities suggest, dialogue of civilizations is the best way toward this goal. Cox himself points to the fact that "the clash of rival collective images provides evidence of the potential for alternative paths of development."[68] Linklater goes even further and sees the possibility of reaching a kind of universality through dialogue.[69]

The question is to what extent dialogue among civilizations can lead to new intersubjectivities in IR. Here the notion of "discourse ethics" in critical theory is helpful. As Devetak rightly argues,

> The resort to discourse ethics is meant to provide a means of resolving situations of social conflict in a just and impartial manner. It offers a basis for advancing the moral point of view wherever there are clashes of culture or morality, that is, wherever there is politics. Against skeptical views, which capitulate to the apparent incommensurability of values, discourse ethics remains committed to . . . generalisability.[70]

Discourse ethics "as a means of consensually deciding upon new principles or institutional arrangements" is the basis of a moral community. This is the closest similarity between the critical approach theory and the idea of dialogue among civilizations. Discourse ethics "is oriented to the establishment and maintenance of the conditions necessary for open and nonexclusionary dialogue." Every individual or group that might be affected by a norm, institution, or principle can participate in a dialogue about it. It is democratic in the sense that everyone has the right to accept or reject any "validity claim." Finally "it is guided by justice."[71] It is also recognized that

> Engaging the systematically excluded in dialogue about the ways in which social practices and policies harm their interests is a key ethical commitment for any society that embarks on this process of change.[72]

This has certain implications for international politics. It engages parties other than the states in setting the international agenda and making decisions about issues of global interest. It is also a means of peaceful conflict resolution through dialogue.[73] Here the institutionalization of dialogue becomes necessary.[74] Multiple frameworks are necessary both at intergovernmental and international nongovernmental levels.

Whether this leads to a more solidaristic or pluralistic international society is not certain. Linklater suggests that there might appear both solidaristic and pluralistic conceptions of world society on the basis of cultural closeness or distance.[75] He says that in the core countries of Europe the emergence of solidarity is more likely. But one may wonder why one cannot conduct dialogues so that a solidarity that accepts plurality may emerge.

Here the impact of cultural differences should be taken into consideration. Certainly a degree of cultural cohesiveness is necessary for conducting dialogues aiming at consensus. As Risse argues, there already exists a minimum international life-world and actors construct this through their shared experiences and shared historical memory.[76] If they enter into a communicative process to reach a shared "definition of the situation" they may also find consensually grounded solutions for common problems of the world. It is through the very process of dialogue that various parties can assess the plausible degree of pluralism or solidarity in world affairs. Of course one may not exaggerate the possibility of the solidaristic ideal in the short run. As Linklater and Macmillan say, "the growing sense that anarchy is what states make [of] it is not coupled with any resounding confidence in the state's capacity to bring about profound and necessary political change."[77] We must not, however, forget that the modern international system with all its advantages and shortcomings is the product of human agency and the same force, especially when exercised in a conscious manner, may lead us to a new more balanced system. And if any "modification of the international system" is to be suggested, it should be "collectively determined through reasoned consensus rather than unilaterally induced by one of the system's more powerful members."[78]

CONCLUSION

The main argument of this article has been that the idea of dialogue of civilizations is in some respects similar to the themes and ideas expressed by critical international theory and that in some other respects it can contribute to this theory. These possibilities were discussed first at the conceptual level of "international public sphere" where dialogue can be considered as the public debate in the Habermasian sense of the term. It might lead to new understandings, alternative agenda settings, and avoiding the implications of power asymmetries at the international level.

By the introduction of the idea of dialogue of civilizations the ontologically static nature of IR is denied. States are not the only actors to be discussed in IR. On the other hand, this is based on the premise that the entities in world politics are not natural givens. States' identities and interests are not fixed and can be changed through interactions. Epistemologically both critical theory and the idea of dialogue of civilizations are based on the premise that there is no single way of knowing the world including the world of IR. The emphasis of critical theorists is more on the historicity of theorizing while the idea of dialogue of civilizations insists on intercultural variations. Thus they both emphasize the legitimacy of counterhegemonic discourses and marginalized voices.

As far as morality and ethics are considered, the existing order is seen as unjust and they seek to change it. Both critical theorists and the proponents of dialogue of civilizations criticize the existing order in terms of inequalities, marginalization, violence, power relations, dominance, etc. Two main strands of critical international theory in this regard can be seen in the work of Andrew Linklater and Robert Cox. While the latter's emphasis (though with little optimism) is on the influence of counter-hegemonic forces, the former seeks a change in the nature of international community by a sort of universality that respects differences. It was argued that the best mechanism to reach either a counter-hegemonic alliance or a new kind of political community at the international level is through dialogue at various levels. Therefore in practice the best way to achieve this goal of change is through dialogue at various levels and the notion of dialogue of civilizations can be seen as a multilevel dialogism.

NOTES

1. B. Hughes, "The Functions of Diplomacy," in W. C. Olson, ed., *Theory and Practice of International Relations* (Englewood Cliffs, NJ: Prentice Hall, 1991), 182.

2. Samuel Huntington, "The Clash of Civilizations," *Foreign Affairs*, vol. 72 (Summer 1993), 22–49.

3. Some authors employ the term "critical theory" in a broad sense or as a generic term comprising various critical approaches such as "Critical Theory" of Frankfurt School, feminism, poststructuralism, postmodernism, identity theory, etc. See, for example, Yosef Lapid, "Sculpting the Academic Identity," in David Puchala, ed., *Visions of International Relations: Assessing an Academic Field* (Columbia: University of South Carolina Press, 2002), 1–15. Following Chris Brown (in "'Turtles All the Way Down': Anti-Foundationalism, Critical Theory and International Relations," *Millennium*, vol. 23,

No. 2 (1994), 213–36, reprinted in Andrew Linklater, ed., *International Relations: Critical Concepts in Political Science* (London and New York: Routledge, 2000), 1655–78), I make a distinction between the Critical Theory inspired by the Frankfurt School and particularly Jürgen Habermas (as well as the more Marxian version inspired by Antonio Gramsci's theory) and the general usage of the term "critical theory." For the purposes of this paper, I confine myself to the limited meaning of the concept even if I do not capitalize "C" and "T." It is clear, nevertheless, that many shared arguments can be found between other critical theories and the critical theory that I use in my discussions.

4. See J. Steans and L. Pettiford, *International Relations: Perspectives and Themes* (London: Longman, 2001).

5. Mohammad Reza Tajik, *Jame'eye amn dar Goftman Khatami* [*Secure Society in Khatami's Discourse*] (Tehran: Nashr Ney, 1379 [2000]), 225.

6. It is worth mentioning that this dimension of critical theory is not so much paid attention to in IR critical theory. The most significant exception is Andrew Linklater who has put forward the idea of dialogue at the international/intercultural level.

7. Jürgen Habermas, *The Structural Transformation of the Public Sphere: An Inquiry into a Category of Bourgeois Society* (Cambridge, MA: MIT Press, 1989), 4.

8. Quoted in Michael Pusey, *Jürgen Habermas* (Chichester, Sussex: Ellis Horwood, 1987), 89.

9. R. C. Holub, *Jürgen Habermas: Critic in the Public Sphere* (London and New York: Routledge, 1991) (references to pages are to the Persian edition, translated by H. Bashireeyeh; Tehran: Nashr-e Ney).

10. Jürgen Habermas, *The Theory of Communicative Action*, trans. Thomas McCarthy (Boston: Beacon Press, 1984).

11. See Pusey, op. cit., 80–81.

12. S. Mohammad Khatami, *Mabani nazari goftoguye tamaddonha: Majmooeh sokhanranihaye Seyyed Mohammad Khatami dar tarh goftoguye tamaddonha* [*Theoretical Foundations of Dialogue of Civilizations: Lectures by S. M. Khatami on Dialogue of Civilizations*] (Tehran: Sogand, 1380 [2001]), 17.

13. Jürgen Habermas, *Knowledge and Human Interests*, trans. Jeremy J. Shapiro (Boston: Beacon Press, 1971).

14. Richard J. Bernstein, *The Restructuring of Social and Political Theory* (New York and London: Harcourt Brace Jovanovich, 1976), 214.

15. Khatami, op. cit., 17.

16. Bernstein, op. cit., 196–97.

17. Khatami, op. cit., 1.

18. See Robert Cox, "Social Forces, States and World Orders: Beyond International Relations Theory," *Millennium*, vol. 10, No. 2 (1981), 126–55 (reprinted in Linklater, ed., *International Relations*, op. cit., 1537–71) and R. K. Ashley, "The Poverty of Neorealism," *International Organization*, vol. 38, No. 2 (1984), 222–86 (reprinted in Linklater, ed., *International Relations*, op. cit., 1572–1632).

19. Steven Smith, "The Discipline of International Relations: Still an American Social Science?" *British Journal of Politics and International Relations*, vol. 2, No. 3

(2000), 374–402, and "The United States and the Discipline of International Relations: 'Hegemonic Country, Hegemonic Discipline.'" *International Studies Review*, vol. 4, No. 2 (2002), 67–86.

20. Richard M. Price and Chris Reus-Smit, "Dangerous Liaisons? Critical International Theory and Constructivism," *European Journal of International Relations*, vol. 4, No. 3 (1998), 261.

21. R. Jackson and G. Sorensen, *Introduction to International Relations* (New York and Oxford: Oxford University Press, 1997), 233.

22. See Cox, op. cit.

23. Richard Devetak "Critical Theory," in Scott Burchill and Andrew Linklater, *Theories of International Relations* (London: Macmillan, 1996), 164.

24. Cox, op. cit.

25. Tajik, op. cit., 227, 229.

26. Margaret Hermann, "One Field, Many Perspectives: Shifting from Debate to Dialogue," in Puchala, ed., op. cit., 16–41.

27. Devetak, op. cit., 149.

28. Price and Reus-Smit, op. cit.

29. Cox, op. cit.

30. Holub, op. cit., 56.

31. See Ashley, op. cit.

32. Holub, op. cit., 59–62, and Jackson and Sorensen, op. cit., 232–33.

33. Ted Hopf, "The Promise of Constructivism in International Relations Theory," *International Security*, vol. 23, No. 1 (1998), 171–200 (reprinted in Linklater, ed., *International Relations*, op. cit., 1756–83, at 1764).

34. Andrew Linklater, *Men and Citizens in the Theory of International Relations* (London: Macmillan, 1982), 11.

35. R. W. Cox and T. J. Sinclair, *Approaches to World Order* (Cambridge, UK: Cambridge University Press, 1996), 90.

36. Cox, "Social Forces . . . ," op. cit.

37. Ibid., 1547.

38. Andrew Linklater, "The Question of the Next Stage in International Relations Theory: A Critical-Theoretical Point of View," *Millennium*, vol. 21, No. 1 (1992), 77–98 (reprinted in Linklater, ed., *International Relations*, 1633–54, at 1644).

39. Ibid.

40. Price and Reus-Smit, op. cit., 262.

41. Brown, op. cit.

42. Ibid., 1668.

43. Ibid.

44. Chris Brown, *International Relations Theory: New Normative Approaches* (New York: Columbia University Press, 1992), 3.

45. Ibid., 7.

46. Richard Devetak, "The Project of Modernity and International Relations Theory," *Millennium*, vol. 24, No. 1 (1995), 27–51 (reprinted in Linklater, ed., *International Relations,* op. cit., 1731–55, at 1738).

47. Price and Reus-Smit, op. cit., 261.

48. Jackson and Sorensen, op. cit., 233–34.

49. R. K. Ashley, "Political Realism and Human Interests," *International Studies Quarterly*, vol. 25 (1981), 227.

50. Devetak, "Critical Theory," 166–67.

51. A. Hasenclever, P. Mayer, and W. Rittberger, *Theories of International Regimes* (Cambridge, UK: Cambridge University Press, 1997), 193–94.

52. Khatami, op. cit. and S. Mohammad Khatami, *Ensan: Moltaqaye mashreq jan va maqreb aql [Human Being: The Nexus of Oriental Spirit and Occidental Reason]* (Tehran: Ministry of Foreign Affairs Publication Center, 1379 [2000]).

53. Khatami, *Ensan . . .* , 84–85, and *Mabani nazari . . .* , 11–20, 45, 74–75.

54. Quoted in Jackson and Sorensen, op. cit., 100.

55. Andrew Linklater, *The Transformation of Political Community* (Oxford: Polity Press, 1998).

56. Devetak, "Critical Theory," 163–64.

57. Andrew Linklater, *Beyond Realism and Marxism: Critical Theory and International Relations* (London: Macmillan, 1990), 138.

58. Linklater, *The Transformation of Political Community*, 3.

59. Cox, "Social Forces . . . ," op. cit.

60. Steans and Pettiford, op. cit., 117.

61. Cox, "Social Forces . . . ," op. cit.

62. Hasenclever et al., op. cit., 196.

63. Steans and Pettiford, op. cit., 117.

64. Linklater, *The Transformation of Political Community*, 3.

65. Thomas Risse, "'Let's Argue': Communicative Action in World Politics," *International Organization*, vol. 54, No. 1 (2000), 2.

66. Cox, "Social Forces," op. cit.

67. Linklater, *The Transformation of Political Community*, 4.

68. Cox, "Social Forces," 1548.

69. Linklater, *The Transformation of Political Community*, 4–5.

70. Devetak, "Critical Theory," 170.

71. Ibid., 171.

72. Linklater, *The Transformation of Political Community*, 7.

73. Devetak, "Critical Theory," 172; see also Khatami, *Mabani nazari . . .* , and *Ensan. . . .*

74. Khatami, *Mabani nazari . . .* , 6.

75. Linklater, *The Transformation of Political Community*, 7–8.

76. Risse, op. cit.

77. Andrew Linklater and J. Macmillan, "Introduction: Boundaries in Question," in J. Macmillan and A. Linklater, eds., *Boundaries in Question: New Directions in International Relations* (London and New York: Pinter Publishers, 1995), 5.

78. Linklater, *Men and Citizens in the Theory of International Relations*, 12.

Chapter Twelve

Between Imperialism and Relativism: The Role of Culture in Defining Universal Human Rights

Karl K. Schonberg

For centuries, human rights discourse in the West has divided thinkers into two broad camps. Universalists, on one hand, have argued that individual freedoms and entitlements emerge from sources external to the individual but applicable to all, usually either God or nature. Relativists, on the other hand, have held that such rights are social constructions, differing between cultures and historical eras, which do not have a basis in reality beyond this context. Clearly, prevailing assumptions about the ways in which individuals can and should behave and the legitimate limits society can impose on their actions, differ greatly across world cultures and have changed dramatically over time within cultures. Equally clearly, conceptions of human rights have been exploited for political purposes, adding to the impression that they are dependent on the perception and perhaps the goals of the observer. At the same time, however, pure relativism produces judgements that are both intellectually unsatisfying and morally unacceptable within any framework, and has in itself been exploited for political purposes. Nobel laureate Aung San Suu Kyi has written that anational culture can become a bizarre graft of carefully selected historical incidents and distorted social values intended to justify the policies and actions of those in power. "It is precisely because of the cultural diversity of the world," she adds, "that it is necessary for different nations and peoples to agree on those basic human values which will act as a unifying factor."[1]

This paper will argue that the assertion of universal human rights has too often failed to distinguish between the practices of governments and the norms and values of societies. This failure has often led to two opposite but equally fallacious conclusions: that individuals should liberally apply their own society's standards of morality to the actions of others; or conversely, that individuals lack any right to voice concerns over practices beyond their

119

borders which they find objectionable. Moral judgements based on universal principles of human rights are possible and necessary, but to a large extent these principles must be framed in the context of the cultural, religious, and historical norms of distinct societies. However, there is a critical distinction between violations of rights that deprive the victim of autonomy of choice altogether, which ought to be viewed as breeches of universal moral norms, and those that do not, which can only be appropriately understood within their particular cultural context. Disregard of universal ideals of human dignity for political purposes can and should be criticized within the world community, but only to the extent that individuals are denied the capacity to exit, or treated in ways that violate prevailing ethical norms of the society in which they live.

UNIVERSALITY AND AGENCY

Concepts of human rights in the premodern era were inevitably connected to the sacred; God had created human beings in his image, and it was therefore an affront to God to defile human dignity. With the modern era, however, came the perceived need in the Western world of the Enlightenment to move philosophy away from this dependence on the divine. In the twentieth century, problems of conflicting standards and interpretations also hindered attempts to connect human rights concepts across distinct cultural and religious traditions. Eleanor Roosevelt reportedly concluded after first convening the UN working group that would draft the 1948 Universal Declaration of Human Rights, that any document which associated human rights with the divine would be politically and philosophically untenable.[2] The neglect of religion apparent in the document which resulted was as much a result of the political reality of its time, and the perceived difficulty of reconciling the notions of human rights held by different faiths, as it was a consequence of the Western movement away from the religious bases of philosophy. However, this does not mean that human rights as defined by the 1948 Declaration are inconsistent with religious faith, only that they were regarded by some of those writing the document as logically independent of any particular faith.

In the decades since 1948, great scholarly attention has been devoted to the question of whether human rights must necessarily be derived from religion, or whether they might result instead from human biology. Elie Wiesel has referred to the 1948 Universal Declaration as the centerpiece of a world-wide secular religion."[3] But other authors have noted that while it resembles religion in some respects, human rights doctrine does not typically offer prescriptions for the good life, as all major world religions do. It does not tell people how to live, but does tell them that they have the freedom to choose how to live, and instructs those who would rule over them that there are strict limits within which this can be justly done. The language of universal human rights does not presume that people should determine solely for themselves how to live, but it does imply that they have wide latitude to decide if, when, how, and to what to subjugate themselves.[4]

Chandra Muzaffar has written that religion "integrates the individual with society in a much more harmonious way," but while this may be true, it is also true that all major world religions rest on the principle of individual self-sacrifice and altruism, which in turn rests on the presumption of individual free will. The very concept of religious faith is fundamentally inconsistent with compulsion.[5]

Michael Perry has argued that logically, human rights are "ineliminably religious," since there is simply no other reason to imagine that all people deserve protection unless one believes that there is some element of the sacred inherent in being human.[6] Without theology, Max Stackhouse has written, why do human beings have a "right to have rights" to begin with?[7] On the other hand, Michael Ignatieff has proposed that human empathy may be enough to justify a universal conception of human rights; the belief that human beings should not be beaten, tortured, coerced, indoctrinated, or in any way sacrificed against their will, he has argued, can be derived from our own experience of pain and our capacity to imagine the pain of others.[8] "For all its individualism," Ignatieff claims, "human rights rhetoric does not require adherents to jettison their other cultural attachments. . . . What the declaration does mandate is the right to choose, and specifically the right to exit a group when choice is denied."[9] This is the case because, while universal human rights doctrine suggests that all people are entitled to certain freedoms, these are primarily comprised of protections against repression—freedoms from, in the language of Isaiah Berlin. But human rights principles are distinct from religious doctrine in that they do not go on to suggest how these freedoms ought to be used; freedom to is not specfied.[10]

The idea of universal human rights, in other words, is built on the assumption of individuals' moral authority to make choices for themselves, and this emphasis on individual volition must therefore be central to the reconciliation of universal human rights and the distinct values of varying cultures. One person or group might regard the practices of another as distasteful, even criminal, with respect to the treatment of individuals. However, the judgment of these practices against universal norms should ask not whether they would be acceptable within the society of the observer, or even whether they are routinely accepted within the society of the observed. Instead, the standard should assess the capacity for volition of the human object of the action. Notions of victimization rooted in empathy—that is, imagining oneself in the "victim's" situation and projecting one's own sensibilities onto her or him—is a natural and laudable human trait, but may be intellectually misguided in situations in which cultural or personal norms create an entirely distinct sense of the situation on the part of the victim.

The core value in human rights philosophy, religious or otherwise, is the value of the individual as possessor of those characteristics which are simultaneously universal and invaluably rare, and therefore to be protected. The value of the individual inevitably presumes the capacity for choice, however; the one principle of human rights that unites all others is the universal requirement that humans be able to choose their political, economic, and spiritual destiny for themselves. But to presume to dictate to another that he or she is a victim of a violation of human rights is therefore a contradiction in terms—if the right to individual choice is paramount, logically only individuals can decide if they are victims or not.

Human rights depend on the capacity of individuals for choice, and if they are incapable of volition, they are not agents fully possessed of human rights. If individuals do posses the capacity for volition—which assumes not only the ability to make informed choices but also the practical ability to act on those choices—then it can be said that their rights as a human being are fully realized. No matter what an individual is subjected to, in other words, and no matter how severe or objectionable it might appear to other observers, as long as the object individual retains the capacity for choice and exit, it cannot be said that his or her human rights are being violated. This is true even if the costs of exit are very high—tremendous personal or social costs accompanying choice do not logically suggest that choice does not exist, only that social groups typically impose expectations as well as conferring benefits on their members. It is the individual's fundamental right to weigh these costs and benefits in the balance, but as long as these freedoms are not impinged, the individual's human rights cannot be said to have been fundamentally undermined.

This is not to suggest that retaining the right to exit should be the only criterion determining the satisfaction of human rights standards. Individuals are sometimes placed in situations where exit and volition are not allowed—as in the case of prisoners, for instance. These individuals do not give up their human rights simply because they have been judged to have violated the rules of their society—they may sacrifice some social and political rights, but they have not ceased being human, and therefore cannot be deprived of the rights entirely, though their choice in exercising these rights is limited. Similarly, it is possible to imagine situations in which choice continues to exist, but where the cost of exercising choice is so high as to limit the freedom of action of an individual beyond fairness. How can what is fair or just be determined in such cases? The standard should be found in the common practices of the society within which the individual exists. These practices should constitute the measure by which the treatment of any member of the society is judged, though this standard should remain secondary and subservient to the broader, universal standard of individual volition and exit. What one might regard as a violation of human rights is clearly less serious if the perceived victim has the ability to exit, has some choice in the matter, even if the cost of exercising that choice is very high, than if there is no choice to be exercised at all.

In the Western world, one standard for the treatment of convicted criminals holds that they should not be subject to cruel and unusual punishment. But it is worth noting that the proscribed punishments must be *both* cruel *and* unusual; cruelty is accepted if it is common practice, and unusual punishments are tolerated as long as they are not cruel. The violation of one's human rights resides first and foremost in the incapacity of an individual to refuse and/or escape the practice, but a violation is clearly more severe if the practice in question is not socially commonplace; that is, if it is being exercised upon the individual arbitrarily and capriciously. At the same time, even a practice from which an individual does have means of escape, but where escape is accompanied by a significant cost, might be regarded as a violation of human rights if the practice was not the norm within that individual's society—that is, if it was being exercised upon him or her by authorities not primarily concerned with social norms but instead with the punishment of the individual.

The perspective of outsiders toward particular practices within societies other than their own can invite misleading and inappropriate judgments about the broader level of respect accorded to universal norms within those societies. It is demeaning to the concept of human rights to label certain practices universally unacceptable without regard to the volition of those affected by them. What is just for one individual might not be for another, even within the same society, depending on whether the individual does or does not willingly accept what is imposed upon them. As long as the individual has a choice, what is done to her or him can be considered an act of personal will, at least in part; but when they do not have the option of accepting or declining, the very same act may be said to constitute a violation of the universal norm of volition. To view human rights as a set of forbidden practices is to ignore the cultural reality of the world, because the violation of norms occurs not in the acts themselves, but in its perception of the individuals affected by them. No matter how cruelly the way I am treated appears to an outside observer, my human rights have not been violated until the point at which I feel I am being subjected to ill treatment without the possibility of refusal. To regard certain actions as violations of human rights without reference to the individuals they affect is to rob human beings of their individuality and humanity as surely as it would be to disregard their human rights altogether.

Violence in all forms implies the absence of volition. The definition of human rights as those needs arising from human nature itself can leave open many questions (are all individuals born wishing to be free, for example, and what does freedom mean in practice?), but it is beyond question that humans as a general rule wish to avoid violence against themselves. If an individual is enduring violence, it therefore stands to reason that they are doing so against their will, and thus their right to exit is not adequately protected. Individuals may freely choose to be subjected to a wide variety of limitations on their actions, and it should not be automatically presumed by others that their submission implies the absence of a choice. But as a general rule, the opposite must be said in cases where an individual is being caused to suffer physical pain—in such cases, the automatic presumption of an observer should be that the victim's right to exit cannot be exercised.

Group rights do not exist as such; only individuals have rights, though they might join together with others to assert them for common political goals. Group rights, Michael Ignatieff has written, "exist to safeguard the collective rights . . . that make individual agency meaningful and valuable."[11] The right to national self-determination, for example, exists only because there are individuals who feel the desire to be separate and independent. As social beings, it may well be the case that humans can only find full self-realization in their association with each other, and that social groups are therefore a critical element in any human life. However, the salutary role of social attachment in the lives of human beings depends on individual freedom to choose it; humans are edified and completed by their willing attachment and even subjugation to ideological or social groups with which they choose to associate themselves consciously and voluntarily, but association with groups which is coerced has exactly the opposite effect—even if individuals become deeply devoted to the group and come to see it as synonymous with their own identity, by compelling this state of being into existence rather than allowing it to emerge through individual consciousness and volition, the group has made a prisoner of the individual. It has not provided them with an avenue through which to become fully human, but instead has robbed them of their humanity and reduced them to brutes.

To suggest that individual rights are the only true rights is not to suggest that communities cannot or should not set standards for individual behavior. Every society in the world enshrines in its laws a code of moral conduct, in effect defining decency and obscenity in ways that are held to be consistent with the norms of the society as a whole. The Universal Declaration explicitly recognizes the propriety of such standards by noting, in Article 29, that individuals' rights shall be subject to limitations necessary to maintain "respect for the rights and freedoms of others and of meeting the just requirements of morality, public order, and the general welfare of democratic society." These standards differ dramatically between societies, but it is not correct to assume on this basis that all such norms are simply culturally relative, any more than it would be to conclude that there is an absolute definition of what is "decent" which can be relevant for all cultures. I would suggest that while what is "decent" or "obscene" is a necessary question in the consideration of universal human rights, it is ultimately a question of secondary importance. Far more critical is the question of whether individuals posses the practical ability to make choices for themselves about whether their conduct falls within the established social norms of decency.

Free expression, for example, is one of the first rights described in the Universal Declaration, but what might be considered legitimate free expression in one society might be considered obscene or treasonous in another. Standards of decency differ from place to place, within societies and particularly between them. While these differences will inevitably produce contention between societies over particular cases of free expression, legal prosecution for such expression does not necessarily mean that the individual's power of volition has been squelched, if the decision to express the ideas labeled as "obscene" was a conscious choice, with a realistic alternative path available. To publicly display a painting which violates common standards of decency is a choice in itself, the punishment of which may well constitute a human rights violation, but one which will likely be inherently tinged with culturally relative value judgements. To have one's *identity* as a human being regarded as indecent, however, does not admit of any choice—if I am prosecuted because my government does not approve of the color of my eyes, for example, my human rights have been violated in a fundamentally different and more profound way than if I display a painting which is considered "obscene," because I did not have the option of choosing my eye color at birth. I did not have the opportunity to exercise volition, and thus my prosecution represents an affront to my human rights more serious than one emerging from my conscious choice.

Human rights have always been thought of as deriving from the core identity of individuals—whether that identity is given to us by God, or results from biology, it is our humanity itself that has been thought of as the source of this category of rights. However, the division between the right of volition and other rights notes an important line of distinction between elements of human identity, and thus suggests a hierarchy between kinds of human rights. Part of our identity is who we are at birth—elements of ourselves which we do not have control over, and our persecution for which thus constitutes, by definition, a deprivation of our primary human right—our right to choose. But there are those elements of our identity which we consciously define for ourselves, and which we also have a right to hold and express. While our persecution on the basis of these beliefs may constitute a violation of our human rights, it does not necessarily amount to a deprivation of our right to choose, and therefore constitutes a real but less profound violation of our individual humanity. Rights violations should be viewed less severe if it is possible for the individuals suffering persecution to remove themselves from the environment in which it is occurring. If they are capable of doing this—even if the cost of doing so is very high—then their decision to stay also amounts to a conscious choice. If they suffer persecution thereafter, while it may still constitute a violation of their human rights, it is a less profound violation than it would have been if they had not had the choice to leave.

This assumes, however, a right to exit, which is more easily conceived in principle than in practice. Just as eighteen and nineteenth century Western liberal thinkers conceived of a society based on the mandate of the governed by imagining an asocial contract which never existed in reality, the right of exit may be a useful intellectual device, but the value of any theory that relies on it must be called into question when the practical difficulty of exercising it is considered. Individuals suffering persecution may have little or no money at their disposal to travel to another place. They will likely have attachments to family, community, and culture, which make such a choice seem not merely painful, but impossible. They may not know that other places exist where such persecution does not occur. And in cases where their biological identity is the object of persecution, that identity in itself may be an overwhelming hindrance to exit. Any or all of these facts may militate against the practical assertion of a right to exit, even where one might be said to exist in principle. This does not mean that this standard loses its relevance as a tool in judging the severity of rights violations, but only that the right to exit must be gauged realistically if it is to have operative meaning. The right to exit cannot mean only the hypothetical freedom to leave or the absence of legal restraints on doing so. If this standard is to have value, the real capacity of individuals to exercise choice, affected by economic power and awareness of the outside world, among other factors, must also be taken into account.

CONCLUSION

The argument made here does not suggest that the rights of individuals to express their own identities are more important than their rights to enjoy social order, or to live in a society where their standards of decency are not routinely offended. It does not suggest that the discourse of human rights is apolitical, or that it should not be colored by discussion of differences in practice between cultures and societies. Nor does it suggest that human beings' ultimate humanity may be found only in their relationship to social groups or their subjugation of themselves to God. But it does rest on the assumption that such subjugation can only be truly meaningful if it emerges from a conscious choice by individuals themselves, and that whoever we understand ourselves to be as individuals, as a species we should find the definition of our humanity primarily in our capacity to reason and to choose our own destinies.

In its details, the language of the UN's Universal Declaration was a matter of negotiation from the start. It was written by fallible and subjective human beings, representing sovereign states with particular interests, and animated in large part by their own cultural perspectives. Its phrases were, and still are, subject to debate and dissent. Of all the principles it enshrines, however, there is one which stands out as the progenitor of all the others, and which, unlike all of its subsidiaries, may be the irreducible notion without which the declaration itself ceases to have any meaning. It is that clause in Article One that suggests, "All human beings are born free and equal in dignity and rights." Though distinct societies may disagree about the laws and institutions appropriate to putting this idea into practice, the principle itself must be nonnegotiable if universal human rights are to be conceived to exist at all.

NOTES

1. Aung San Suu Kyi, "Freedom, Development, and Human Worth," *Journal of Democracy*, vol. 6, no. 2 (April 1995), 16, 17.

2. The secularism of modern human rights discourse is a result of the difficulty of resolving this question, which was encountered by the framers of the 1948 UN Declaration, who found that any language that suggested the origin of human rights ideas in the divine became immensely problematic due to conflicting religious doctrines. Johannes Morsink has noted that Eleanor Roosevelt, after hearing an argument over the divine origins of human rights between a Lebanese Thomist and a Chinese Confucian, concluded that any universal principles which could be established between the array of world cultures would have to be premised on an agreement to disagree about their bases. References to the divine in the declaration were studiously and conspicuously avoided. Johannes Morsink, *The Universal Declaration of Human Rights: Origins, Drafting and Intent*. (Philadelphia: University of Pennsylvania Press, 1999).

3. Elie Wiesel, "A Tribute to Human Rights," in Yael Danieli et al. eds., *The Universal Declaration of Human Rights: Fifty Years and Beyond*, (Amityville, N.Y.: Baywood Publ Co., 1999), 3.

4. Michael Ignatieff, "Human Rights: the Midlife Crisis." *New York Review*, May 20, 1999, 58–62.

5. Chandra Muzaffer, "Asian Economies: Development, Democracy, and Human Rights," unpublished conference paper quoted in Jack Donnely, "Human Rights and Asian Values: A Defense of Western Universalism," in Joanne R. Bauer and Daniel A. Bell, eds., *The East Asian Challenge for Human Rights* (Cambridge, UK: Cambridge University Press, 1999), 81.

6. M. J. Perry, *The Idea of Human Rights* (Oxford: Oxford University, 1998), 11–14.

7. Max L. Stackhouse, "Human Rights and Public Theology: The Basic Validation of Human Rights," in Carrie Gustafson and Peter Juviler, eds., *Religion and Human Rights* (New York: M.E. Sharpe, 1998), 13, 16.

8. Michael Ignatieff, "Human Rights: the Midlife Crisis." *New York Review*, May 20, 1999, 58–62.

9. Michael Ignatieff, "The Attack on Human Rights," *Foreign Affairs*, vol. 80, no. 6 (Nov./Dec. 2001), 102–16.

10. Isaiah Berlin, "Two Concepts of Liberty," in Henry Hardy, ed., *The Proper Study of Mankind: An Anthology of Essays* (New York: Farrar, Stresses and Giroux, 2000), 191–243.

11. Michael Ignatieff, "The Attack on Human Rights," *Foreign Affairs*, vol. 80, no. 6 (Nov./Dec. 2001), 102–16.

Chapter Thirteen

Citizenship in a Globalizing World: The Role of Civilizational Dialogue

Joseph A. Camilleri

Citizenship is hardly a new idea. The meaning we attribute to it today still carries the imprint of the diverse moral and intellectual influences that have shaped the Western tradition. From its philosophical and practical origins in the Greek city-state to the legal norms developed by Republican and later Imperial Rome, the ethical impulses of the Judeo-Christian worldview, and the secularist leanings of the Enlightenment, citizenship has served as a central ordering concept in the organization of human affairs.

Legitimate doubts have nevertheless surfaced as to its current and future relevance. Several questions readily come to mind: Can an idea rooted in the history of the territorially bound state, be it the city-state, the imperial state, the feudal state, or the nation-state, still have relevance in the era of globalization? Can the ethos of citizenship respond to the multiple crises of contemporary life? Is it possible or even desirable to breathe new life into a concept that many identify with the particularist identities and allegiances of a bygone age? This paper argues that both the theory and practice of citizenship can be usefully adapted to meet the challenges of the contemporary human predicament. But such a project is necessarily fraught with difficulty.

To have any chance of success, it will need to tap into the extraordinarily rich resource that is the world's civilizational inheritance. As we shall see, the key to this journey—acquiring a clearer sense of the destination and of the signposts along the way—lies in enhancing the dialogical dynamic between different parts of that inheritance. Put simply, citizenship as both idea and practice must be recast in ways that draw sustenance from the dialogue of civilizations.

The argument to be advanced here proceeds in three stages. First, we revisit the discourse of citizenship to identify the major landmarks of its historical trajectory and determine whether and how it can be adapted to meet the vastly altered conditions of a rapidly globalizing world. The second stage logically follows from the first. To assess the contemporary appropriateness and emancipatory potential of citizenship, we need also to probe the multifaceted character of the present human predicament and its far-reaching implications for the individual, for human collectivities of different size and function, not just the state, but for the world as a whole. Having established the complex interconnections between the citizenship ideal and global reality—but also the distance that separates them—we should be better placed to inquire into the possible contribution that civilization dialogue might make to bridging that distance and establishing a better fit between normative concerns and economic, social, and political exigencies.

THE EVOLUTION OF CITIZENSHIP

Though "citizen" derives from the Latin word *civitas*, the idea itself has a much older history, which we can trace back to Hellenic civilization. More specifically, we associate citizenship with the emergence of the Greek *polis* and the development of the twin notions of freedom and equality, which, though barely discernible in Homer's writings, become fully visible in Solon's Athens in the sixth century BC.[1] Athenian citizenship was in practice reserved for the few, but the privilege and status, which it implied rested on a profound understanding of the relationship between politics and humanity, between the public and the private. To be truly human life had to be lived inside the polis. Citizenship meant participation in the life of the community and in the decisions that vitally affect its future. In this important sense the private and private spheres became inextricably intertwined.

While it inherited the Greek legacy of citizenship, Rome substantially modified it. Civic virtue remained a distinguishing characteristic but the participatory ethos was replaced by the rule of law. As Pocock has aptly put it,

A "citizen" came to mean someone free to act by law, free to ask and expect the law's protection, a citizen of such and such legal community and such a legal standing in that community. . . . The ideal of citizenship has come to denote a legal status, which is not quite the same thing as a political status and which will, in due course, modify the meaning of the term "political" itself.[2]

Both Greek and Roman conceptions of citizenship survived the decline of the Roman Empire, but medieval Christendom shifted the understanding of the person "into the domain of religion and metaphysics," in part by establishing a division between the temporal and the supernatural, between "an earthly city that glorified itself, and a heavenly city that glorified god."[3] The corollary of this shift, implicit in Augustine's doctrine of the two cities,[4] was that the profane should be ultimately subordinate to the sacred. In time the shift was made explicit with the concerted efforts of the church to make secular power subservient to papal power. Paradoxically, at the very time that the Catholic Church seemed at the zenith of its power, its most influential theologian, Thomas Aquinas, countenanced a different path to humane governance. He argued that human law could be perverted if the intention of the lawgiver is not fixed on true good, understood as "the common good regulated according to divine justice." In that event, the tyrannical law is not consistent with reason, and therefore not worthy of obedience by the citizen. The lawgiver may be resisted by dint not of papal edict but of human reason.

Embryonically at least, Aquinas had foreshadowed the decisive shift to human reason as the governing principle in the ordering of human affairs, which several centuries later the Enlightenment would take to its ultimate and secular conclusion. Citizenship became a central plank of the project of modernity. The Greek principles of equality and freedom were resurrected but by grounding them in the existence of a secular state and the development of universalistic norms of participation in civil society. Though the state had a claim on the obedience of its citizens, its authority was in reality indistinguishable from the authority of the citizenry. In other words, state authority was legitimate to the extent that it represented the democratically expressed will of the people. State authority rested not on subjection but citizenship.[5]

THE ENLIGHTENMENT PROJECT: SCOPE AND LIMITATIONS

There is no denying that the twin impulses of democracy and nationalism in the late eighteenth century gave rise to a new conception of citizenship of considerable emancipatory potential. A new sense of belonging emerged, which, though simultaneously inclusive and exclusive, gave rise to an understanding of the citizen as "universal man," a species being endowed with inalienable "human" rights, destined to make his own history rather than be made by it.

However, when viewed in all its theoretical and practical complexity, the Enlightenment idea becomes far more ambiguous. Rousseau and Kant may have envisaged a new form of citizenship, predicated on notions of self-determination and "popular sovereignty."[6] Authoritarian power exercised from above was to be transformed into "self-legislated" power arising from the general will (Rousseau) or the "concurring and unified will" of the citizenry (Kant). The democratic impulse, which made participation in the community the defining quality of citizenship, was not, however, either universally understood or practiced. Maximalist interpretations of democratic citizenship were consistently questioned and often thwarted by minimalist conceptions. In this latter view, the individual remained external to the state, "contributing only in a certain manner to its reproduction in return for the benefits of organizational membership."[7] The participatory, communitarian ethic of shared values and intersubjective discourse was replaced by a concept of "private" or "passive" citizenship, in which the affairs of government are safely left to a periodically elected elite, citizens concentrate on their individual rights and preferences, and institutions perform a largely instrumental function.[8]

Citizenship, as it actually developed in Western liberal democracies, was gradually deprived of its participatory impulse. Daniel Skubik describes the Western, and more specifically Anglo-American, understanding of the rights of the citizen in terms of the following key attributes: (1) individuality (each human being is considered to be a separate, distinct whole; (2) moral agency (each person, is a free, autonomous agency); (3) moral equality (each individual is deemed inherently equal); (4) rationality (each individual has access to reason); (5) individual integrity (each person has an inherent dignity concomitant with his or her individuality) [Skubik 1992, 31]. It is primarily these attributes that explain the western preoccupation with negative rights understood as freedom from undue interference or repression by political authority.

Negative rights, which stress personal autonomy, are often contrasted with positive rights (freedom to) that emphasize the needs of others and support principles of justice. Though the Western conception of rights has its origins in the Judeo-Christian notion that all men are equal in the sight of God, its modern expression is inextricably linked to the growth of capitalism and to the rise of the merchant and manufacturing classes that gradually displaced the power of monarchs and feudal lords. Over time it became an integral part of the culture of modernity with its emphasis on rationality, efficiency, predictability, scientific advance, and productivity. The net effect has been to rupture the traditional attachments to local community and to create instead mobile and atomized populations whose claim to humanity rests primarily on the assertion of individual rights vis-à-vis an impersonal, distant, and bureaucratized governmental apparatus.

Though some continued to point to the preeminent role of community as the basis of individual identity and stability of character, the attractions of individual choice offered by the consumer society assumed increasing importance. Even when the conception of citizenship was widened to encompass the social and economic as well as political dimensions of public life, the stress remained very much on the rights and choices of the individual. In what became a highly influential interpretation, T. H. Marshall's *Citizenship and Social Class* written in 1949 characterized citizenship in England as having traversed three distinct phases: the emergence of civil rights in the eighteenth century, political rights in the nineteenth century, and social rights, including public education, health care, and social security, in the twentieth century. Paralleling the extension of rights was the extension of citizenship to a wide range of previously excluded groups, including women, workers, Jews, Catholics, and blacks.[9] But their inclusion was primarily as individual voters, as claimants of rights in the public domain and consumers of goods and services in the marketplace, in short as members of an atomized society. The function of the state was to guarantee the stability of both domains and so ensure in each case relatively satisfied customers.

This project, which we associate with the development of the welfare state and policies of Keynesian demand management, benefited from the unprecedented rates of economic growth registered in much of the Western world between the late 1940s and early 1970s. However, even during the heyday of capitalist peace and prosperity, several voices could be heard questioning the adequacy of political arrangements which reduced citizenship to the relatively passive enjoyment of entitlements.[10] To begin with, an entitlement to something did not necessarily mean a capacity to exercise that entitlement. Legal, political, and social rights could not be delivered by mere constitutional or legislative fiat. Such delivery would inevitably depend on appropriate political, social, and economic arrangements. In the political arena, constitutional guarantees had to be buttressed by a plurality of power centers, the open and balanced dissemination of information and opinion, and effective access to the protection of the law, especially for the less affluent social strata. In few societies were these requirements wholly or even largely met.

Liberal democratic practice is in any case vulnerable to a more radical critique. The welfare state might somehow be "democratized" through the separation of powers, the decentralization of authority, and even the establishment of a substantial set of legally enforceable rights. But such democratization is still open to the charge that the citizen may end up functioning more as an atomized individual than a member of an organic whole. By the end of the 1960s many had drawn attention to the glaring gap between an individualistic conception of rights and the participatory ethic required of the democratic society. More tellingly perhaps, some began to question whether the theory and practice of democracy, and its corollary citizenship, could be confined to the domain of the national state. Could democratic arrangements established within a state coexist with external relationships predicated on violence and domination? Were the rights and obligations of the citizen confined to the political space constituted by the state's sovereign jurisdiction?

These and other questions, highlighted as much by practical experience as by academic disputation, have in recent years encouraged many to revisit the notion of citizenship. Several developments have been important contributing factors. The first and most obvious is globalization, a complex and multifaceted phenomenon involving successive waves of technical innovation. With it has come the retooling and reorganization of production, large-scale reshaping of transportation and communication systems, and profound changes to rural and urban life. The result is a highly interconnected system of social and economic relationships, with production, trade, and finance brought increasingly under the unifying logic of the world market. Social change can now be said to be global. It unfolds over global space with key actors exercising global reach, reflects a global architecture of power, and gives rise to global norms and principles.[11] In a world of cars, planes, televisions, telephones, and computers—or, as Agnes Heller describes it, a world of "geographic promiscuity"—we are simultaneously at home everywhere and nowhere.[12]

A second and closely related development is the rapid movement of people, goods, technologies, money, ideas, images, and information. A globalizing world is by necessity a fragmenting world—a world of traveling cultures, global refugee flows, mushrooming diasporas, and new forms of religious and ethnic polarization. The erosion of existing boundaries and the creation of new ones suggest a third and crucial trend: the diminishing capacity of most societies to draw together their citizens as one, to endow them with a national identity, or enable them to speak with a single voice. At stake is the very capacity of the state to "govern." As Urry puts it, "globalization seems to involve some weakening of the power of the social and a corresponding development of 'postnational' citizenship."[13] To put it simply, the state, as both a political and legal institution, is being squeezed from above, from below, indeed from all sides. Supranational fusion, subnational fission, and transnational interconnectedness are the three dominant trends that are shaping the social, cultural, economic, and ecological landscape. The complex dynamic of these interconnected trends is calling into question both the state as exclusive ordering principle in the organization of human affairs and state-centric citizenship as the exclusive form of cultural identification and political allegiance. It is doubtful to say the least whether the idea of citizenship can continue to rest on the theory and practice of the nationally bounded society. As Bryan Turner has incisively characterized the trend,

> The processes of globalization undermine . . . the emotive commitment to membership within the nation-state. . . . The traditional language of nation-state citizenship is confronted by the alternative discourse of human rights and human-

ity as the normatively superior paradigm of political loyalty. The idea of human rights is itself partly a product of this globalization of political issues.[14]

It is not, however, a case of one discourse replacing another, or of some kind of global ethic displacing national loyalties. The net effect of contemporary trends is not to obliterate cultural and political difference, but to highlight the need for a new synthesis that somehow incorporates the universality of human rights and human needs discourse into the complex mosaic that is postmodern cultural and political life.

ADDRESSING THE MULTIPLE CRISES OF MODERNITY

Here we need to pause, if only for a moment, to remind ourselves that any attempt to reassess citizenship must do more than bring about a readjustment consistent with the structural logic of a globalizing world. It is not merely a question of ameliorating the problematic relationship between state and citizen, but of addressing the deeper psychosocial, political, and ecological imbalances which that relationship mirrors and reinforces. A new conception of citizenship is needed which can more effectively guide the reorganization of authority and power on a global scale. An emerging consensus suggests that globalization, understood as the technological, economic, and cultural integration of the world, is proceeding in ways and at a pace which our social and political institutions do not adequately comprehend, let alone guide or manage. Expressed a little more crudely, the organization of human affairs is suffering from a growing legitimation deficit. The vicissitudes of the Kyoto Protocol, last year's Johannesburg Summit, September 11, the war on terror, the unlawful use of force in Iraq are but the outward manifestations of this deficit and its radically destabilizing consequences.

It is not just that we are failing to feed the world's hungry, eradicate common diseases, bring HIV/AIDS under control, stem the tide of human rights abuse, or curb the destructiveness of weapons systems, but that in responding to this multidimensional crisis we are creating new faultlines or deepening existing ones. These assume different forms at different times, but in the present conjuncture four seem particularly deep and threatening: geopolitical faultlines that pit one major center of power against another (e.g., the United States against the Soviet Union yesterday, against China tomorrow); economic faultlines that pit the North against the South; identity faultlines that polarize states (e.g., India and Pakistan), or more often communities within states (e.g., Indonesia, Philippines, Sri Lanka), civilizational faultlines, most dramatically between the West and Islam, that seemingly validate Hunting-ton's bleak prognosis.[15]

The question arises: can we over the next several decades give shape to a transformed concept of citizenship capable of navigating the highly treach-erous seas ahead? What might such transformation involve? To begin with, citizenship can no longer be understood as the privileged, not to say exclu-sive, relationship between state and individual. The principle of "public sov-ereignty," which has since the seventeenth century been equated with the ab-solute authority of the state is in need of urgent reappraisal. The state, it is now generally conceded, is not as central to the shaping of political out-comes as was once thought, and its function is as much to keep the public will or public opinion at bay as it is to give it legal and political expression. Fearful of subjecting the workings of the global market and the profoundly altered conditions of political life to sustained public scrutiny, the legislative, administrative, and judicial arms of the state are increasingly used to obscure the diminishing efficacy of state action and to limit wherever possible the arena of normative discourse. Citizenship must therefore function not merely as a body of entitlements, which protects the individual against the encroachments of state power, but as a vehicle for connecting individuals, thereby extending the arena of public discourse and deepening the participa-tory ethic of civil society.

Civil society is in effect the missing link in much that passes for democratic theory or democratic practice in official discourse in the West. Michael Walzer is surely right to remind us "the words 'civil society' name the space of uncoerced human association and also the set of relational networks—formed for the sake of family, faith, interest, and ideology—that fill this space."[16] Citizenship, then, is best understood as a relational concept—one that connects the citizen not only to the state, but to other citizens and to civil society as a whole. To quote Walzer again:

> The picture here is of people freely associating and communicating with one an-other, forming and reforming groups of all sorts, not for the sake of any partic-ular formation—family, tribe, nation, religion, commune, brotherhood or sister-hood, interest group or ideological movement—but for the sake of sociability itself. For we are by nature social, before we are political or economic, beings.[17]

To the extent that Walzer is right to make sociability the centerpiece of civil society, it follows that citizenship must connect with all relevant forms of so-cial and political organization. Of particular importance here is the radical no-tion of "differentiated citizenship."[18] In contrast to universal conceptions of citizenship, which treat the citizen as the individual repository of universal rights, group-differentiated citizenship affirms the importance of group identity. To this end, a range of political mechanisms are envisaged, designed to provide minority groups of various kinds with access to public funds for purposes of advocacy, guaranteed representation in decision-making bodies, and veto rights over policies of direct interest to them. Understood in this sense, citizenship serves as an antidote to the propensity of many societies to privilege socially or culturally dominant groups at the expense of marginalized ones. Differentiated citizenship becomes an institutional device for "the explicit recognition and representation of oppressed groups."[19]

Group identification is not, however, the only emerging limitation on state-centric citizenship. Human security in the era of globalization is subject to a much wider and more complex range of problems, whose origin or solution can no longer be equated with the military capabilities of states. It is now generally acknowledged that many of the most pressing threats to security, including large and unregulated population movements, illicit arms transfers, drug trafficking, money laundering, and other forms of transnational organized crime, piracy on the high seas, global warming, and transboundary pollution of various kinds, global epidemics, and international terrorism, cannot be understood, let alone resolved, in primarily state-centric terms.[20] Indeed, as many Third-World countries have recently discovered, including the well performing economies of East Asia, currency and stock values can drastically fall in the wake of large, sudden, and unexpected financial flows dictated by erratic markets and the herd-like behavior of hedge funds.[21]

Given these unprecedented challenges to human survival and well-being, it is hardly surprising that a growing body of informed world opinion should be calling for major policy adjustments in the areas of trade, finance, energy consumption and production, environment, law, and health. Such adjustments, however, cannot be made purely within the traditional confines of national politics. Increasingly, the values and principles which should guide policy, and the laws, institutions and decision-making processes through which such policies are to be developed and applied must also be considered regionally and globally. New forms of ethical discourse and political behavior are called for which operate simultaneously at several levels.

A series of multifaceted and mutually reinforcing imbalances have buffeted the world system during this past century, in particular the phenomenon of "total war" as reflected in two world wars and a putative nuclear war, the profound and seemingly unbridgeable gap that separates the industrialized and less developed economies, and the increasingly dangerous disruption of planetary ecosystems of which global warming is but the most dramatic manifestation. To this must be added the organized mass slaughter of innocents, which is at the center of much contemporary experience—one need only mention the German Holocaust, Hiroshima and Nagasaki, the Cambodian "killing fields," the ethnic cleansing practices that followed the break-up of the former Yugoslavia, and the Rwandan genocide. These indelible stains on the collective human conscience have inevitably given added poignancy to the human predicament, and paradoxically enough engendered a steadily expanding consciousness of a shared human destiny.

There is much evidence to suggest that since the end of the Second World War we have seen the slow but steady rise of "world opinion," which has focused on the major problems confronting humanity: disease and epidemics; famine and humanitarian emergencies; unresolved conflicts, wars, and war crimes; pollution of the air and the seas; gross human rights violations and more generally the abuse of power. The extraordinary speed and intensity with which a peace movement of global proportions responded to the illegal actions of the U.S.-led invasion of Iraq is but the most recent manifestation of a multifaceted trend that has been long in the making. The communications revolution, itself the product of the globalization of market forces, has provided the material basis for a vastly expanded arena of ethical discourse that cuts across national, cultural, and religious boundaries. As a consequence, we are seeing, at least embryonically, the growth of a new set of allegiances and forms of political action that do not replace but complement those of the past. National citizenship continues to serve as an important form of self-identification and political participation, but increasingly it interacts with new forms of "postnational citizenship" in which political expression and activity center as much on local, regional, transnational, and global as on national space.[22]

Both the market and civil society are playing a critical role in providing the ideational and material conditions for the emergence of new forms of consciousness. Civil society, in its diverse functional and geographic manifestations, the rapidly internationalizing intellectual communities that it spawns, the expanding international civil service, and to a lesser degree the state, or at least particular states and state agencies, will form the major sites of the emerging global dialogue. Such a dialogue will be mediated by words and actions, but above all by symbols. The September 11 attacks on the World Trade Centre and the Pentagon derive their power from their symbolism. They are the latest in a series of events that dramatize three concurrent trends: the vulnerability of the state (even the world's most powerful state), the reflex and often destructive reactions of states when confronted with their own insecurity, and the growing realization that no state, however powerful, can adequately cope with that insecurity.

Key elements of the current dialogue include: the changing face of terrorism, its social and political roots, and the appropriateness of the antiterrorist policies pursued by the world's only superpower; effective and acceptable approaches to the administration of criminal justice on a global scale; the legitimacy of so-called humanitarian intervention; the unstable balance between nuclear haves and nuclear have-nots, the relationship between Islam and the West; the Arab-Israeli conflict and its possible resolution; the role of unilateralist coalitions on the one hand and of regional and global institutions on the other. At stake in this dialogue is the rediscovery, renegotiation, and reinvigoration of the twin notions of governance and citizenship.

THE RICHNESS OF OUR CIVILIZATIONAL INHERITANCE

It may well be that in this emerging dialogue the dominant Western discourse is less potent and less useful than is often assumed. Partly as a consequence of its global economic, political, and military dominance the West has come to believe in the universality of its culture and to measure progress in the light of its own achievements. Western epistemology, with its bias for analytical thinking, has tended to segment and interpret society in zero-sum or adversarial terms where one of the primary functions of conflict is to identify winners and losers. Galtung has characterized "Western social cosmology" as a complex process of fragmentation and marginalization, which separates one individual from another, material from nonmaterial needs, and the private from the public sphere. Though civil and political freedoms are considered the norm in the public sphere, they can coexist, both normatively and practically, with the widespread incidence of poverty and inequality in the private sphere.[23]

To draw attention to these shortcomings is not to ignore the very substantial contribution of the Western citizenship tradition and the associated conception of human rights, but rather to indicate that it does not hold a monopoly on citizenship and rights discourse. Vincent rightly reminds us that the West has given expression to "three worlds of democracy": one modeled on civil and political rights (Locke); the second on social and economic rights (Marx); and the third on collective rights (Rousseau).[24] While all three tendencies have left their mark, it is fair to say that the Lockean view has been predominant. The same three tendencies are also to be found in different civilizations, but here the mix has often assumed a different and subtler complexion. The contemporary international discourse on governance has, of course, developed largely under Western leadership, which helps to explain the dominance of the liberal democratic tradition. Much of the post-1945 institutional fabric not only of international relations but also of national politics in postcolonial societies were shaped by the West. Even in the aftermath of political independence, most Third-World countries, though formally participating in international fora and negotiations, could exercise only limited leverage over a process that was still driven largely by Western perceptions and priorities.

It is against this backdrop that the "Asian versus Western values" debate of the late 1980s and 1990s assumes particular significance. Though their motives varied widely, East Asian elites, encouraged by their economic success, found it useful to challenge the assumption of a universal human rights consensus, hence of a universal conception of citizenship. Whether they judged the prevailing Western discourse as prejudicial to their political and economic interests, or whether they hoped to use cultural and civilizational arguments to advance alternative conceptions of regional integration, the net effect was to call into question the hegemonic control of Western discourse.

The ensuing acrimony, for example, between the United States and China or between the European Union and the Association of Southeast Asian Nations (ASEAN), seemed at first sight to give added weight to Huntington's notion of an impending clash of civilizations.[25] On closer inspection, the notion of an unbridgeable civilizational divide between cultures that privilege rights and those that privilege duties is unsustainable. The point of the exercise, it should be stressed, is not to establish some fictitious identity between Asian and Western cultural traditions, but rather to explore the implications of differences, commonalities, and complementarities for the emerging dialogue. The question to be addressed here is: can civilizational differences, commonalities and complementarities contribute to the renewal of citizenship and governance—locally, nationally, regionally, and globally?

To illuminate this question we shall briefly survey the social cosmology of four of Asia's most influential religious and ethical systems, namely Hinduism, Buddhism, Confucianism, and Islam. Though it has a substantial presence in many parts of Asia, Christianity is omitted because we have already considered it implicitly and explicitly. The normative structure of any culture is, of course, a complex phenomenon that cannot be reduced to a religious or ethical tradition, however dominant it may be. On the other hand, for most of the societies under consideration the religious and ethical worldview is so closely interconnected with other social and cultural variables as to offer useful insights into the dynamics of social and political discourse.

Hinduism

The Hindu faith, one of the oldest world religions, still holds a remarkable sway over the cultural and political life of modern India. The Hindu tradition and the caste system that it sustains and legitimizes are, it would seem, fundamentally at odds with notions of freedom and equality. Duties and privileges are assigned on the basis of status or position as specified by caste, age, and sex. On the other hand, the Hindu tradition has tolerated and even encouraged periodic challenges to the prevailing hierarchical order. The caste system itself represents an intricate set of reciprocal relationships, with each group in theory at least respecting "the rights and dignity of the others."[26] The notion of right, it is true, remains wedded to the concept of duty or *dharma*, one of the four values, the others being wealth (*artha*), happiness (*kama*), and liberation (moksha). For many in the Hindu tradition, however, *dharma* is not only an end in itself, but the necessary means for the achievement of the other three values. *Dharma* represents an ideal of society, including "the righting of injustices, the restoring of balance which men in their ignorance or out of selfish passions had disturbed."[27]

It is instructive to note that modern Hinduism has sought to breathe new life into the five social freedoms and five individual virtues derived from an older Hindu tradition. The five freedoms refer to freedom from violence, freedom from want, freedom from exploitation, freedom from violation or dishonor, and freedom from early death or disease. The five individual virtues comprise absence of intolerance, compassion or fellow feeling, knowledge, freedom of thought and conscience, and freedom of fear and frustration or despair.[28] These are not, it is true, the standard liberal formulation of individual freedoms, but a delicately balanced framework of norms in which rights exist in relation to obligations.[29] Set in the context of ancient India, it required the king to uphold the law but also to be subject to the law. By virtue of his duties, as enshrined in sacred and customary laws, the king administered a system of justice based "on equality before the law and equal protection of law."[30]

Complementing these ancient strands in Hindu thought has been the influence of British law and education, the combined effect of which was reflected in the agenda of various social change movements, notably the Indian independence movement. Especially revealing in this respect is the contribution of Mohandas Karamchand Gandhi. Though a Hindu by birth, Gandhi could not but be influenced by the many other religious traditions with which he came into contact from early childhood. Especially influential was his Jainist friend and guide, Rajchandra Mehta, for whom religion was a "discipline of spiritual self-perfection [*sadhana*] through which we are able to know ourselves."[31] Gandhi concluded that Hinduism was consistent with such a view of religion, but from his understanding of the Hindu metaphysic he derived a social morality based on certain key principles, in particular the unity of man, life and creation, noninjury or nonviolence [*ahimsa*], and the indivisibility of humanity and of human salvation.[32]

For Gandhi man was an integral part of the cosmos, which consisted of "different orders of being ranging from the material to the human, each autonomous and standing in a complex pattern of relationship with the rest within a larger framework."[33] The cosmic order was a cooperative product that depended upon each of these orders, not least the human order, playing its part. So, while remaining faithful to the Hindu notion of *dharma* and drawing on "an ethic of community, responsibility and loyalty," he was able to establish the principle that each human being is entitled to equal consideration and concern, and "has an equal right to the necessaries of life."[34] Obedience of the law was, for Gandhi, "necessarily willed and reasoned."[35] He subordinated political obligation to a moral standard, to "loyalty to God and His Constitution."[36] The State's authority could be accepted only to the extent that its laws were just and its actions nonrepressive. Where laws were unjust and the state's conduct repressive, the citizen could appeal to his conception of truth [*satya*] to challenge the authority of the State so long as the means chosen where consistent with *ahimsa*. From these principles Gandhi derived a long list of rights, including the right to vote, the right to participate in the affairs of government, the right to resist bad government, and the right to liberate one's country from foreign rule.[37]

The Gandhian legacy represents an uneasy blending of the cosmic harmony of *dharma* and the doctrine of individual rights. Elements of that synthesis are evident in the Indian constitution, although some have interpreted its elaborate statement of fundamental rights (e.g., liberty of thought, expression, belief, faith, and worship; equality of status and of opportunity; right against exploitation) as tilting the balance too far in favor of rights and neglecting ethical notions of self-discipline, cooperation, and responsibility.[38]

Buddhism

Buddhism, which emerged as an alternative faith to Hinduism in the fifth century BC, took one strand in Hindu thought, namely the renunciation of self, to its ultimate conclusion. In opposition to the class or caste system, Gautama Buddha established the community of practitioners as a society of equals. The new religion undermined the status of the high-born priestly caste and the metaphysical system on which it was based. Accordingly, Buddha's teaching stressed impermanence rather than permanent being, radical ignorance rather than knowledge, and suffering rather than bliss.[39] The Buddhist vision of reality is of "innumerable, incalculable universes in infinite expanse, all filled with sentient beings, hellions, hungry ghosts, beasts, humans, titans, and the many gods. . . ."[40] Though Buddhas do not create these universes, they enter into all of them, and in so doing create an environment conducive to the liberation and enlightenment of sentient beings.

For our purposes several salient features of Buddhist teaching are worth highlighting. The process of evolution (*karma*) that produces human beings represents a series of successful adaptations, in which each individual is the product of countless generations of personal achievement. Upon this evolutionary foundation is built the edifice of "responsible individualism," namely the notion that every individual must take responsibility for his or her actions, since the consequences of those actions will form an integral part of his or her future experience. The knowledge that evolution can be negative as well as positive provides the incentive in the continuing quest for enlightenment, that is the cultivation of intelligence or wisdom to the transcendent degree. The accumulation of positive *karma* is made possible by the "eightfold noble path" which in ascending order consists of right views, right thought, right speech, right action, right livelihood, right effort, right mindfulness, and right contemplation.[41] There are two important points to note here: first, we are all endowed with the potential for enlightenment and liberation; secondly, the radical transformation (or renunciation) of self "does not mean the loss of personality, individuality, or moral responsibility," but the realization of an egoless but truly human personhood.[42]

There is, then, in Buddhist thought a delicate balance between the achievement of individual enlightenment and the interdependence and interconnectedness of all existence. On the one hand, human beings are viewed not anthropocentrically, but as an integral part of all existence, sentient and nonsentient. That is why they are seen as transient or impermanent, and why any notion of absolute self-identity or enduring selfhood is an illusion. On the other hand, the life of the individual is a unique experience, a unique combination of past and present relationships and experiences. Just as a person is a historical product, being born, living and dying in the world, so the historical world is affected by the creative powers of the individual. As Taitetsu Unno puts it, "here we find the absolute affirmation of the individual, irreplaceable and unique, but at the same time subservient to all things for the good of the many."[43] It is precisely this understanding which has helped to make the associated notions of noninjury [*avihimsa*] and compassion central to Buddhist teaching on the treatment of sentient beings.[44]

Writing in the third century BC, the Indian emperor Ashoka, a convert to Buddhism, stressed that all sects deserved reverence:

> For he who does reverence to his own sect while disparaging the sects of others wholly from attachment to his own, with intent to enhance the splendour of his own sect, in reality by such conduct inflicts the severest injury on his own sect.[45]

For Ashoka the object of government was noninjury, restraint, impartiality, and mild behavior applied to all creatures. We may not find in Buddhist cultures the Western liberal notion of individual rights—though some have argued that we do find in Buddhism the right to fair and equal treatment, as well as freedom from discrimination on the basis of race, creed, economic class, or gender,[46] but we do find a highly developed sense of the dignity of human life and of the responsibility that each person has as a free and rational moral agent to construct his or her life. The fulfillment of each individual is the purpose of the whole, provided that fulfillment is understood not as material acquisition but as enlightenment and liberation. In this context, culture and language are especially valued insofar as they contribute to the communication and sharing of understanding over time and space.

The monastic, spiritually centered institutions, which assumed responsibility for government in Tibet from the fifteenth to the seventeenth centuries, are perhaps the most significant attempt to date to give practical application to Buddhist teaching. A policy of nonviolence (no army, few police), unfettered access to learning, wide social mobility and universal commitment to the enlightenment of each individual became the hallmarks of this Buddhist experiment.[47] The main thrust of Buddhist political principles can also be gleaned from frequent advice offered to rulers. These principles have been described in terms of (1) individualistic transcendentalism, (2) nonviolent pacifism, (3) religious pluralism with an educational emphasis, (4) compassionate welfare paternalism, and (5) reliance on a powerful central authority to affirm the rights of individuals.[48] It is the failure of the Burmese government to abide by these principles that prompted Aung San Suu Kyi to conclude in her essay "In Quest of Democracy" that a fundamental contradiction existed between Buddhism and the Burmese dictatorship. Conversely, she saw no contradiction between "indigenous values" and "concepts which recognize the inherent dignity and equal and inalienable rights of human beings, which accept that all men are endowed with reason and conscience and which recommend a universal spirit of brotherhood."[49]

One concluding observation is especially pertinent to our analysis. Whereas Western liberalism treats each individual as a disparate, static, almost closed entity, the Buddhist conception considers human experience as a totally open, holistic phenomenon which transcends the division between the mental and the physical and aspires to an emptiness which is not sheer nothingness but openness to everything. As such it offers a healthy antidote to the crude rationalism and psychological reductionism, which have so profoundly influenced the modern liberal conception of citizenship.

Confucianism

The Confucian ethical code, as expressed in the *Four Books*: *The Analects*, *The Great Learning*, *The Doctrine of the Mean*, and *The Book of Mencius,* has largely shaped the Chinese understanding of social relationships. Its two most important contributions were to affirm the perfectibility and educability of the individual and to extend to the commoner a code that was principally derived from the rules and rituals governing the conduct of nobility in Feudal China.[50] As with the Hindu and Buddhist traditions, though without reference to their supernatural or metaphysical cosmology, the Confucian notion of human dignity is embedded not so much in the abstract, purely rational, calculating, autonomous individual favored by Western liberalism as in the person considered in relationship to other persons. It is the set of complex interpersonal relationships, that is the social context, which confers on personhood its meaning and content, hence the importance of manners, customs, and traditions in defining obligations and inextricably linking personal histories.

The Confucian ethic is not, as we shall see, antithetical to notions of justice, but the primary function of law is the maintenance of social harmony. There is considerable scope for individual lives to be aesthetically enriched, but such enrichment stems from a profound sense of shared humanity which connects the individual with others, that is with contemporaries across space, but also across time, with elders and ancestors on the one hand, and children and descendants on the other.[51] Such spatiotemporal continuities reflect and nurture the "humaneness" or "humanity" of Confucian ethics and help to explain the subordinate role of law itself.

Human relationships and expectations, whether in the context of family or community, are normally governed not by law but by reciprocity based on civility, respect, affection, and tradition. Recourse to the law, in the sense of penal codification and administration of punishment, is only a last resort, a less than optimal method of resolving conflict, since it represents "official interference in the normal processes of community life and . . . the violence or coercion of externally imposed rule."[52] The organization of human relations generally and the satisfaction of human needs in particular revolve around *rites* rather than laws. Indeed rites or *li*, understood as "the formal definition and concrete embodiment of principle,"[53] are the closest Confucian approximation to the Western conception of rights. It is *li* or the system of rites that orders five basic status relationships: ruler-subject, father-son, husband-wife, elder brother-younger brother, and friend-friend. By ordering and providing standards of rightness for these relationships, *li* orders society as a whole. The function of ritual is to socialize each member of society into his or her role, to coordinate the different roles in society, in short to preserve and transmit culture.

In ritualized behavior lies the key to the Confucian vision of social harmony, not simply because it fosters social cohesion, but in the more important sense that social relationships allow individual persons to express their uniqueness and develop their creativity. The ritual-ordered community envisaged by Confucius has been aptly described as "programmatic—a future goal that is constantly pursued . . . an open-ended aesthetic achievement, contingent upon particular ingredients and inspiration like a work of art."[54] The emphasis on ritual as an alternative to law is designed to provide more flexible, less adversarial mechanisms for the resolution of conflict. It also opens up the possibility of a social system that is both more diverse and more inclusive.

To complete this brief sketch, it remains to say a word about the function and importance of duties and obligations. Much has been written about the Confucian insistence on the need for harmony in social relationships, notably the kind of harmony which rests on hierarchy, status, deference, and uniformity, which is, in other words, preoccupied with duties as opposed to rights.[55] Yet there is in Confucian thought and practice a strong commitment to legitimacy. To put it differently, there are clear expectations as to how authority is to be exercised, for duties apply at least as much to those of high rank as they do to those of lower rank. In the neo-Confucian context, the principles of reciprocity and humaneness required officials to "govern the people with humaneness," "clean up the penal system," "be fair in administering tax collections," and "establish charitable granaries."[56] The Mandate of Heaven made it incumbent on any ruler or regime to respect the universal life-giving principles constitutive of human nature, notably the inherent dignity of man. For Kim Dae-Jung the ultimate goal of government in Confucian political philosophy is to bring peace under heaven [*pingtianxia*]. Such key government functions as "public safety, national security, and water and forest management" are subsumed under the wider concept of "peace under heaven," which includes "peaceful living and existence for all things under heaven."[57]

The neo-Confucian scholar, Lu Liu-Liang, described the moral imperative of rulership in the following terms: "The Son of Heaven occupies Heaven's position [*t'ien wei*] in order to bring together the common human family within the Four Seas, not just to serve the self-interest of one family. . . ."[58] Here we have, at least by implication, something akin to the Lockean view of natural rights, which government must respect if it is to have legitimacy, except that in this case the term "rite" is used to denote fundamental institutions and principles, whereas "right" is reserved for conduct appropriate to particular times, places, and circumstances. Where these rites are violated, where rulers ignore or thwart the ordinances of heaven, the legitimacy of rulership is thereby undermined. The duties of rulers to take care of the interests of their people imply a corresponding right on the part of the people to overthrow tyranny, a notion which finds clear and repeated expression in several Confucian classics, not least in the works of Mencius. Rulers who live up to their duties cannot be assailed, but those who do not forfeit their claim to power and may even be executed for their misdemeanors.[59] Here de Bary rightly reminds us that for Mencius the ruler-minister relation may be more telling than the ruler-subject relation. For the minister the critical consideration is adherence to what is right—"undying loyalty attaches to principle not rights."[60] To refer to this doctrine as the "right of revolution" is an unwarranted modern reinterpretation, but "remonstration against an erring monarch" is considered a paramount duty of the responsible official. To this extent at least we may legitimately speak of an incipient doctrine of rights and responsibilities.

So far as the relationship of Confucianism to Chinese political life is concerned, the most notable institutional development was the introduction by the Han Dynasty of the examination system that was to underpin a vast administrative empire and provide a major vehicle for social mobility.[61] By expanding the opportunities for political participation, and dispensing more widely the distribution of rewards, the examination system may be said to have created an incipient welfare system, which helps to explain the longevity of Confucian institutions and the absence of the kind of intellectual and political ferment that was to engulf Europe from the Renaissance and Reformation through to the Enlightenment. A number of writers have also attributed to the Confucian legacy the observable tendency of modern China, as of other East Asian societies, to fashion a highly organized social order intent on delivering job security, social welfare, and public safety.[62] The preoccupation with social and economic rights and relative neglect of civil and political rights are said to be part of the same legacy. Reference is also made in this context to several features of the contemporary Chinese constitution, in particular the inseparability of rights and duties and the practice of deriving rights from one's ongoing membership of society. By withdrawing from community participation or failing to perform certain duties, individuals can disqualify themselves from the exercise of certain rights. The same principle, namely the emphasis on wholeness rather than individuality, on the rights of all parties as distinct from one person's rights against another's, is said to characterize more generally the East Asian consensual tradition, hence the dislike of industrial strikes, trade union militancy, and adversarial politics.

There is an element of truth in all these claims, but it should not be assumed that the Confucian influence alone accounts for all or any of these aspects of contemporary political life. In China's case, several influences are at work. For example, the legalist school of thought, while still embracing social harmony as a key objective, substantially deviates from the Confucian analysis, emphasizing laws [*fa*] rather than rites [*li*], and the consistent and predictable application of codified rewards and punishments without regard to status. The more recent and profound influence has been that of Marxism, with its stress on community over individuality and on centralized planning as a legal form of state control.[63] Equally important has been the preoccupation with social and economic rights (e.g., work, education), often defined in terms of duties, but also with collective rights (e.g., right of self-determination, right to development) usually presented as part of a larger international campaign against colonialism, racism, imperialism, and hegemonism.[64]

What emerges from this discussion is that the contemporary Chinese state has merely appropriated those cultural influences and ethical prescriptions, which most closely approximate its own organizational interests, ideology, and political vocabulary. The Chinese Communist state does not embody, any more than any other state, the diversity of religious and ethical traditions that make up its cultural inheritance. To give one example, the Jiang Zemin leadership was keen to exploit the nationalist theme insofar as it could strengthen and legitimize the state and indirectly at least the Communist Party, but much less keen to explore the relationship between nation and citizenry. Yet, that connection had been integral to the awakening of national sentiment in early twentieth-century China, to which neo-Confucianism made an important intellectual contribution.

Writing at the time, Liang Qichao, a leading neo-Confucian scholar, argued for a new "public morality" that would enable people to fulfill their responsibilities toward others and toward themselves. In his essay on "Renewing the People," he referred explicitly to the citizenry as "an assemblage of individual persons" whose strength was constitutive of the strength of the state. Describing the state as "a tree" and the consciousness of rights as "its roots," he warned that "if the roots are destroyed, the tree will wither and die no matter how strong its trunk or vigorous its leaves."[65]

The moral of this story is clear enough. There exists within any civilization, especially one as large and as rich as China's, a wealth of normative tendencies, some of which at least pose a challenge to the prevailing political orthodoxy. So it is with Confucianism. There are important elements of its social cosmology, not least its view of moral human nature, its conception of rites and reciprocity, its emphasis on the need for humane and legitimate governance, which are only marginally reflected in contemporary Chinese political practice, but have considerable relevance for the future development of citizenship discourse and the application of conflict resolution norms and procedures both nationally and internationally.

Islam

Though Islam is often associated with the societies of North Africa and the Middle East its demographic center of gravity lies in South and Southeast

Asia, with its adherents accounting for the majority of the population in Pakistan, Bangladesh, Malaysia, Brunei, and Indonesia, and for significant minorities in India and the Philippines. Notwithstanding the image of political extremism, which Islamic fundamentalism conjures up in the Western mind, and much of the ill-informed stereotyping prevalent in the Western media, the closely related concepts of rights and duties are an integral part of the Islamic faith. Islamic scriptures, beliefs, and traditions may not entirely accord with the Western secular philosophy of the rights of citizens, but a spate of pronouncements and declarations by religious and political leaders suggest that the connections are both numerous and illuminating.

Of particular interest is the Memorandum prepared in 1970 by the Saudi Ministry of Foreign Affairs in response to a United Nations request. The Saudi government, not noted for its democratic credentials, had been asked to clarify its position on the 1948 Universal Declaration and the International Covenant on Social, Economic, and Cultural Rights.[66] The memorandum cited the following rights as safeguarded in Islamic law: the dignity of the human person, prohibition of racial discrimination, unity and dignity of the family, freedom of conscience, protection of the goods of others, inviolability of the home, concern for the poor, the right to knowledge, and health. Reservations were expressed in relation to three issues raised by UN statements: the right of a Muslim woman to marry a non-Muslim man; the right of Muslims to change their religion, and the right to strike and form unions. The document became the subject of extensive discussions between Saudi and European jurists as well as with officials of the Catholic Church.

Another indication of Islamic attitudes to human rights came with the 1980 Colloquium of Kuwait jointly sponsored by the International Commission of Jurists, the Union of Arab Advocates and the University of Kuwait. In his inaugural address, the Emir of Kuwait reaffirmed the Islamic commitment to human rights: "To preserve the dignity of man, it is necessary that society guarantees him food, drink, lodging, clothing, education and employment as well as his right to express his opinion, participate in the political life of his country and to be assured of his own security and his kin."[67] The colloquium reached the following conclusions: (1) the *Qur'an* and the *Sunna* present a total way of life which assures both men and women their freedom and their rights; (2) minorities in Islamic countries have the right to practice their faith, to engage in work of their choice, and to avail themselves of public resources; (3) Islam gives learning and science an honored place in the community and recognizes freedom of opinion and expression; (4) Islamic law is based on the principle of social equality; (5) in the area of penal law Islamic principles have in regard to individual security (e.g., prohibition of torture and false arrest) and the well-being of society. The colloquium conceded that Islamic practice did not always match Islamic law, and insisted on the need for a periodic review of the *Shari'ah* (i.e., codification of Islamic law) to deal with the unforeseen circumstances of modern life.[68]

A more conservative statement, prepared by the Foreign Ministers of the Organisation of the Islamic Conference for consideration by the 1981 summit meeting, affirmed the principle of human equality, without distinction of race, color, language, religion, sex, political affiliation, or social situation.[69] Numerous other Islamic scholars, jurists, and religious leaders have since returned to the same theme, arguing for the compatibility of human rights and Islamic faith, and setting out the basic principles in Islam which define and legitimate these rights.[70] These individual affirmations are to varying degrees mirrored in the constitutions of Islamic states and in their endorsement of the Universal Declaration.

It is nevertheless the *Qur'an* that remains the most authoritative source of Islamic support for the concept of rights. The right to life and property ("Your blood and your property are sacrosanct until you meet your Lord"), the right to freedom and expression, the right to freedom of religion and conscience ("There is no compulsion in religion"), the right to equality ("No Arab has superiority over a non-Arab as no non-Arab has superiority over an Arab"), equality before the law, and protection of social and economic rights, find sustenance in the *Qur'an* and the *Sunna* of the Prophet.[71] So does the overarching principle of legitimate governance:

> The nation that lived before you were destroyed by God because they punished the common man for their offences and let their dignitaries go unpunished for their crimes. . . . It is not considered obedience to God to obey a person who acts against the Good people.[72]

Yet, in seeking to liberate human beings from servitude and grant them equal status, Islam, it is true does not share the liberal passion for individual rights. For Islam human rights are not merely or even primarily the rights of individuals, but the rights of the community. In Islamic democracy freedom is affirmed as the necessary foundation for the establishment of a stable community, in which people cooperate for the sake of the common good. Conversely, the function of the stable community and of the resultant political system is to utilize resources so as to satisfy human needs and promote human creativity. The four types of freedom identified by Islam (personal freedom, freedom of expression, freedom of religious beliefs, and freedom of private ownership) form part of an "egalitarian, community-oriented approach to freedom," which distances itself from individualistic liberalism in order to stress participation in cultural creation.[73]

There is one other important difference. Whereas the modern Western conception of democracy is often associated with the notion of popular sovereignty, in Islamic theory, as indeed in medieval Christendom, rulers are but God's representatives on earth; their rule ultimately rests on divine authority. The Islamic state becomes a vehicle for God's will, which among other things requires it to prevent all forms of exploitation and injustice and to nurture instead qualities of purity, beauty, goodness, virtue, success, and prosperity.[74] While it affirms the principle of human dignity and recognizes the concepts of participation, consultation, and justice, Islamic law interprets these as much in terms of duties as of rights. The emphasis on obligation, which derives from the twin ideas of obedience to God and attachment to the collective good, translates into a range of specific duties, for example, the duty of a ruler to his people, the duty of the rich to the poor, or the duty of the individual to the community, notably the community of believers.

These duties and obligations draw their inspiration from the principles of the *Shari'ah,* that is the laws derived from the *Qur'an, the Sunna* (the way of life based on Muhammad's example), the *Hadith* (sayings and actions attributed to the Prophet), *Ijma* (the consensus of opinion shared by religious scholars), and the *Ijtihad* (the counsel of judges on a particular case). The state enjoys legitimacy to the extent that its laws and policies are in accord with the principles of the *Shari'ah.* There are two aspects of the Islamic conception of legitimacy, namely consultation and accountability, which are worth noting because they are central to governance and, by implication, to the complex relationship between human rights and conflict resolution. On matters other than those regulated by the *Qur'an* or the *Hadith* consultation *(Shura)* is considered a prerequisite for the functioning of government. The leader is required to consult with the people on all community affairs, and to do so in honesty and good faith. The duty to consult (and the right to be consulted) is closely connected to the notion of accountability, that is, in exchange for accepting leadership the leader must exercise power within the limits laid down by the *Shari'ah.* Once leaders fail to perform their functions or duties (e.g., internal and external security, proper management of public property, administration of social justice) on behalf of the community, their authority lapses and so does the community's duty to obey.[75] Here we come remarkably close to the Lockean conception of the social contract.

The place accorded the notion of rights within the Islamic tradition is impressive to say the least, yet, judged from the vantage point of liberal individualism, it seems deficient. The rights of women, the right to strike and to form unions, and freedom of religion for both Muslims and religious minorities are often cited in this respect. We confine our attention to two categories: women and religious minorities. So far as women are concerned, veiling,

seclusion, and noncontact with marriageable males are just a few of the restrictions which, it is argued, seriously violate the rights of women in Islamic
societies, hence their capacity to act as fully-fledged citizens. Three reservations are relevant here. First, such restrictions are not confined to the Islamic
world; they have been prevalent in a number of Middle Eastern and Mediterranean civilizations from ancient to rather recent times. Secondly, the *Qur'an*
may be credited with the introduction of several reforms (e.g., the obligation
on husbands to provide a dowry, thereby creating a contract between a
woman and her husband; the prohibition of female infanticide; recognition of
property rights for women before and after marriage).[76] Thirdly, many societies where Islam predominates have moved decisively to extend the economic, social, and political rights and opportunities available to women. The
treatment of women under the Taliban in Afghanistan or even in Saudi Ara-
bia differs markedly from prevailing mores and practices in Lebanon, Egypt,
Indonesia, or Malaysia.

As for the question of religious minorities in Muslim countries, the traditional understanding is that if they submit to Muslim sovereignty they can
reach an agreement for a charter of rights and duties with the Islamic state,
known as a compact of *dhimmh*. Under this compact, they may be expected
to pay a special poll tax, but are in exchange guaranteed the right to security
of life and property, freedom of worship, and a degree of internal autonomy
to conduct their personal affairs in accordance with their religious beliefs.[77]
Religious tolerance, it should be noted, was a distinguishing feature of the
reign of Moghul emperor Akbar (1556–1605). One of his enactments proclaimed: "No man should be interfered with on account of religion, and anyone [is] to be allowed to go over to a religion he pleased."[78] Akbar was no
democrat, but he was careful to organize his court in ways that respected different religions and combined their respective artistic talents and intellectual
insights. It is nevertheless true that where modern nation-states have sought
to translate *Shari'ah* principles into constitutional and legislative arrangements, the net effect has often been to place serious limitations on the exercise of religious freedom. As a generalization, guarantees for freedom of conscience appear to have fared better in those countries where Islam, though it
may be the majority religion, is not accorded official status.

In concluding this cursory analysis of the relationship of Islam to governance and rights, it is worth highlighting the severe and rising tensions that
exist between tradition and modernity within the Islamic faith. The reasser-
tion of traditional symbols, norms, and institutions is in large measure a response to long years of Western political and cultural domination and to widespread disillusionment with Western lifestyles and the Western model of
development.[79] It would appear that jumping onto the "traditional" band-

wagon might be a convenient strategy used by clerical and political elites to advance their power and influence in society. In this sense, Islamic resistance to liberal democratic theory and practice may be symbolic of larger political or cultural undercurrents.

The fact remains that within most Islamic countries there are reformist tendencies—some religious, others secular—committed to the institutionalization of new forms of governance and citizenship. These tendencies are well exemplified in the pronouncements and actions of prominent Southeast Asian leaders, including Mahathir and Anwar Ibrahim in Malaysia, and Abdurrahman Wahid in Indonesia, and President Khatami in Iran. Equally instructive are the attempts of Islamic movements to nurture reform by developing "a comprehensive and coherent Islamic methodology." Central to this project is the advocacy of a return to the earliest sources of the Islamic faith, the *Qur'an* and the *Hadith*—a parallel tendency is observable in the contemporary efforts to renew the Christian tradition—with a view to stressing their egalitarian and reformist ethos. A second but closely related strategy seeks to question the validity of certain literal prescriptions of the *Qur'an,* which, it is argued, may have made sense in the context of "the reformist possibilities of its own times,"[80] but are clearly out of step with the vastly altered circumstances of modern life. For many in the Islamic world, reform of the *Shari'ah* is an entirely feasible project, which can draw its inspiration and validation from the fundamental sources of Islam itself. Placed in this context, Islam's capacity to participate in the emerging political discourse may be much greater than is often assumed in the West.[81]

CONCLUSION

The preceding analysis has hardly done justice to the complexity of the citizenship problématique as it currently confronts the peoples and states of Asia, let alone the world. To begin with, the four traditions we have surveyed by no means exhaust the cultural or religious diversity either of the region as a whole or of its constituent societies. Secondly, civilizational discourse is not static. The multiplicity of influences, both indigenous and external, which are helping to shape the political culture of these countries, are furiously interacting with each other and are, in the process, contributing to the slow but steady transformation of norms and expectations. Enough has been said, however, to suggest that, for all their differences, Hinduism, Buddhism, Confucianism, and Islam share with Western liberalism and the Judeo-Christian tradition from which it springs a sense of the dignity of human life, a commitment to human fulfillment, and a concern for standards of "rightness" in human conduct.[82] Common to all traditions is the notion of humane and legitimate governance, although the criteria used to measure legitimacy may vary considerably from one tradition to another. There is, one may reasonably conclude, sufficient common ground between these religious and ethical worldviews to make possible an ongoing regional conversation about human ethics in general, and political ethics in particular.[83]

This is not to deny or obscure the many unique characteristics that distinguish each of the civilizational currents and cultural formations. However, it does not necessarily follow from this that differences are inimical to normative discourse either within or between the major civilizational traditions. One of the key contentions of this paper is that the emerging dialogue may benefit as much from complementarity as from commonality. Indeed, it is arguable that each of the four traditions we have reviewed can richly contribute to the universality and comprehensiveness of the evolving global governance regime. While it is true that each tradition has its own distinctive ethos and symbolism, five dimensions may be said to characterize their collective contribution. First, they provide a richer and more varied conception of political space, by establishing a closer connection between human rights and human needs, notably those of the disadvantaged (hence the emphasis on social and economic rights). Secondly, they offer a more holistic understanding of the human condition by establishing a closer connection between rights and obligations and between the individual and the community (hence the dual emphasis on rights and responsibilities). Thirdly, they help to situate citizenship within a larger social context, opening up new possibilities whereby the individual can think and act not as a disaggregated atom but as a member of several overlapping collectivities (hence the emphasis on the rights of peoples — not only the right to self-determination but the right to a healthy environment, the right to food, the right to security, the right to a share of the common heritage of humanity).

The other two dimensions flow from the preceding three but have an importance of their own. The first involves a rejection of Western hegemony, that is, a rejection of the view that the West enjoys a monopoly on the definition of human needs and human rights. Western liberal formulations (and the idea of progress on which they rest) are not seen as applying universally across time and space. Human rights standards may be universal in scope at a given moment, but how these standards are understood and applied is likely to change over time. This brings us to the last aspect of the non-Western contribution to human rights discourse, namely the emphasis on consensual decision making. If participation is one of the criteria of legitimate governance of a nation's affairs, then presumably the same criterion applies when the arena shifts from national to international governance, be it regional or global. In other words, an international system of law is more likely to command universal respect to the extent that it proceeds by way of negotiation, involves all parties concerned, and incorporates the insights of their respective traditions.

If citizens of the future are to address the immense challenges of the next several decades, they will have to participate in a dialogue of global proportions—global not simply or even primarily in geographic terms, but global in the sense that it cultivates a "global spirituality." Such a dialogue will have to point to the transcendental, yet natural unity of the human family, indeed of all life. Such unity may converge with, but at times also diverge from, the material unification of a shrinking, consuming and self-consuming, globalizing, yet fragmenting world. This will be a dialogue tailored to a new conception of citizenship that puts an entirely different complexion on unity and difference, and allows them to coexist, illuminate, and reinforce each other. Individual citizens will be exalted, not because they are at the center of the political universe, but because they are engaged in an ongoing journey of personal transformation inextricably entwined with and contributing to the transformation of social, political, and economic life. Such citizenship will understand that religious and cultural differences are not necessarily a cause for alarm. If properly understood and placed in context, they can be a source of great enrichment. In many ways the challenge of the new citizen is to practice a dialogue that appreciates and celebrates the diversity of our civilizational inheritance.

None of this is to suggest that the theory and practice of citizenship and the wider normative framework governing state conduct are likely to evolve without pain or confusion. For citizens and the various communities to which they belong must come to terms with the difficult task of reconciliation. Many communities have suffered from past violence, some continue to suffer today. Yet, we also know that many of these same communities have been the perpetrators of violence. Reconciliation will require citizens of different communities to share their stories, to listen to one another's experience of pain, to confess past wrongs, and to acknowledge collective responsibility for righting the wrongs of the past. Civilizational dialogue can become a force for healing to the extent that it nurtures a radical ethic in the evolving organization of human affairs. The implications for states and international organizations, be they the UN, the IMF, or the WTO, are equally far-reaching. These institutions have a tendency to appropriate normative and ethical ideas and symbols in the pursuit of vested interests. Official rhetoric is often used to find favor with powerful constituencies, be they domestic or international. The new citizenship will have to subject all formal structures to probing scrutiny.

The preceding analysis offers no more than a map for the possible trajectory of civilizational dialogue. Such a possibility may or may not materialize depending on two equally important and interdependent variables: the extent to which the state allows the voices of civil society sufficient political space to express themselves, and conversely the extent to which the discursive practices of civil society can draw on the deepest civilizational insights to influence the political processes of states, but also the international rule of law and the constantly expanding network of regional and global institutions.

NOTES

1. Ronald Beiner, ed., *Theorizing Citizenship* (Albany: State University of New York Press, 1995), 4–6.

2. J. G. A. Pocock, "The Ideal of Citizenship since Classical Times," in Beiner, *Theorizing Citizenship*, 35–36.

3. See Paul Barry Clarke, *Citizenship* (London: Pluto Press, 1994), 11.

4. Marcus Dods, ed., *The Works of Aurelius Augustine, Bishop of Hippo*, vol. 2: *The City of God* (Edinburgh: T. & T. Clarke, 1871–76), 326–28.

5. Clarke, *Citizenship*, 22.

6. See Jürgen Habermas, "Citizenship and National Identity: Some Reflections on the Future of Europe," in Beiner, *Theorizing Citizenship*, 259–60.

7. Habermas, "Citizenship and National Identity," 261.

8. See Charles Taylor, "The Liberal-Communitarian Debate," in Nancy L. Rosenblum, ed., *Liberalism and the Moral Life* (Cambride, MA: Harvard University Press, 1989), 178.

9. T. H. Marshall, *Class, Citizenship and Social Development* (New York: Anchor Books, 1965), 78–80.

10. C. B. Macpherson, *The Political Theory of Possessive Individualism* (London: Oxford University Press, 1962).

11. Joseph A. Camilleri, "State, Civil Society, and Economy," in Joseph A. Camilleri, Anthony P. Jarvis, and Albert J. Paolini, eds., *The State in Transition: Reimagining Political Space* (Boulder, CO: Lynne Rienner, 1995), 211.

12. Agnes Heller, "Where Are We at Home," *Thesis Eleven*, no. 41 (1995), 16.

13. John Urry, "Globalization and Citizenship," *Journal of World-Systems Research*, vol. 5 (Spring 1999), 265.

14. Bryan Turner, "Postmodern Culture/Modern Citizens," in Bart van Steenbergen, ed., *The Condition of Citizenship* (London: Sage, 1994), 157.

15. Samuel P. Huntington, *The Clash of Civilizations and the Remaking of World Order* (New York: Simon and Schuster, 1996).

16. Michael Walzer, "The Civil Society Argument," in Beiner, *Theorizing Citizenship*, 153.

17. Walzer, "The Civil Society Argument, 162.

18. Will Kymlicka and Wayne Norman, "Return of the Citizen: A Survey of Recent Work on Citizenship Theory," in Beiner, *Theorizing Citizenship*, 194.

19. Iris Marion Young, "Polity and Group Difference: A Critique of the Ideal of Universal Citizenship," in Beiner, *Theorizing Citizenship*, 175–208.

20. Joseph A. Camilleri, "Security: Old Dilemmas and New Challenges in the Post-Cold War Environment," *GeoJournal* (October 1994), 1–11.

21. Adam Harmes, "The Role of Portfolio Investors in the Asian Financial Crisis," in E. Aksu and J. Camilleri, eds., *Democratizing Global Governance* (Basingstoke, UK: Palgrave Macmillan, 2002), 117–23.

22. See Urry, "Globalization and Citizenship," 266.

23. See Johan Galtung, "International Development in Human Perspective," in John W. Burton, ed., *Conflict: Human Needs Theory* (London: Macmillan, 1993), 313.

24. See R. J. Vincent, *Human Rights and International Relations* (Cambridge, UK: Cambridge University Press, 1986), 51–52.

25. See Huntington, *The Clash of Civilizations*.

26. See Kenneth W. Thompson, ed., *The Moral Imperatives of Human Rights: A World Survey* (Washington, DC: University Press of America, 1980); and Adamantia Pollis and Peter Schwab, eds., *Human Rights: Cultural and Ideological Perspectives* (New York: Praeger, 1980).

27. Margaret Chatterjee, *Gandhi's Religious Thought* (London: Macmillan, 1983), 19.

28. Mark Juergensmeyer, cited in Robert Traer, *Faith in Human Rights: Support in Religious Traditions for a Global Struggle* (Washington, DC: Georgetown University Press, 1991), 129.

29. See Peter Bailey, *Human Rights: Australia in an International Context* (Sydney: Butterworths, 1990), 43.

30. Yougindra Koushalani, "Human Rights in Asia and Africa," *Human Rights Law Journal*, vol. 4 (1983), 407–8.

31. Sibnarayan Ray, *Gandhi and the World* (Melbourne: Hawthorn Press, 1970), 35.

32. See Bhikhu Parekh, *Gandhi's Political Philosophy* (Delhi: Ajanta, 1989), 104.

33. Parekh, *Gandhi's Political Philosophy*, 86.

34. Louis Fischer, ed., *The Essential Gandhi: His Life, Work and Ideas* (New York: Vintage Books, 1983), 284.

35. Ram Rattan, *Gandhi's Concept of Political Obligation* (Calcutta: Minerva Associates, 1972), 73.

36. Mohandas Gandhi, *The Collected Works of Mahatma Gandhi*, vol. 9 (Delhi: Ministry of Information and Broadcasting, Government of India, 1963), 107.

37. Rattan, *Gandhi's Concept of Political Obligation*, 91–92, 95.

38. See P. V. Kane, *History of Dharmashastras*, 2nd ed. (Poona: Bhandarkar Oriental Research Institute, 1968), 169; and John B. Carman, "Duties and Rights in Hindu Society," in Leroy S. Rouner, ed., *Human Rights and the World's Religions* (Notre Dame, IN: University of Notre Dame Press, 1988), 126–27.

39. Taitetsu Unno, "Personal Rights and Contemporary Buddhism," in Leroy S. Rouner, *Human Rights and the World's Religions*, 131.

40. T. Unno, "Personal Rights and Contemporary Buddhism," in Leroy S. Rouner, *Human Rights and the World's Religions*, 133–34.

41. Arthur Danto, *Mysticism and Morality: Oriental Thought and Moral Philosophy* (Harmondsworth, Middlesex: Penguin, 1987), 74.

42. Unno, "Personal Rights and Contemporary Buddhism," 140.

43. Unno, 161.

44. Ian Mabbet, "Buddhism and Freedom," in David Kelly and Anthony Reid, eds., *Asian Freedoms: The Idea of Freedom in East and Southeast Asian Societies* (Cambridge, UK: Cambridge University Press, 1998), 21.

45. Amartya Sen, "Human Rights and Asian Values," *The New Republic*, vol. 217 (14 July 1997), 37.

46. John M. Peek, "Buddhism, Human Rights and the Japanese State," *Human Rights Quarterly*, vol. 17 (1955), 527–40.

47. Unno, "Personal Rights and Contemporary Buddhism," 156.

48. Kenneth K. Ineda, "A Buddhist Response to the Nature of Human Rights," in Claude E. Welch and Virginia A. Leary, eds., *Asian Perspectives of Human Rights* (Boulder, CO: Westview Press, 1990), 94–98.

49. See Josef Silverstein, "The Idea of Freedom in Burma and the Political Thought of Daw Aung San Suu Kyi," in Kelly and Reid, eds., *Asian Freedoms*, 199.

50. Hung-Chao Tai, "Human Rights in Taiwan: Convergence of Two Political Cultures," in James C. Hsiung, ed., *Human Rights in Asia: A Cultural Perpective* (New York: Paragon House, 1985), 90.

51. Henry J. Rosemont, Jr., "Why Take Rights Seriously? A Confucian Critique," in Rouner, ed., *Human Rights and the World's Religions*, 178.

52. W. Theodore de Bary, "Neo-Confucianism and Human Rights," in Rouner, ed., *Human Rights and the World's Religions*, 187.

53. de Bary, 196.

54. Roger T. Amus, "Rites as Rights: The Confucian Alternative," in Rouner, ed., *Human Rights and the World's Religions*, 201.

55. R. J. Vincent, *Human Rights and International Relations*, 41.

56. de Bary, 191.

57. Kim Dae-Jung, "Is Culture Destiny? The Myth of Asia's Anti-Democratic Values," *Foreign Affairs*, vol. 73 (November-December 1994), 194.

58. de Bary, 195.

59. *The Chinese Classics*, vol. 2: *The Works of Mencius*, trans. James Legge (Hong Kong: Hong Kong University, 1970), 167.

60. W. Theodore de Bary, *Asian Values and Human Rights* (Cambridge, MA: Harvard University Press, 1998), 19.

61. James C. Hsiung, "Human Rights in an East Asian Perspective," in Hsiung, ed., *Human Rights in Asia*, 7–8.

62. Hsiung, 2–22.

63. See Daniel W. Skubik, "Two Perspectives on Human Rights and the Rule of Law: Chinese East and Anglo-Amerian West," *World Review*, vol. 3 (June 1992), 38–39; and Richard W. Wilson, "Rights in the People's Republic in China," in Hsiung, *Human Rights in Asia*, 109–28.

64. *Beijing Review* (July 26, 1982), 13–17, 22.

65. de Bary, "Neo-Confucianism and Human Rights," 114.

66. L. R. Fitzgerald, *The Justice God Wants: Islam and Human Rights* (Melbourne: Collins Dove, 1993), 19–21.

67. *Human Rights in Islam* (Geneva: International Commission of Jurists, 1982, 25.

68. Ibid., pp. 22–25; Traer, *Faith in Human Rights*, 111–12.

69. Fitzgerald, *The Justice of God Wants*, 26–27.

70. Traer, *Faith in Human Rights*, 113–14.

71. Allabbuksh K. Brohi, "Human Rights and Duties in Islam: A Philosophic Approach," in Salim Azzam, ed., *Islam and Contemporary Society* (London: Longman, 1982), 231–52.

72. Abdul Aziz Said and Jamil Nasser, "The Use and Abuse of Democracy in Islam," in J. L. Nelson and V. M. Green, eds., *International Human Rights: Contemporary Issues* (New York: Human Rights Publishing Group, 1980), 64.

73. Ibid., 75–76.

74. Abdul Ala Mawdudi, *Human Rights in Islam* (London: Islamic Foundation, 1982), 9–11.

75. Said and Nasser, 68–71.

76. Abdullahi A. An Na'im, "Religious Minorities under Islamic Law and the Limits of Cultural Relativism," *Human Rights Quarterly*, vol. 9 (February 1987), 10–14.

77. Kathleen Taparell, "Islam and Human Rights," *Australian Foreign Affairs* 7. Sen, "Human Rights and Asian Values," 8.

78. Sen, "Human Rights and Asian Values," 8.

79. Elizabeth Mayer, "The Dilemmas of Islamic Identity," in Rouner, ed., *Human Rights and the World's Religions*, 99–100.

80. Nikki R. Keddie, "The Rights of Women in Contemporary Islam," in Rouner, ed., *Human Rights and the World's Religions*.

81. See An Na'im, 14–18.

82. Chandra Muzaffer, "From Human Rights to Human Dignity," in Peter Van Ness, ed., *Debating Human Rights* (London: Routlege, 1999), 25–31.

83. See Edward Friedman, "Asia as a Fount of Universal Human Rights," in Van Ness, ed., *Debating Human Rights*, 32–55.

Chapter Fourteen

Khatami's Dialogue among Civilizations as International Political Theory

Fabio Petito

On November 4, 1998, the General Assembly of the United Nations unanimously adopted the resolution proposed by the president of the Islamic Republic of Iran Mohammad Khatami, and designated the year 2001 as the United Nations Year of the Dialogue among Civilizations. Since then the idea of dialogue among civilizations has been made the object of a plethora of conferences and international meetings but very little attention has been devoted by international relations and political theorists to clarify and articulate its possible meaning as a framework for the future of international relations and this is even more regretful since Khatami explicitly put forward this vision with this aim in mind. Academics with an interest in global issues, however, found the notion of dialogue among civilizations a useful rhetorical antithesis to the widely discussed and popular thesis of the clash of civilizations. In other words, the dialogue among civilizations initiative provided something like an occasion for criticizing Huntington or a fitting rhetorical device to refer to some kind of normative political dimension opposite to the clash.[1]

There are theoretical reasons that can explain this Western intellectual indifference—my favorite candidate being the supremacy of liberalism as a set of analytical and normative assumptions structuring our academic discourses; however, the fact that it was the president of the Islamic Republic of Iran, arguably the representative of the most anti-Western revolution since the emergence of the Westphalian system, to launch this political initiative, constitutes in my view another significant element in the explanation. "Why should our research agenda be designed by a rhetorical *escamotage* used for strategic reasons by some illiberal politician?," this question captures the more or less explicit, often unsaid, political assessment of the academia; but, I would argue, we miss the point if we are not able to move beyond this position. If the president of the theocracy founded by Khomeini, the real Other for the West is serious about the necessity of a dialogue among civilizations, as I believe he is, we might be confronting a paradoxical situation worthy of some thought. How is it possible that the intrinsically antiliberal leader of political Islam is calling for a global dialogue with the liberal West? Why is the tolerant liberal West not receptive to this invitation, and why is this especially true of those thinkers, scholars, and intellectuals to whom this invitation has been primarily directed?

To move beyond the predominant position of indifference and to give back intellectual dignity to Khatami's project, I will analyze his idea of dialogue among civilizations and argue, contrary to any interest-oriented and realist interpretation that sees this political discourse as nothing but a rhetorical escamotage used for strategic reasons, that its originality lies in its implicit international political theory that envisages a normative structure for a peaceful (multicultural and globalized) international society beyond the intellectual constraints of the post–1989 dominant global political discourses of the "end of history" (or globalization of liberalism) and the "clash of civilizations." Furthermore—and perhaps even politically more relevant given the too many misperceptions of Western intellectual and political circles vis à vis the Muslim world—I will suggest that Khatami's idealist-normative tension is the result of an original fusion of recent developments in Western philosophy and political theory (dialogism) with the tradition of Islamic spirituality and doctrine known as Sufism. Before turning to Khatami's vision, however, a brief note on the idea of dialogue among civilizations in the post–1989 context is called for.

"DIALOGUE AMONG CIVILIZATIONS" AS A GLOBAL POLITICAL DISCOURSE

The end of the cold war bipolar opposition, strategically organized around spheres of influence and managed through the common language of a realist ethics of statecraft, brought about, among many other things, a large debate on the future of world politics and, more importantly for our discussion, the need to rethink afresh the moral basis upon which a new international coexistence should be constructed. In this context, two intellectual reactions soon became the unavoidable opposite references for any discourse on post–cold war international order: Francis Fukuyama's "end of history" and Samuel Huntington's clash of civilizations.[2]

For Fukuyama world history, after the defeat of Communism, had reached its end as a dialectical process and liberalism, now the only game in town, represented the only *rational* model available worldwide in the now final consolidation of the linear progress of mankind. From this perspective, the problem of the new moral basis of international coexistence is greatly simplified—if not finally resolved—by the globalization of liberalism: the greater international homogeneity based on the liberal values of free market, democracy, and human rights provides the conditions to develop some form of cosmopolitan polity (here the recipes are varied) and fulfill the Kantian ideal of a perpetual peace; in the international relations jargon, the final victory of liberalism, by expelling or at least substantially mitigating the two defining features of the modern international society, anarchy, and war, marks *the end of history* of international relations as we have known them.

For Huntington the ideological conflicts that had characterized the cold war would be substituted by cultural conflicts occurring along the faultlines of civilizations. The "clash of civilizations" thesis puts forward not only a framework, what Huntington describes as the best available geopolitical map, to understand post–cold war international relations, but also an argument for a new moral basis of international relations: an international order based on a plurality of civilizations and grounded in a minimalist morality of coexistence, mainly understood as an ethics of prudence and reciprocal noninterference to prevent the threat of the clash of civilizations.[3] To have a full grasp of this recipe for world order we have to consider its two main intellectual components: first, the idea that global politics has been experiencing in the last decades of the twentieth century a return of culture and religion as determinant factors in the formation of political identity; and secondly, a realist notion of politics with its focus on conflict, security, and threat to be balanced by an ethics of responsibility and prudence exemplified by the classical principles of "balance of power," noninterference, and deterrence now applied not at the state level—as in the classical realist version—but at the civilization level.

These two theses, formulated as academic arguments, soon became powerful political frames used by key political actors to justify political choices and decisions. In particular, one knows about the association of the "end of history" with the policies of important economic organizations such as the IMF and the WTO, the view of the executives of MNCs as well as with the democracy promotion strategy supported, for example, by the Clinton administration. In a similar fashion, the clash of civilizations has been often associated with NATO's new strategies, U.S. conservative foreign policy attitudes toward China and the so-called rogue states as well as political organizations campaigning against the idea of a multicultural society. Of course, after 9/11, the clash of civilizations was again at the center of the debate on how to explain and make sense of this tragic event.

I take the idea of the dialogue among civilizations as being a third political reaction to the end of the cold war that, while not being a synthesis of the two first ones, could be set and framed, I would contend, only against the background of these two intellectually and politically powerful theses.[4] If the Islamic Revolution in Iran and the global resurgence of political Islam in the last quarter of the twentieth century are the most visible exemplification of this return of culture and religion in international politics—what Hedley Bull has aptly called the "cultural revolt against the West," after the political revolt of the decolonization struggle and economic revolt of the Third World[5]—is Khatami's initiative then really a sign of the non-Western world finally hoisting a white flag or is it the beginning of a historical *nemesis* for the arrogant liberal self-proclaimed *Last Man* announcing the *End of History*? It is to the analysis of Khatami's ideas that I now want to turn.

UNDERSTANDING KHATAMI'S DIALOGUE AMONG CIVILIZATIONS

Since the election as president of the Islamic Republic of Iran in 1997, Khatami has articulated his proposal for a dialogue among civilizations. Kathami's starting point is that "[t]oday's world is searching for a new basis on which to regulate human and social relations";[6] and it is in order "[t]o respond to this evolving global climate" that Khatami, in his 1998 speech at the UN General Assembly, proposed "that the United Nations, as a first step, designate the Year 2001 as the "Year of the Dialogue among Civilizations.""[7]

Interpreting Dialogue among Civilizations: The Post–1989 Context

The main sources of this evolving global climate can be traced to two most discussed topics in contemporary international relations: the end of the cold war and the phenomenon of globalization. Kathami, however, provides a particular reading of these issues. First of all, in his view, the collapse of the bipolar order opens up the possibility for a new and more just world order based on pluralism, one that will not be the monopoly of any single power.[8] Khatami's rejection of any unipolar form of international order goes hand in hand with his critique of the prevalent realist paradigm of international relations—as exemplified by the cold war mind-set and American foreign policy—and his commitment to the logic of dialogue. Using, as has been noted, discernibly Habermasian language,[9] Khatami in his famous interview on the CNN called for "American foreign policy [to] abandon its instrumental rationality and stop considering others as objects [and instead] respect the rights of others and adopt an approach based on communicative rationality."[10]

In a key passage of his speech at the UN General Assembly, just after having officially proposed the designation of 2001 as the "Year of Dialogue among Civilizations," Khatami, in a striking as well as unexpected praise of Western values, articulates more comprehensively his view:

> Among the worthiest achievements of this century are the acceptance of the necessity and significance of dialogue and rejection of force, promotion of understanding in culture, economic and political fields, and strengthening of the foundations of liberty, justice and human rights. Establishment and enhancement of civility, whether at national or international level, is contingent upon dialogue among societies and civilizations representing various views, inclinations and approaches.[11]

From these extracts, it is clear how the idea of dialogue among civilizations entails a critique of power politics (and in particular a rejection of the clash of civilizations thesis) combined with a commitment to a paradigm for conducting international relations where morality has a prominent role. In one of his most recent speech, on the occasion of the Conference at the UN launching the "Year of Dialogue among Civilizations," Khatami has more clearly spelled out this dimension:

> We ought to critically examine the prevalent paradigm in international relations based on the discourse of power, and the glorification of might. . . . From an ethical perspective, the paradigm of Dialogue among Civilizations requires that we give up the will-to-power and instead appeal to will-to-empathy and compassion. Without the will-to-empathy, compassion and understanding, there would be no hope for the prevalence of order in our world. We ought to gallantly combat this dearth of compassion and empathy in our world. The ultimate goal of Dialogue among Civilizations is not dialogue in and of itself, but attaining empathy and compassion.[12]

The other key dimension of Khatami's view of dialogue among civilizations is more directly related to the rise of globalization and consists of two apparently contrasting elements: on one side, the acknowledgment of the increasing economic, political, and cultural interconnectedness and its inherent push toward a convergence of people's mind-sets and ways of life; and on the other side, the rejection of the superiority of Western liberalism (in particular as formulated by the "end of history" thesis) as well as of any notion of "world culture" that is monolithic and overlooks indigenous cultures.[13] Actually, this tension represents one of the main challenges to which the dialogue among civilizations wants to respond. At a first approximation and in a politically simplified language, this search for "unity in diversity" takes the form, in Khatami's words, of statements like "we want a world that has commonalties, coexistence, but that also has differences and variety."[14] As I said, however, this issue is at the heart of Khatami's elaboration of the idea of dialogue among civilizations and I now want to show where, in my reading, the originality and depth of his vision lie.

At this stage, however, a reminder is in order: as I mentioned above, I do not take Khatami's dialogue among civilizations initiative as a foreign political discourse *strictu sensu*, that is, as discursive strategy to justify Iranian foreign policy or to protect Iranian national interests, rather as a genuine vision on how to construct a more peaceful and just world order after the end of the cold war. Statesmen are indeed sometimes at the origin of political visions aiming at the common international good—especially when they are intellectuals, as is the case for Khatami. I would recognize, however, that, also in this case, statesmen continue to speak from a specific "national" viewpoint and that the particular international vision they support does often envisage a "special" role for the State they represent. Nevertheless, tracing and reconstructing the intellectual and political arguments of Khatami's vision will help me to provide a reading opposite to the interest-oriented and strategic interpretation that emphasizes Khatami's role as foreign policymaker. But before turning to that, I want to briefly present another alternative—though always sympathetic—reading of Khatami's proposal of dialogue among civilizations.[15]

According to John Esposito and John Voll, Khatami's opening to the West must be put in the context of his world historical view on the fall and rise of civilizations and the emergence of new leading civilizations.[16] From this perspective it follows that dialogue is not a passive policy of accommodation, it is a competitive strategy for strengthening and transforming Islamic civilization because, as the West itself evolves and possibly declines, there is the opportunity for Islam to regain its position as the leading progressive world civilization.[17]

This interpretation of dialogue among civilizations as a learning strategy that has to be enacted by the Islamic world in order to catch up with the technological and economic achievements of the West can well find justifications in some passages of Khatami's writing and public speeches, but I would contend that it is not enough to explain the full meaning and rationale of his initiative. Instead of a means-ends logic, my reading of Khatami's proposal gives key importance to the broader philosophical and religious frame within which, I want to argue, the dialogue among civilizations initiative has been articulated. In order to do that, I look at three defining elements of this "dialogue"—the participants, the philosophical nature, and the aim—with an eye to make more explicit and unpack what Khatami has synthetically expressed in his public interventions.

The Participants in the Dialogue among Civilizations

The issue of the participants in the dialogue among civilizations has raised several questions. Who are the direct recipients of this call for dialogue? States, individuals, international organizations, non-state actors, such as NGOs, universities, churches? Who—assuming that we can agree on the meaningfulness of such a problematic category as civilization and, as a consequence, identify a plurality of civilizations—is supposed to legitimately represent the different civilizations in this dialogue? It could be argued that in Khatami's formulation there is a degree of ambiguity on this issue: on one side, he presents this proposal as an alternative paradigm for international relations and emphasizes the important role states are called to play, on the other, he stresses how intellectuals (and strangely enough also artists, poets, and mystics) should be central to this enterprise.[18] This ambiguity at a closer look turns out to be only apparent. In fact these two dimensions or levels—the relationships among states and among individuals (belonging to different civilizations)—become irreconcilables only if we believe international relations to be the domain realists describes to be: a competitive arena inhabited by strange—though anthropomorphic—creatures called states condemned by their nature or by impalpable (systemic) force to behave according to their national interest.[19] Khatami's rejection of power politics entails not only the refusal of politics without morality and the consequential reestablishment of the dignity of human being (will-to-empathy and compassion) as the measure for (just) world order, but also the belief that ideas and values, embedded in cultures and civilizations, inform in a determinant way all the political process on a *continuum* that goes from the singular individual to the state apparatus. As a consequence for Khatami the role of intellectuals in general and in particular with reference to the dialogue among civilizations becomes very important:

> It should not be doubted that the central role in true dialogue between cultures and Civilizations is played by the learned, by thinkers and the formers of public opinion. Scientists, artists and intellectual elites are the listening ears and communicating medium of nations, representing their spirit and psyche. They can chart new paths towards a new horizon in the dialogue between East and West.[20]

This emphasis on the embeddedness of values in national communities and civilizations and the idea that thinkers are representing the spirit and psyche

of these communities can be regarded, particularly in our positivistic globalized age, as both analytically problematic and politically dangerous, but I
think Alasdair MacIntyre has persuasively elaborated on this essential connection by developing the notion of "social tradition" as a set of practices embedded in a community.[21] For MacIntyre, every notion of morality (virtue)—
as well as any notion of justice and practical rationality (of politics, in other
words)—is embedded in a social tradition as a set of practices of a particular
community. As a consequence, there is a necessary link between a moral and
political philosophy as articulated by a thinker and the broader social and cultural context within which this view has been elaborated. This is why MacIntyre can argue that:

> There is a history yet to be written in which the Medici princes, Henry VIII and
> Thomas Cromwell, Frederick the Great and Napoleon, Walpole and Wilberforce,
> Jefferson and Robespierre are understood as expressing in their actions, often
> partially and in a variety of different ways, the very same conceptual changes
> which at the level of philosophical theory are articulated by Machiavelli and
> Hobbes, by Diderot and Condorcet, by Hume and Adam Smith and Kant.[22]

Moreover "a moral philosophy . . . characteristically presupposes a sociology" and, therefore particular values, ethical conceptions and even political
visions presuppose a social content and a social context.[23] This set of issues,
however, is beyond my present concern and at this stage my aim was only to
show how this point cannot be simply and easily dismissed as nonscientific,
given that contemporary "communitarian" philosophy has given back to it academic dignity.[24]

What I want now to underline is the kind of thinkers to whom Khatami is especially entrusting the duty of engaging in a dialogue among civilizations: "together with philosophers, scholars and theologians . . . great artists (and also poets and mystics) should undoubtedly get due recognition [in this dialogue]."[25] I
want to argue that this apparently minor or even politically irrelevant point reveals a lot about the nature of dialogue Khatami is envisaging: this is a dialogue
that aspires to be a "thick conversation," opposing both antifoundationalist or
relativist approaches that prioritize ethics and politics to ontology and a social-
scientific engineering of dialogue based on negotiation methodologies to reach
technical-limited agreements.[26] This dialogue is always and, in different ways,
a search for truth and, as such, it does not hide the deepest differences of the
participants and cannot separate the political and social realm from the existential condition of human being. In Khatami's words:

> [T]alking and listening combine to make up a bipartite—sometimes multipar-
> tite—effort to approach the truth and to reach a mutual understanding. That is

why dialogue has nothing to do with the sceptics and is not a property of those who think they are the sole proprietors of Truth. It rather reveals its beautiful but covered face only to those wayfarers who are bound on their journey of discovery hand in hand with other human beings.[27]

Who can represent or incarnate those *wayfarers* on their journey of discovery hand in hand with other human beings better than the artist, the poet, and the mystic? In another passage in a more direct way Khatami expands on this aspect:

Indeed, meta-historical discussion of such eternal human questions as the ultimate meaning of life and death, or goodness and evil ought to substantiate and enlighten any dialogue in political and social issues. Without a discussion of fundamentals, and by simply confining attention to superficial issues, dialogue would not get us far from where we currently stand. When superficial issues masquerading as "real," "urgent" and "essential" prevail, and where no agreement or at least mutual understanding concerning what is truly fundamental is obtained among parties to dialogue, in all likelihood misunderstanding and confusion would proliferate instead of empathy and compassion.[28]

THE PHILOSOPHICAL NATURE OF DIALOGUE

These elements allow us to expand the analysis on the philosophical underpinnings of the notion of dialogue put forward by Khatami. First of all, it is interesting to note how this dialogue does not demand the use of a neutral language. In particular, the Rawlsian idea of "public reason" as the only legitimate language—in the public political forum of liberal democratic societies as well as of international society—in which discussions among "irreconcilable comprehensive doctrines" can take place is implicitly rejected in favor of a political discussion that does not neutralize or hide the metaphysical backgrounds behind the idea of "the politically reasonable" but that, in a way, pushes them to the forefront searching for an understanding at this deeper level.[29]

Secondly, although sometimes unequivocally phrased in Habermasian language with strong emphasis on "the argumentative authority of reason," Khatami maintains that "dialogue, before anything else, is a search for emotional contact and sincere trust."[30] In this respect, the dialogue among civilizations envisaged by Khatami closely resembles the model of "global conversation" articulated by Fred Dallmayr building on "Michael Oakeshott's association of conversation with interpersonal friendship."[31] Expanding on Charles Taylor's discussion of the deficit of vernacular experience in the

Habermasian discourse model, Dallmayr describes a "thick conversation" or "thick dialogue" as

> a communicative exchange willing to delve into the rich fabric of different lifeworlds and cultures. The appeal in such exchange is no longer merely to the rational-cognitive capacity of participants, but rather to the full range of their situated humanity, including their hopes, aspirations, moral and spiritual convictions, as well as their agonies and frustrations. In this respect thick dialogue remains closely attentive to the "sufferings of vulnerable creatures."[32]

Does this close attentiveness to the suffering of vulnerable creatures not imply that empathy and compassion that Khatami sees as the ultimate goal of the dialogue among civilizations?

Finally, another element of the dialogical model put forward by Khatami is worth mentioning: this dialogical engagement is not only a process through which a deeper mutual understanding can emerge among different civilizations and compassion and empathy be attained, but it is also a process of discovery of the "Self" through the meeting of the "Other" and as a consequence, I would contend, it is potentially a deeply transformative event. In a recent speech, Khatami has expressed this point in a rather literary rich and politically daring way:

> One goal of dialogue among cultures and civilizations is to recognise and understand not only cultures and civilizations of others, but those of "one's own." We could know ourselves by taking a step away from ourselves and embarking on a journey away from self and homeland and eventually attaining a more profound appreciation of our true identity. It is only through immersion into another existential dimension that we could attain mediated and acquired knowledge of ourselves in addition to the immediate and direct knowledge of ourselves that we commonly possess. Through seeing others we attain a hitherto impossible knowledge of ourselves.[33]

Similar paths have been explored in theoretical terms by Hans-Georg Gadamer and Charles Taylor and recently their reflections have been applied to the specific issue of dialogue among civilizations by Dallmayr.[34] These theoretical elaborations share an emphasis on the tranformative dimension of the dialogical engagement. The outcome of dialogue so conceptualized, however, is not some form of consensualism or rationally reached agreement but rather what Gadamer refers to as a "fusion of horizons," a possible enriching change of the "prejudgements" that we carry with us as an indispensable and unavoidable starting point in any dialogical engagement. MacIntyre has expressed the huge challenge that is at stake in this essentially transgressive attempt of going beyond the moral boundaries of one's own horizon or tradition:

> [T]he fact that the self has to find its moral identity in and through its membership in communities . . . does not entail that the self has to accept the moral limitations of the particularity of those forms of community. Without those moral particularities to begin from there would never be anywhere to begin; but it is in moving forward from such particularity that the search for the good, the universal, consists. Yet particularity can never be simply left behind or obliterated. The notion of escaping from it into a realm of entirely universal maxims which belong to man as such, whether its eighteen century Kantian form or in the presentation of some modern analytical moral philosophies, is an illusion and an illusion with painful consequences. When men and women identify their partial and particular causes too easily and too completely with the cause of some universal principle, they usually behave worse than they would otherwise do.[35]

In this respect, it can be argued that the dialogue among civilizations takes MacIntyre's warning seriously by carefully, respectfully, and even critically walking the narrow and steep path of search for "unity in diversity."

THE AIM OF DIALOGUE AMONG CIVILIZATIONS

After examining the philosophical nature of the dialogue among civilizations as proposed by Khatami, I want to conclude by asking what is the aim, the real end, the rationale of this call for a dialogue among civilizations: what is really this initiative aspiring to? By answering to this final question, this concluding section rejoins the beginning of this analysis where a reading of this initiative opposite to the interest-focused interpretations—either pointing to Iran's national interest as the decisive factor in explaining this move or to a broader civilizational interest in the context of the world historical view on the fall and rise of civilizations—was announced. I want to suggest that Khatami's proposal for a dialogue among civilizations is driven by the belief that, at this particular stage in the history of humankind, getting closer to the truth—whether its ethical, political, social, or even religious dimension is concerned—inescapably requires a dialogical encounter between "East and West" (on a large scale). In religious (Abrahamic) language, that we can reasonably assume to be familiar to Khatami, there is a kind of *prophetic call* on humankind to find that deep ontological and humane unity that has been lost and this can only be attained by recognizing that "[m]an is in fact the meeting point of the soul's East and the reason's West."[36]

That is why Khatami has gone as far as saying, in a politically unusual fashion, that "[o]ne of the issues that should be on the agenda of dialogue is: is there truth or not?"; and continuing along these lines of reasoning, "if we accept these two assumptions—that truth exists and that man can generally get to the truth—then the real aim of dialogue is understanding," he reaches the conclusion that "[I]n dialogue based on understanding and sincerity, I believe we can get closer to the truth."[37] As stated before, this dialogue in Khatami's view must have as main protagonists East and West since:

> West and East are not only geographical regions, but also kinds of worldviews and ontologies. In genuine dialogue, one can accept what is true in each outlook, highlight the better truths in each by accepting their capacities, values and developments, and in a changing world look for the common human element in the median between material and spirit.[38]

This quotation contains all the main elements of the argument put forward by Khatami. In a simplified and schematic way, Khatami is presenting us with a series of three related dichotomies: West and East, modernity and tradition, materialism and spirituality. It is his belief that in this particular historical context, the path for human progress and for the construction of a more just and peaceful world order necessarily lies on the border between these dichotomies. In several passages of his speeches Khatami stresses, on one side, the imbalance suffered by the West with its overreliance on rationality and its fascination with materialism, on the other, the need for the East to embark on a critique of tradition and gain true knowledge of the critical approach of Western culture.[39]

This analysis is supplemented by the firm belief that the Western techno-political hegemony grounded in its intellectual overreliance on rationality is already experiencing a deep crisis at different levels—intellectual, political, and social—and if "the establishment of peace, security and justice in the world" must be achieved "[t]he next century should be a century for turning to a kind of spirituality that the Oriental Man has several thousand years of experience in its pursuit."[40] Referring to a wide range of problems that beset the world today such as the crisis in the relationship of man and nature, the ethical crisis that has developed in scientific research and the family crisis, Khatami reaffirms the centrality of the dialogue among civilizations also in finding practical solutions since "[I]t now appears that the Cartesian-Faustian narrative of Western civilizations should give way and begin to listen to other narratives proposed by other human cultures."[41] Along similar lines, William Johnston has remarked that at the beginning of the twentieth century the Jewish thinker Simone Weil (1909–1943) spoke prophetically of Europe's need for Eastern spirituality: "It seems that Europe requires genuine contacts with the East in order to remain spiritually alive. It is also true that there is something in Europe that opposes the Oriental spirit, something specifically Western . . . and we are in danger of being devoured by it."[42]

These criticisms, however, are always balanced by Khatami's praise for Western culture and its achievements. In this respect it might not seem easy to make sense of how Khatami reconciles his own strong foundational starting point with an unconditional openness to the transformative dimension of dialogue and to its unpredictability in terms of result as expressed, for example, in the following passage: "Dialogue is a bi-lateral or even multi-lateral process in which the end result is not manifest from the beginning. We ought to prepare ourselves for surprising outcomes as every dialogue provides grounds for human creativity to flourish."[43]

INTERPRETING KHATAMI'S VISION
OF DIALOGUE AMONG CIVILIZATIONS:
THE ROLE OF SUFISM AND DIALOGICAL THEORY

The just-mentioned apparent contradiction might well be resolved by pointing to the "insincere" or strategic nature of the call for a dialogue among civilizations in one of the two versions that I have already mentioned. From this standpoint, the declared openness to the surprising outcomes of the dialogue is nothing less than a costless rhetorical device. How can someone who believes to be the possessor of Truth—in this case as revealed in Islam—truly show such an openness to the dialogical contribution of the Other? I think I have already shown that the understanding Khatami has of Truth and the access man has to it is much more philosophically rich and nuanced than we tend to expect—in the Western world—from an Islamic thinker! (This could also be said, perhaps to a lesser degree, for a religious thinker *tout court*).[44]

An answer to this apparent paradox—of great political relevance given the many misperceptions of Western intellectual and political circles vis à vis the Muslim world—is to trace the roots of Khatami's arguments to the very rich and ancient philosophical tradition of doctrinal Sufism. Sufism is "an interpretation of Islam that prioritizes the religious and spiritual dimension, focusing on man's interior walk of perfection." Grown in the world of the Muslim confraternities in the very first centuries of Islamic expansion, it has suffered a major setback in the twentieth century as a result of the international rise of Wahhabism and the criticisms of various Islamic reformers,[45] but is today the object of a new attention by a number of Muslim reformists such as Abdolkarim Soroush in Iran, Maulana Wahiduddin Khan in India, and Syed Muhammad Naquib al-Attas in Malaysia. These Islamic intellectuals have been exploring new perspectives in the spirit of what another Iranian Islamic reformer, Ali Shari'ati, has called "the war of religion against religion."[46] This religious matrix, it seems to me, is an essential reference to locate intellectually Khatami's argument and to make sense of passages like the following one:

> There was a time when poets who promoted colonialism, such as Rudyard Kipling, used to say that "East is East and West is West and never the twain shall meet." Today, the vision of a unipolar world and the dissolution of all cultures and civilizations into the dominant culture of the world is another expression of such a prejudiced and nation-oriented view. Goethe said, "The East is God's, the West is God's," and Iqbal, as if to indicate the origin of the German poet's inspiration, adorned his Message of the East with the Qur'anic verse that "East and West belong to God." The objective of both poets is to show a point where East and West meet. This common point of contact, in both views, is the divine origin of humanity. The feeling of estrangement the East and West have towards each other will be dissolved when each stops viewing itself as an absolute phenomenon and see its "self" in relation to the "other" and in relation to this common origin. This is how East and West help each other towards perfection.[47]

Here the Sufi sources and inspirations are evident for, as Andrey Smirnov has recently argued with specific reference to Ibn Arabi, Sufism maintains that the beautiful plurality of religious beliefs finds a deep harmonious unification in the ungraspable and uncontainable greatness of God.[48] This also explains why many authors have pointed to the intrinsically well-disposed attitude of Sufism vis à vis the process of inter-religious dialogue.[49]

Furthermore, as I have sporadically indicated in my analysis, Khatami's initiative seems to express in the international sphere the very same conceptual changes, which at the level of philosophical theory have been articulated by the dialogical approaches that have critically analyzed the logocentric assumptions of our philosophical thinking and tried to overcome the stalemate of the communitarian/cosmopolitan (liberal) divide. This communitarian path to cosmopolitanism, to use Richard Shapcott's formulation, has been primarily outlined by Gadamer in his model of dialogue as "fusion of horizons" and it is therefore not surprising that in the post–1989 era, the father of hermeneutics and perhaps the greatest witness of twentieth century European philosophy could talk in the following terms on the need of creating "new global solidarities:"[50]

> [t]he human solidarity that I envisage is not a global uniformity but unity in diversity. We must learn to appreciate and tolerate pluralities, multiplicities, and cultural differences. . . . Unity in diversity, and not uniformity and hegemony— that is the heritage of Europe. Such unity-in-diversity has to be extended to the whole world—to include Japan, China, India, and also Muslim cultures. Every

culture, every people has something distinctive to offer for the solidarity and welfare of humanity.[51]

Khatami's initiative of dialogue among civilizations can therefore be, in some way, interpreted as a transgressive and transformative dialogical journey open to unpredictable outcomes and inspired by this "contemplation in action or mysticism of everyday life" that Fred Dallmayr sees as the kind of spirituality urgently needed for the creation of a more peaceful and humane global order.[52]

SKETCHING DIALOGUE AMONG CIVILIZATIONS AS INTERNATIONAL POLITICAL THEORY

As I have argued, dialogue among civilizations as global political discourse was set and framed by Khatami against the background of the end of history and the clash of civilizations theses. We can start from here to sketch dialogue among civilizations as international political theory, that is, an argument for the moral basis of a multicultural and globalized international society. In a simplified and schematic way, it can be said that the dialogue among civilizations shares *analytically* essential assumptions with the thesis of the clash of civilizations while *normatively* is closer to the approach endorsed by the end of history.

In fact, against the analytical and empirical argument about the globalization of liberalism being the last stage of the modernization and secularization of the world, the dialogue among civilizations stresses the global resurgence of culture and religion in world politics and identifies in the quest for cultural authenticity the main present political issue in the relationship between the Western and non-Western world. But where Huntington sees the clash of civilizations scenario as mainly a social-scientific *prediction*, the dialogue among civilizations sees it as a dangerous *possibility* produced by wrong policies that need to be opposed.

On the normative side, it is self-evident that the proposal for a dialogue among civilizations is formulated as a reaction to the clash of civilizations thesis. In simple terms, the former is designed to prevent and avoid the latter. The reason that explains why from rather convergent empirical considerations and analyses, the supporters of the dialogue strategy reach very different conclusions from Huntington has to do, in my view, with the very different notion of (international) politics these two positions assume: where Huntington subscribes to a *realist* political framework, the dialogue strategy is committed to a more *idealist* framework closer to the notion of politics implicit in the end of

a history thesis. In the first case, struggle for power is perceived to be the unavoidable necessity of politics and this condemns international politics to be
the realm of conflict *recurrence and repetition* that can only be partially miti-
gated by a *consequentialist* ethics of statecraft based on noninterference. In the
second case, an idealist commitment to politics as a search for *justice* and for
mutual understanding through *conversation* prevails, and as a consequence, international politics is perceived as a realm where *progress*, however difficult,
is nonetheless possible on the basis of an ethics of *ends*.

Saying this, however, does not imply that the dialogue among civilizations
as an argument for the moral basis of contemporary international society can
be interpreted as a via media theoretical position between the clash of civilizations and the end of history; rather I have suggested that if the attention is
shifted from theory to practice, the radical distance of the dialogue among
civilizations from the other two theses becomes apparent. In particular, while
the two share a pragmatic political commitment to what I call a Western-centric and liberal global order, the dialogue among civilizations points toward
and calls for the reopening and rediscussion of the core Western-centric and
liberal assumptions upon which the normative structure of the contemporary
international society is based.

From this perspective, the idea of a dialogue among civilizations as an argument for the moral basis of a multicultural and globalized international society represents the only powerful normative challenge to the contemporary
political orthodoxy, not only in the sense that it opposes Western political
hegemony but also, and more importantly, because it calls for the reopening
and rediscussion of the core Western-centric and liberal assumptions upon
which the normative structure of the contemporary international society is
based. By way of conclusion and following Khatami's intuitions I want to
point to some theoretical and political lines that need to be included by any
reflection on the normative structure of contemporary international society
that want to be sensitive to this call.

First, if the normative structure—the global ethos—of future global coexistence is to be genuinely universal, it cannot only be liberal and Western-
centric. Genuine universality requires a thick conception of the presence of
different cultures and civilizations in world affairs; in many ways it must also
spring from there. A fundamental void looms when this global ethos reflects
the tenets of a cosmopolitan liberalism, a political tradition that forecloses the
centrality of cultural and religious identity in the everyday practices of "really existing communities."[53]

Secondly, any reflection on a principled world order based on dialogue
among civilizations has to acknowledge something like a fundamental ethical
and political crisis of the secularized and liberal Western civilization. To this

critical situation, the dialogue among civilizations seems to bring the promise of an answer, or better, a way, a path on which to start walking in search for an answer through the dialogical encounter with the premodern humanistic wisdom of the great world civilizations and traditions.

Finally, the present situation of international politics imposes on us all a moral and political obligation to pursue a politics of intercivilizational understanding since it cannot be ignored that on September 11, 2001, during the year designated by the United Nations as the "Year of Dialogue among Civilizations," the shadow of a future clash of civilizations has expanded incredibly fast in the world and brought a growing atmosphere of fear and war in which we have been enveloped since those terrible terrorist attacks. Not only that: the search for a new global ethos, that is unity in diversity, is today even more necessary to defend the plurality of world politics against any imperial temptation; for in the words of Hans Georg Gadamer "[t]he hegemony or unchallengeable power of any one single nation . . . is dangerous for humanity. It would go against human freedom."[54] With this context in mind, a politics of understanding would already be a great achievement. But to really face this challenge at its roots we need to imagine a way out of this strict grid of choices imposed by the contemporary Western-centric and liberal global order toward the construction of a multicultural peaceful international society. For this we need to criticize the present unipolar Western-centric and liberal global order and support a politics of intercivilizational dialogue; in the hopeful expectation that the future might see the emergence of unpredictable and heterodox political alliances in the spirit of dialogue among civilizations.

NOTES

Earlier versions of this paper were presented at the LSE IR Theory Workshop in November 2001 and at the conference on "Political Science and Dialogue among Civilizations," hosted by the International Centre for Dialogue among Civilizations, Teheran, Iran, in May 2003. I want to thank Pavlos Hatzopoulos, Joseph Camilleri, Alain Chong, Abbas Manoochehri, Louiza Odysseos, John L. Esposito, and Alberto Ventura for their comments and pertinent suggestions.

1. Samuel Huntington, "The Clash of Civilizations?," *Foreign Affairs*, vol. 72 (1993), 22–49.

2. Francis Fukuyama, *The End of History and the Last Man* (New York: Free Press, 1992) and Huntington, "The Clash of Civilizations?"

3. This argument is more clearly articulated in the book that followed his article. See Samuel Huntington, *The Clash of Civilizations and the Remaking of World Order* (London: Simon & Schuster, 1996).

4. Here it is fair to mention that Khatami has not been the only political proponents of such a vision although he has to get much of the credit for its politicization. For example, Václav Havel, moving from a very different political and intellectual starting point, has developed a very similar vision though under the different rubrics of "multipolar and multicultural civilization" and "search for unity in diversity," see Fabio Petito, "Havel and the Future of International Relations," *World Affairs*, vol. 7, no. 4, 106–19.

5. For the return of culture and identity in International Relations, see Yosef Lapid and Friedrich Kratochwil, *The Return of Culture and Identity in International Relations Theory* (London: Lynne Rienner, 1996). For the global resurgence of religion and its implications for International Relations see Fabio Petito and Pavlos Hatzopoulos, eds., *Religion in International Relations: The Return from Exile* (New York: Palgrave, 2003); and Hedley Bull, "The Revolt against the West," in *The Expansion of International Society*, eds. H. Bull and A. Watson (Oxford: Clarendon Press, 1984).

6. Mohammad Khatami, remarks at the Symposium on "Islam, Iran and the Dialogue of Civilizations," Palace of Weimar, Berlin, July 12, 2000; an edited transcript of the discussion can be found in Mohammad Khatami, Josef van Ess, and Hans Küng, "Symposium: Islam, Iran and the Dialogue of Civilizations," *Global Dialogue* 3 (2001), 1–13.

7. Mohammad Khatami, speech at the United Nations General Assembly, New York, September 21, 1998.

8. Mohammad Khatami, statement at the Eighth Session of the Islamic Summit Conference, Tehran, December 9, 1997 [www.persia.org/] (24 September 2001).

9. Mark Lynch, "The Dialogue of Civilizations and International Public Spheres," *Millennium: Journal of International Studies* 29, no. 2 (2000), 307.

10. Mohammad Khatami, interview by Christiane Amanpour, CNN, January 7, 1998, transcript found in [www.persia.org/khatami/s_khatami06.html] (September 24, 2001).

11. Mohammad Khatami, speech at the United Nations General Assembly, New York, 21 September 1998.

12. Mohammad Khatami, address at the "Dialogue among Civilizations" Conference at the United Nations, New York, September 5, 2000 [http://www.un.int/iran/dialog05.html] (September 20, 2001).

13. Ibid.

14. Khatami, "Symposium," 12.

15. John L. Esposito and John O. Voll, "Islam and the West: Muslim Voices of Dialogue," in *Religion in International Relations: The Return from Exile*, eds. Fabio Petito and Pavlos Hatzopoulos (New York: Palgrave, 2003), 237–69.

16. This view has been extensively articulated by Khatami in his *Islam, Liberty and Development* (Binghamton, NY: Institute of Global Cultural Studies at Binghamton University, 1998). In this respect, a change of emphasis in the public speeches following the publication of this book can well be explained by the fact that Khatami's initiative is work in progress open to reelaboration and rethinking.

17. Ibid., 629.

18. Khatami, address at the "Dialogue among Civilizations" Conference.

19. Probably this statement can be generalized to all state-centric and interest-driven theories of international relations that exclude a central role for ideational and normative factors, in particular the rational choice approach. For a classical *locus* see Kenneth Waltz, *Theory of International Politics* (Reading, MA: Addison-Wesley, 1979).

20. Khatami, "Symposium," 2, italics added.

21. Alasdair MacIntyre, *After Virtue*, 2nd ed. (London: Duckworth, 1985). For a discussion of MacIntyre's notion of social tradition in the context of the IR debate on international society see Scott Thomas, "Taking Religious and Cultural Pluralism Seriously: The Global Resurgence of Religion and the Transformation of International Society," *Religion in International Relations*, 21–53.

22. Alasdair MacIntyre, *After Virtue*, 2nd Edition (London: Duckworth, 1985), 61.

23. MacIntyre, *After Virtue*, 23.

24. A similar approach can be found, in my view, in what has been described as the "theology of nations" of Pope John Paul II; see Andrea Riccardi, *Governo carismatico. 25 anni di pontificato* (Milano: Mondadori, 2003) as well as in the role that according to Arnold Toynbee "creative minorities" have in the birth and flourishing of civilizations. See D. C. Somervell, *A Study of History: Abridgement of Vols I–X in one volume*, with a new preface by Toynbee (Oxford: Oxford University Press, 1960).

25. Khatami, address at the "Dialogue among Civilizations" Conference.

26. On "thick conversation" see Fred Dallmayr, "Conversation across Boundaries: Political Theory and Global Diversity," *Millennium: Journal of International Studies*, vol. 30, (2001), 331–47 and also Thomas, "Taking Religious and Cultural Pluralism Seriously."

27. Mohammad Khatami, speech at the European University Institute, Fiesole, Florence, 15 March 1999 [http://www.] (2001), emphasis added.

28. Khatami, address at the "Dialogue among Civilizations" Conference.

29. John Rawls *Political Liberalism* (New York: Columbia University Press, 1993) and *The Law of Peoples* (Cambridge, MA: Harvard University Press, 1999).

30. For the centrality of reason in dialogue see Khatami, speech at the European University Institute; Khatami, "Symposium," 1.

31. Dallmayr, "Conversation across Boundaries," 332. In a similar move, Dallmayr rejects a strong separation or distance between his model of conversation and the neo-Kantian model of cosmopolitan discourse proposed by Habermas.

32. Dallmayr, "Conversation across Boundaries," 346. For Charles Taylor's discussion along similar lines see Taylor, *Sources of the Self: The Making of Modern Identity* (Cambridge, MA: Harvard University Press, 1989) and "The Politics of Recognition," in *Multiculturalism*, ed. Amy Gutmann (Princeton, NJ: Princeton University Press, 1994).

33. Khatami, address at the "Dialogue among Civilizations" Conference.

34. Hans-Georg Gadamer, *Truth and Method*, 2nd rev. ed., trans. Joel Weinsheimer and Donald G. Marshall (New York: Crossroad, 1989); Taylor, *Sources of the Self*; Fred Dallmayr, "A Gadamerian Perspective on Civilizational Dialogue," *Global Dialogue*, vol. 3 (2001), 64–75, and *Dialogue among Civilizations: Some Exemplary Voices* (New York: Palgrave, 2002).

35. MacIntyre, *After Virtue*, 221, emphasis in original.

36. Mohammad Khatami, speech at the European University Institute, Fiesole.

37. Khatami, "Symposium," 5.

38. Khatami, "Symposium," 2.

39. For the critique of the West see in particular, Khatami, "Symposium," 7 and the speech at the European University Institute. For a critique of the East it is also interesting to look at the speeches that Khatami has delivered in the context of the Islamic Conference Organization.

40. Khatami, speech at the European University Institute. For the same argument made from a Christian standpoint see William Johnston, *"Arise, My Love . . .": Mysticism for a New Era* (Marykoll, NY: Orbis Books, 2000).

41. Khatami, address at the "Dialogue among Civilizations" Conference.

42. Simone Weil, cited in William Johnston, *"Arise, My Love . . .": Mysticism for a New Era* (Maryknoll, NY: Orbis Books, 2000), 40.

43. Ibid.

44. For example see this statement: "The understanding of Truth is historical-bound and complete truth is never acquired but rather genuine and constant search is the attitude that is more proper to it," Khatami, Eighth Session of the Islamic Summit Conference.

45. Marietta Stepanyants, "Introduzione," in Marietta Stepanyants, ed., *Sufismo e confraternite nell'Islam contemporaneo. Il difficile equilibrio tra mistica e politica* (Torino: Edizioni Fondazione Agnelli, 2003), x. See also the chapter by Alberto Ventura in the same volume.

46. Marietta Stepanyants, "Il sufismo nel contesto delle dinamiche politiche contemporanee," in Marietta Stepanyants, ed., *Sufismo e confraternite nell'Islam contemporaneo*, 341. Ali Shari'ati is cited there.

47. Khatami, "Symposium," 3–4.

48. Andrey Smirnov, "Il concetto di 'essere' nel sufismo: quale spazio per una tolleranza universale? Il problema della diversità religiosa" in Marietta Stepanyants, ed., *Sufismo e confraternite nell'Islam contemporaneo*.

49. See the chapters by Scattolin, Gursory, Rafique, and Murata in Marietta Stepanyants, *Sufismo e confraternite nell'Islam contemporaneo*.

50. Richard Shapcott, *Justice, Community and Dialogue in International Relations* (Cambridge: Cambridge University Press, 2001). See also Fred Dallmayr, "A Gadamerian Perspective on Civilizational Dialogue," *Global Dialogue*, vol. 3, (2001), 64–75, reprinted in Dallmayr, *Dialogue among Civilizations: Some Exemplary Voices*, (New York: Palgrave, 2002), Ch. 1.

51. Thomas Pantham, "Some Dimensions of Universality of Philosophical Hermeneutics: A Conversation with Hans-Georg Gadamer," *Journal of Indian Council of Philosophical Research*, vol. 9 (1992), 132 quoted in Dallmayr, *Beyond Orientalism*, xiii.

52. Fred Dallmayr, "A Global Spiritual Resurgence? On Christian and Islamic Spiritualities," in F. Petito and P. Hatzopoulos, eds., *Religion in International Relations*, 209–36.

53. Jean Bethke Elshtain, "Really Existing Communities," *Review of International Studies*, vol. 25 (1999), 141–46.

54. Thomas Pantham, "Some Dimensions of Universality of Philosophical Hermeneutics: A Conversation with Hans-Georg Gadamer," *Journal of Indian Council of Philosophical Research*, vol. 9 (1992), 132.

Index

About the Contributors

Seyed Ali Reza Hosseini Beheshti is senior lecturer in political thought at Tarbiat Modares University (Tehran). He teaches Medieval Political Thought and Contemporary Political Theory and is interested in multiculturalism, identity, and politics of cultural diversity. His publications include *Theoretical Aspects of Toleration* (1998 in Persian), *Postmodernism and Contemporary Iran* (1998 in Persian), *Theoretical Aspects of the Theory of Justice* (2000 in Persian), *Foundations of Politics in Multicultural Societies* (2002 in Persian and Arabic), and *Surveys of Western Political Thought* (2004).

Joseph A. Camilleri is professor of international relations and director of the Centre for Dialogue at La Trobe University. He has written and lectured extensively on international relations, governance and globalization, human rights, North-South relations, international organizations, the United Nations, and the Asia-Pacific region. His most recent books include: *Regionalism in the New Asia Pacific Order* (Edward Elgar 2003); coedited *Democratizing Global Governance* (Palgrave Macmillan 2002); edited *Religion and Culture in Asia Pacific: Violence or Healing?* (Vista 2001); *States, Markets and Civil Society in Asia Pacific* (Edward Elgar 2000). He is a fellow of the Australian Academy of Social Sciences, and the recipient of St. Michael's Award for Distinguished Service to the Community.

Fred Dallmayr is Packey J. Dee Professor in the departments of philosophy and political science at the University of Notre Dame. He holds a Doctor of Law degree from the University of Munich (1955) and a Ph.D. in political science from Duke University (1960). He has been a visiting professor at Hamburg University in Germany and at the New School for Social Research in New York, and a fellow at Nuffield College in Oxford. He has been teaching at Notre Dame University since 1978. During 1991–1992 he was in India on a Fulbright research grant. Some of his recent publications are: *Between Freiburg and Frankfurt* (1991); *The Other Heidegger* (1993); *Beyond Orientalism: Essays on Cross-Cultural Encounter* (1996; Japanese translation 2001); *Alternative Visions: Paths in the Global Village* (1998: Persian translation 2005); *Achieving Our World: Toward a Global and Plural Democracy* (2001); *Dialogue among Civilizations: Some Exemplary Voices* (2002; Italian translation forthcoming); *Hegel: Modernity and Politics* (new ed. 2002); *Peace Talks—Who Will Listen?* (2004); and *Small Wonder: Global Power and Its Discontents* (2005).

Ahmad Golmohammadi is assistant professor of political science at Allame Tabatabaee University (Iran). He teaches history and political sociology of modern Iran. His publications include *Globalization, Culture and Identity* (1381/2002), *"Fadaeian e Eslam": a Documentary Narrative* (1382/2003), *Iran between Two Revolutions* (translation 1998).

Hadi Khaniki, Ph.D. in communication, is a member of the scientific staff of Allameh Tabatabaee University (Tehran). He has published several books, including: *Power, Civil Society and the Media* and *In the World of Dialogue*. Khaniki has also conducted 16 researches and published 53 scientific articles. He has held the following scientific positions: Director and Chief Editor of *Resaneh*, a quarterly journal on the media; chief editor of the quarterly journal *Nameyeh Farhang*; and the quarterly journal *Daftare Danesh*. He has been cultural advisor to Mr. Khatami, the former president of Iran, and a member of the High Council of National Committee of UNESCO in Iran; cultural deputy of Ministry of Higher Education, and director of the Research Center of Cultural and Social Studies. Now he is a member of the board and director of the committee of the International Institute of Dialogue among Cultures and Civilizations. His main field of specialization is media, cultural studies, and more specifically dialogue among cultures and recent social developments of Iran.

Abbas Manoochehri is senior lecturer in political theory at the Tarbiat Modares University in Tehran. He received his Ph.D. in political theory in 1988 from the University of Missouri at Columbia (USA). His research interests include comparative contemporary political theory, intercultural philosophy and world peace, postcolonial thought, and contemporary Iranian political thought. He is a member of the board of directors of the Iranian Political Science Association, and the chief editor of the *Iranian Journal of Political Research*. Among his works are: "Enrique Dussel and Ali Shari'ati on Cultural Imperialism," in *Cultural Imperialism* (Broadview Press, 2006, with German translation forthcoming), *Theories of Revolution* (2001, in Farsi, Arabic translation forthcoming), *Ali Shari'ati: Hermeneutic of Liberation and Civic Mysticism* (2004, in Farsi), *Hermeneutics, Knowledge and Emancipation* (2002, in Persian).

Homeira Moshirzadeh (Ph.D. University of Tehran 1999) is an assistant professor in the Department of International Relations (IR) and an adjunct faculty at the Center for Women's Studies, University of Tehran. Her main scholarly interests are international relations theory, theories of social movements, and women's studies. She has published several books in Persian, including: *Social Movements: A Theoretical Introduction* (2001), *From a Social Movement to a Social Theory: History of Feminism* (2002), *An Introduction to Women's Studies* (2005), and *Theories of International Relations* (2006). She has edited the books *Caspian Sea: An Overview* (2002) and *Dialogue of Civilizations* (2005), and has translated some of the major IR texts into Persian, including Hans Morgenthau's *Politics among Nations* and Alexander Wendt's *Social Theory of International Politics*. Her articles on international relations, feminism, Iran's foreign policy, dialogue of civilizations, etc., have been published in Persian and English journals, including *Siasat Khareji* (*Foreign Policy*), *Majalleh Daneshkadeh Hoghoogh va Olum Siasi* (*Journal of the Faculty of Law and Political Science*) and the *Iranian Journal of International Affairs*.

Norma Claire Moruzzi is associate professor of political science and gender and women's studies at the University of Illinois at Chicago. She received a Ph.D. in political science from the John Hopkins University in 1990. Her research interests focus on the intersections of gender, religion, and national identity, particularly for Jewish and Muslim women. Her book *Speaking through the Mask: Hannah Arendt and the Politics of Social Identity* (2000) won the 2002 Gradiva Award. She has published articles on Iranian cinema, politicized veiling in France and Algeria, contemporary feminist approaches to female circumcision, and nineteenth-century intersections of religious revivalism and imperial policy. Her current project is a book analyzing transformations in Iranian women's lives since the 1979 Revolution, tentatively titled *Tied up in Tehran: Women, Social Change, and the Politics of Daily Life*. Since 1998 she has been regularly conducting fieldwork in Iran, as well as participating in and conducting workshops and contributing to local journals.

Fabio Petito teaches International Relations at the School of Oriental and African Studies (SOAS) in London and at the University "L'Orientale" in

Napoli. His research interests lie in International Political Theory, the theory and practice of dialogue among civilizations, the return of religion in international politics and the international politics of the Mediterranean. He is co-editor of *Religion in International Relations: The Return from Exile* (2003; Italian translation, 2006) and of *The International Political Thought of Carl Schmitt: Towards a New Global Nomos?* (2007). Together with John L. Esposito, he is directing the "Mediterranean, Europe and Islam: Actors in Dialogue" Programe at the Fondazione Mediterraneo in Naples.

Fateme Sadeghi is a graduate of Azad Islamic University (B.A., 1992, and M.A., 1996) and Tarbiat Modares University (Ph.D. 2004), and currently an assistant professor of politics in the Department of Political Science at Azad Islamic University in Karaj, Iran. She teaches courses on political sociology, gender studies, and political thought. She has taught previously at the University of Tehran, where she was teaching Western and Islamic feminist theories in the Department of Women Studies. She recently published a book in Persian called *Gender, Nationalism, and Modernization in the First Pahlavi Iran* (2006) and translated Fred Dallmayr's *Alternative Visions* and Agnes Heller's *A Theory of Modernity* into Persian (the latter is forthcoming).

Seyed Kazem Sajjadpour is a graduate of Tehran University (B.A. and M.A.), George Washington University (Ph.D. in Political Science, 1991) and Post-Doctoral Fellow, Harvard University, 1991–1993. He currently is a faculty member of the Iranian School of International Relations and Ambassador to the UN in Geneva.

Hossein Salimi is associate professor of international relations and political science in Allame Tabatabaee University of Tehran. He has received B.A. in political science and M.A. in international relations from Tehran University and Ph.D. in international relations from Tarbiat Modares University. His main academic interests are in the field of theories of international relations, cultural studies and Islamic studies. These books were written and published by him: *Culturalism, Globalization and Human Rights* (Persian); *Moslems in Balkan, Seeking for Identity* (Persian); *Islamic Views on Human Rights*, edited (Persian and English); *Politics in Imam Ali's View: The Bases of Democracy in Islamic Thought* (Persian); *Contending Theories on Globalization* (Persian); *Understanding of Iranian Reformist Mentality* (Persian). He has published twelve articles in academic quarterlies and thirteen articles in scientific meetings. He had been deputy of president of the university for two years and Dean of Faculty of Law and Political Science for two years. Now he is the editor of *Research Letter of Political Science Quarterly* and member of the board of directors of Iranian Political Science Association.

Karl Schonberg is a graduate of Colgate University (B.A., 1990) and the University of Virginia (Ph.D., 1998), and is currently an associate professor of international relations in the Department of Government at St. Lawrence University in Canton, New York. He teaches courses on topics including U.S. foreign and national security policy, international conflict and security, international law and organization, and political and economic globalization. He has taught previously at the University of Virginia, James Madison University, and Dickinson College, and has been the recipient of a variety of fellowships and teaching awards, including a Research Fellowship at the Brookings Institution in 1994–1995. His recent publications include: *Pursuing the National Interest: Moments of Transition in Twentieth-Century American Foreign Policy* (Praeger, 2003) and "Global Security and Legal Restraint: Reconsidering War Powers after September 11," *Political Science Quarterly* (Spring 2004).

Mostafa Younesie studied classical Western political philosophy at the Tarbiat Modares University, Tehran. He wrote his dissertation on the relation of political philosophy and language philosophy in Plato. He is assistant professor of classical and medieval intercultural and comparative political thought in Tarbiat Modares University. He has published research articles on different aspects of intercultural thinking. His special research interests include intercultural classical and medieval political philosophy, language philosophy, and hermeneutics. He is currently working on projects about Platonic readings of Plato's writings; a translation of Homer's Iliad and Odyssey with the poet Pegahe Mosleh; and a Greek-Persian Lexicon with Professor L. Bargeliotes.